INCREDIBLE ICE CREAM

Making It Your Way with Passion!

INCREDIBLE ICE CREAM
Making It Your Way with Passion!

For Professional Ice Cream Artisans
and
Home Ice Cream Junkies

MALCOLM STOGO

Ice Cream University Press
The Educational Arm Of
Malcolm Stogo Associates
79 Edgewood Avenue
West Orange, New Jersey 07052
TEL: 1-973-669-1060   **FAX:** 1-973-669-1062
E-MAIL: Malcolm@icecreamuniversity.org
WEBSITES: www.malcolmstogo.com; www.icecreamuniversity.org

Library of Congress Cataloging-in-Publication Data
Library of Congress Control Number: 2009902831
Stogo, Malcolm
       Incredible ice cream: making it your way with passion!
       for professional ice cream artisans and home ice cream junkies/Malcolm Stogo

       Includes bibliographical references and index. 304 pages
       ISBN 978-0-615-28965-6
       Printed in the United States of America, 2009

CONTENTS

PREFACE

The idea for this book has been swirling around in my head for years: how to take a basic ice cream recipe and reconfigure it to the size of the batch freezer (ice cream machine) being used, so that anyone— a chef in a large restaurant or a home chef— can make the same great ice cream flavor and have fun doing it. The most important ingredient you bring to this experience is passion which, I strongly believe, drives everything we do in life. So, how can you take your passion from your everyday life and eating experiences to create great ice cream?

Passion has been the hallmark of my success for 35 years when I first turned Oreo cookies into an ice cream flavor and cut up Milky Way candy bars to create Milky Way ice cream! I took a simple-looking waffle cone and turned it into something very special by wrapping chocolate around the top. In everything I do, it is passion that drives my creativity!

While many of the recipes in this book come from my other books and newsletters, I also share the flavors that have come out of my seminars around the country from my students' ideas and experimentation. At our seminars we encourage our students to brainstorm—the result being many new and exciting flavors.

The first part of this book is technical knowledge about ice cream production. The second part offers 300 recipes to which you, your customers, family and friends will say "WOW."

FOREWORD

When Malcolm asked me to write the Foreword to his latest book, I was honored. Here was my opportunity to articulate things that I've thought about ever since our first encounter about ice cream desserts in 1994 when Malcolm came to my bakery to show me how larger-size ice cream production could be made with a ready-made ice cream mix. It was quite an experience. That day I became his schlepper (his helper). He said "do this, do that" all day long, and by the end of the day I was exhausted and laughing at the same time—but it was worth it! I learned so much. We became friends and associates and are now partners in his seminar business.

The expression "opposites attract" is perfect to describe our working relationship. It's almost like "The Odd Couple!" My training came from European and American culinary schooling and apprenticeships; Malcolm is self-taught and his knowledge comes out of an entrepreneurial spirit, instinct, drive and the willingness to take risks.

As anyone who has had the pleasure to meet and learn from Malcolm knows, ice cream is his *passion*. Actually, his philosophy is that if you have passion you can do anything. He is a genius at what he has accomplished with his passion, drive and sharing ideas with others. This latest book is another example in his repertoire of accomplishments.

Malcolm's books are bibles—American Ice Cream bibles—in the frozen desserts industry, and are different from other books in the field. This new book, a compilation of his work over many years, plus hundreds of new recipes, continues the tradition. What makes this book *unique* is its inclusion of recipes in different size batches for the professional ice cream maker with many that have been adjusted for home use by the amateur chef.

Malcolm is a person who truly makes things happen! As a reader of this book, you will enjoy the knowledge he imparts and the recipes he shares. *Happy ice cream making!*

Robert Ellinger, C.M.B., C.E.P.C.
Founder, Baked to Perfection
Port Washington, New York

ACKNOWLEDGMENTS

This book has turned into a family collaboration: myself, Carole and Carole's sister Beverly Lozoff, our editor. It's been three years in the making but fun to write, although dealing with family does take a little extra effort! When we first started out on this book-writing adventure and we asked Bev, who is a professional editor, to join our team, she knew nothing about how to make ice cream, only how to eat it (like most people)! Lucky for me, her many questions forced me to be very precise with each recipe and ingredient, thus causing me to really think about what makes an ice cream flavor and how people not in the business interpret a recipe. Bev has done an amazing job editing this book. She really knows her vocation well. Bev, thanks so much! I also want to thank Richard Goldstein of Northshore Designs who designed the book cover. I know I have been a pain, but who ever thought creative geniuses were normal? In the end, it all worked out.

While I have written this book, it really is a combination of ideas and knowledge that I have gained from many different people in this incredible business.

Let's start from the beginning. My mother, Rose, taught me about cooking early on, when I was eight years old. While she never made ice cream, I know my mom would have been an incredible ice cream maker. Her technique was "a little of this and a little of that," which has also been *my* trademark. In other words, don't be afraid to experiment.

Bill Lambert is a big part of my life. He is my partner, mentor and friend. He is also the most knowledgeable ice cream person I know. So when I say thank you to Bill, it's really deep down from the bottom of my heart. And, Sally Lambert, ditto to you too.

In every one of my books I have to thank my daughter, Emily, who, at the age of six, cracked the eggs that were used in the first ice cream I ever produced and sold.

I thank my seminar partners, Robert Ellinger and Lisa Tanner, for being such terrific partners and teachers and keeping me informed on what's really happening in our retail ice cream industry. And, thanks Robert for writing the forward for the book.

My pal, Tony Lana, has been my "secret weapon" for over twenty-five years. We talk almost every week about ice cream and life. When I need an answer fast, he's just a telephone call away.

Steve Thompson, of Emery Thompson, continues to be my one man booster club for many years; thanks for enabling me to expand my ice cream production seminar business to a new and larger facility in Florida where many of the ice cream recipes were developed.

A very special thank you to Gino Cocchi of Carpigiani Group, Bologna, Italy, for friendship and wonderful support in sponsoring our successful Gelato Tours to Italy and making them an incredible learning experience for everyone. Thank you also for graciously allowing me to use Carpigiani batch freezing and pasteurizing equipment at our seminar locations where many of the gelato recipes have been created. He is my very special buddy.

A special thanks to my consulting clients around the world where I have discovered many of the ideas for flavors that were later developed into recipes that appear in this book.

But the best thanks of all goes to Carole, an incredible spark of life, who, from the very beginning of our relationship, has made my life richer and more fulfilling every day we are together. In a funny kind of way, she is also my mentor. We have traveled and tasted together many exotic flavors that have now been incorporated into our business seminars and into this book. We even share a four-ounce cup of many of our new flavors in bed every night! I call her Chairman of the Board of the many Malcolm Stogo enterprises because, while I always thought it was possible to do anything, Carole was the one who encouraged me to make it happen.

So, enjoy these recipes and have fun making great ice cream for your customers, friends and family.

INTRODUCTION

THE LANGUAGE OF ICE CREAM MAKING

Ice cream, something we encounter almost daily, is one of those food items we purchase, consume and enjoy without thinking too much about the details of how it actually came to us. This lack of knowledge may surround a product with mystery, and the "secret" jargon of a particular industry only adds to the mystery. Do you recall thinking that your mother's home cooking was mysterious until you tried it yourself? Once you *know* what to do, the mystery disappears! Certainly, procedures will seem difficult and the terms hard to understand until you've been introduced to them and become familiar with their purposes and explanations. Then you're on your way to becoming a master! The mystery lies only in not knowing.

So here is your introduction to the terms used in the everyday world of ice cream making. The ice cream industry isn't a mystery; it's just another business or hobby that can be understood through common sense and familiarity.

ICE CREAM PRODUCTS:
STANDARDS AND DEFINITIONS

French ice cream A rich version of ice cream that contains at least 1.4 percent egg-yolk solids. Most superpremium ice cream made today contains egg yolks. (*See also* Ice cream)

Frozen custard A frozen dessert with egg yolks as the predominant ingredient in its base, making it similar to French ice cream.

Gelato Italian ice cream that is low in butterfat (5 to 10 percent) with intense flavor and usually served in a softer state than regular ice cream.

Granita Made with the same ingredients as an ice, granita is a coarser version with ice crystals formed as part of the final product.

Ice cream A frozen dessert made from dairy products containing a minimum of 10 percent butterfat, with the exception of Chocolate ice cream which requires only 8 percent butterfat. If the product contains 1.4 percent or more of egg-yolk solids, it is considered Frozen custard or French ice cream. (*See also* Philadelphia ice cream, Variegated ice cream)

Ice cream, lowfat Any ice cream product that has a butterfat content of 0.5 to 2 percent.

Ice cream, nonfat Any ice cream product containing less than 0.5 percent butterfat.

Ice cream, premium Any ice cream product that has at least 12 percent butterfat in the mix. Generally it indicates a butterfat content of 12 to 18 percent and can be more dense (less overrun) than other types of ice cream.

Ice cream, superpremium Any ice cream product that has at least 14 percent butterfat in the mix.

Ice milk Any ice cream product containing a butterfat content of 2 to 7 percent; now referred to as reduced-fat ice cream.

Neapolitan ice cream A product having at least two flavors, usually fruit, in the same container.

Philadelphia ice cream Ice cream usually without eggs in the mix.

Sherbet (Cream ice) A frozen product, sometimes confused with ices, made with fruit and containing 1 to 2 percent butterfat.

Sorbet All sorbets are water based and contain no butterfat, but they generally contain egg whites. Almost all sorbets are prepared with fruit and can be produced in a batch freezer.

Yogurt, frozen A creamy frozen dairy product that usually has fewer calories and lower sodium and cholesterol than regular ice cream. A 4-ounce serving has 100 to 120 calories and at least 2 to 4 grams of butterfat. Some frozen yogurts have no yogurt cultures in the product.

Yogurt, nonfat Yogurt that contains less than 0.5 percent fat.

Water ice A lightly sweetened product that is usually made with an extract flavoring (as opposed to American or French sorbet that sometimes uses pieces of fruit).

ICE CREAM PRODUCTION:
TERMINOLOGY AND DEFINITIONS

Air A term used in conjunction with *overrun*. Air is incorporated into ice cream by the whipping action of the dasher inside the barrel of the batch freezer.

Bulk ice cream Ice cream usually packed in a 2½- or 3-gallon paper or plastic tub that is purchased by retailers for resale to the consumer as individual servings.

Butterfat An ingredient made from rich sweet cream. Egg-yolk solids and cocoa are sometimes included in calculating the percentage of butterfat in a product, but those ingredients should not be confused with the fat from the cream. The specific percentage of butterfat is a unique characteristic of various frozen desserts. The most frequently asked question in the industry is about the percentage of butterfat in the ice cream being produced. (*See also* Ice Cream)

Confectioners' sugar A very fine sugar, also known as 10-X, sometimes used in producing ices or sorbets. It will produce a smoother scooping product, but it will not make a sugar syrup solution.

Corn syrup A liquid sweetener that provides a firm, heavy body to finished ice cream and improves shelf life. It is considered an inexpensive substitute for sugar, but approximately twice as much corn syrup as sugar is needed to obtain the right taste. Corn syrup (liquid or dry) is regularly labeled with a description of DE, such as 36 DE corn syrup. DE stands for "Dextrose Equivalent." 36 DE indicates that the product is 36 percent as sweet as dextrose. Dextrose is about 80 percent as sweet as sugar. Corn syrups are used in ice cream mixes to add solids (and improve body and texture); so the amount of sweetness they contribute has to be considered and the sugar has to be adjusted accordingly.

Cream, heavy Cream that has a butterfat content of 35 percent and can be whipped into a thick froth.

Cream, light Cream that has a butterfat content of 20 percent and cannot be whipped into a thick froth.

Dasher The main part inside the barrel of a batch freezer. It uses two main components, the blades and the beater, to agitate the ice cream mix into a partially frozen state.

Dietary frozen dessert A product that must contain less than 2 percent fat.

Egg yolks An ingredient used in ice cream to produce richness and smoothness. Too much egg yolk inhibits the freezing process and should be avoided.

Egg-yolk solids An emulsifier that improves the texture and body of the ice cream. It is also sometimes considered a sweetener.

Emulsifier An additive used to create smoothly textured ice cream to facilitate scooping and provide control during the various stages in manufacturing.

Extrusion Removing the product from the freezing barrel at the end of the production process.

Flavorings All the ingredients added to an ice cream mix to provide flavor. They can be fresh ingredients such as fruits and nuts, or packaged substances such as extracts and concentrates. All nonfresh flavoring substances are classified as category I (pure extracts), II (pure extracts with a synthetic component) or III (artificial flavors).

Freezer, batch A piece of equipment that makes a single flavor and specified quantity of ice cream using measured flavorings and ice cream mix.

Freezer, blast (hardening cabinet) A piece of equipment that reduces the freezing point of the semifrozen ice cream product extruded from the batch freezer from 26 degrees to minus 30–40 degrees Fahrenheit in approximately 8 hours or overnight.

Freezer, continuous Ice cream production equipment in which a continuous amount of ice cream mix is fed into one end of the freezing chamber with the partially frozen product coming out the other end.

Freezing point The temperature at which ice cream mix will freeze (approximately 27–28 degrees Fahrenheit, depending on the sugar content of the mix); a mix with a lower sugar content will freeze at a slightly higher temperature.

Fructose A white crystalline powder that is very sweet and sometimes used as a substitute for sugar, but only half as much is needed. Some diabetics can use fructose on the advice of a doctor.

Hardening The process during which ice cream freezes to at least -25 degrees Fahrenheit after the product has been removed from the batch freezer. This fast freezing process usually takes 8 to 12 hours in a blast freezer.

Homogenization Homogenization of ice cream mixes reduces the size of fat globules in the mix from 7–9 microns to 1 or 2 microns. This reduces the risk of churning or buttering in the freezer. In the case of pasteurizing an ice cream mix in the small Italian-style gelato units, no homogenization occurs. When making a normal gelato mix, the fat content is normally about 3 to 7 percent. The milk that is used is already homogenized, so churning is not a serious problem. Making higher fat (10 to 16 percent) mixes in these units requires the use of heavy cream, which is not homogenized. Churning in these mixes can become a serious problem; however, using half-and-half—cream that is homogenized—will greatly improve the production of either a gelato or ice cream mix made in a pasteurizer (mixer).

Ice cream mix An unfrozen prepared mix of cream, water, and sugar and/or other sweeteners. It can include egg yolks and other solids.

Ice crystals The frozen portion of water in the ice cream mix. Crystals are formed when ice cream is exposed to air (either external or air pockets within the product itself) when out of the freezer or in a freezer that is above 0 degree Fahrenheit.

Locust bean gum A stabilizer used in the production of sherbet, sorbet and ices.

Overrun The increase in the volume amount of finished ice cream over the volume of mix used. It results from the amount of air whipped into the product during the freezing process.

Skim milk Milk having very little or no fat content that is widely used in commercial ice cream production because it is an inexpensive way to acquire the necessary milk solids.

Stabilizer A substance added to an ice cream mix to produce smoothness and uniformity in the finished product and enhance resistance to melting. It also reduces or retards the formation of ice crystals resulting from heat shock (change in temperature from cold to hot and back to cold again) during storage.

Sugar syrup A solution made from hot water and cane sugar that is used in making ices and sorbets. The ratio of water to sugar (usually 2 or 3 quarts water to 1 pound sugar) varies depending on the fruits used. (*see also* Corn Syrup)

Sweeteners Any ingredients used to sweeten the unfrozen ice cream product; mainly sugar, fructose, honey, maple syrup or a corn sweetener.

Variegated ice cream An ice cream mixed with fudge or syrup to create a marbled effect in the finished product.

REFERENCE

Stogo, Malcolm. *Ice Cream and Frozen Desserts: A Commercial Guide to Production and Marketing.* New York: John Wiley & Sons, Inc., 1998.

1

PASSION AND QUALITY
GO HAND IN HAND

Passion and *Quality* are two words that are linked together—you can't have one without the other. As I have said many times before, it's pretty hard to achieve any kind of success without passion. You can't even get close to acquiring quality without it. So how does one define *quality*, and what are the steps to getting there?

PASSION

What is passion? Webster's Dictionary defines *passion* as "intense desire or being emotional about something." Both definitions are correct, but to me passion is simply loving what I am doing and doing it all the time. While passion is the desire, carrying out that passion is hard work—thinking and creating—and, when all is said and done, looking back and feeling very proud.

QUALITY

The issue of determining quality—"the general standard or grade of something"—is a lot more complicated than you might think, and this is especially true for newcomers versus those who are experienced in the ice cream business. Quality is determined by a number of factors:

- Passion about your concept
- Ingredients you use
- Where you buy them
- How you use them
- What they cost

How you make these critical decisions will determine the quality of your product. And never underestimate the reaction of your customers to your product. This will tell you whether you have achieved *quality*.

Quality and Cost

How do you define the quality of your ice cream and determine the costs associated with it? In many instances, an experienced salesperson from a flavor house or ice cream distributor dominates a novice's thinking, resulting in your purchase of all ingredients and/or equipment from that one source. While every flavor house or distributor has many good ingredients, each has its downside, and, for the novice, this can be both dangerous and costly. How many products do you have sitting on a shelf that you used only once and never again?

People who come to me wanting to enter the ice cream business talk about passion for making great ice cream. And many in fact strive to make a great product once they open their business. But what does *great* mean? Does it mean "someone says your ice cream tastes good," or "this is incredible"? When you hear the words *great* and *incredible* two or three times a day the first month you are in business, you know you have achieved something very special. When you hear that the ice cream tastes "good," you should listen hard and take stock. Is the customer just being nice? You really need to find out, so simply ask. If you don't, you may be fooled into thinking your ice cream is better than it actually is. At the end of the day, it is *quality* that will define your business.

Don't get me wrong. I don't mean that you should spend without regard to the real costs of creating your ice cream flavors, sundaes, shakes, ice cream cakes and so on. The issue of cost is directly related to the selling price of your products and what the market will bear. But the reality is that most newcomers have no idea what it costs to create a great flavor, and what to charge for it. Many look at the cost per pound of a particular ingredient and forget to price out its cost to the end product, meaning an ice cream cup or cone. Also, someone may look at the change in cost over a few years and think that the product will have to cost that much more, but this is not necessarily so. Let's use vanilla extract as an example. Because of a tornado in Madagascar three years ago, a batch of ice cream required $9.25 worth of pure vanilla extract at a cost of $296.00 per gallon versus the cost today of about $65.00 per gallon. This meant that the amount of vanilla in a 5-ounce serving of ice cream was about 14 cents versus 3 cents today—a difference of 11 cents. While this may seem like a big increase, the difference in cost per serving represents less than one percentage point.

When producing ice cream, the most important thing to remember is to equate the cost of your add-on ingredients with the selling price of your ice cream. Most novice ice cream makers are confused about this. They think that adding ingredients will drive up the cost, but this is not true. If you add 2 pounds of cocoa and 1 pound of sugar to our chocolate ice cream base recipe, the costs of these two ingredients is approximately $4.05. You've now added 48 ounces to your batch. If your average size scoop is 4½ ounces and your selling price is $2.75 per serving, you have now garnered $27.50 with 10 additional servings against a cost of $4.05. What does this mean? The cost of add-ons actually made you money with only a small increase in cost. So always strive to make the best product regardless of what you add on. You will be pleasantly surprised!

To be successful today, an operation must be both good *and* unique. There is no incentive for customers to seek you out if you don't provide something different. That's one reason why we stress quality so much. To be quality-minded means working in a clean, sanitary environment and using the best ingredients along with proper processing methods to produce a superior product. Being organized, using proven standardized written recipes and instilling good work habits in your employees contribute greatly to obtaining and maintaining quality control. Be patient—achieving quality takes both effort and time.

HOW TO MAINTAIN QUALITY CONTROL

The most important aspect of ice cream production is maintaining quality control. Here are some things to keep in mind.

- Each new employee must be trained to have a thorough knowledge of how each piece of production equipment operates.

- All ingredients must be handled in a sanitary manner consistent with the health department's policies regarding proper sanitary procedures.

- All ingredients must be marked with the date received, and manufacturers' expiration dates must be adhered to. Throw out expired ingredients.

- The net weight of each ice cream pan or tub meets the operation's standard for acceptability.

- All products manufactured must be taste-tested by the person in charge of production and from time to time by all employees to assure consistency of quality.

- Be careful to guard against the overproduction of flavors that don't sell as well as others.

- Products served from the open display case must be checked constantly for flavor, body, texture and distribution of chips, nuts and fruit within the tubs.

QUALITY AND GOOD PURCHASING PRACTICES

When I think about purchasing an ingredient, quality is the first thought that comes to mind. But it is a learning-over-time process. Before purchasing, always ask for samples and never buy an ingredient without first doing a taste test. Run small test batches of ingredients that you will be using to produce products, and compile a final list of the items you decide on. Help yourself by documenting the results of your tests and maintaining good bookkeeping procedures and records. A purchase or suppliers journal listing each supplier's products, prices, and quality and quantity of packages makes purchasing ingredients and supplies an orderly function of everyday business.

When choosing suppliers, consider the following:

- **Availability of quality ingredients** Do your suppliers maintain an adequate inventory that will satisfy your needs *or* are you restricted because they produce ingredients on a batch basis only and you are therefore required to purchase the whole batch?

- **Price** Are their prices competitive?

- **Service** Do your suppliers answer your questions about their products and how you can use them in your business?

- **Packaging** Will their products be shipped in clearly marked containers that will arrive in good condition?

- **Delivery** Do they have a specific policy about delivery schedules that does not conflict with your business hours?

- **Payment** Are their payment terms clear and can they be counted on to be understanding if problems arise?

Purchasing ingredients for a batch-freezer operation is in some ways quite different from purchasing for a large continuous-freezing operation. Most often because of size minimums and freight costs, a small ice cream manufacturer cannot obtain the same ingredients, due mostly to how they are packaged. For batch-freezer operations, the perfect package is #10 cans, usually packed 6 to a case. This means that an operator is able to use just what is needed. Many manufacturers pack only in 5-gallon pails, and once the pail is opened it must be refrigerated. If an operation has limited refrigeration capabilities, the pail option is not a good one.

Why should you know about packaging? Simply, it is important to know the makeup and size of your ingredients and have a full understanding of pricing. By the end of your first season in business, you will have learned that there are no bargains and that the price paid, in most cases, separates good quality from bad. Sometimes, though, a high-quality artificial ingredient will nearly duplicate the taste, texture and color characteristics of its natural counterpart but will be much less expensive. The price you need to set on your product to be competitive in the marketplace will determine whether or not you can afford to use an expensive all-natural ingredient.

Sometimes the difference in price between one level of quality and another is not substantial and for a few cents more, you might be able to buy a much higher grade. The extra expense could mean the difference between a good product and an outstanding one.

QUALITY STANDARD OPERATING PROCEDURES

A day's ice cream production should always begin with vanilla-based flavors. (*See* Chapter 7) After the vanillas are produced, proceed with coffee and chocolate, then clean the machine. Follow this with fruit, then clean the machine. Finally you can make nut flavors, then clean the machine once again. Chocolate can be produced after coffee without cleaning if you are careful to extract as much of the finished coffee ice cream product as you can.

Clean ice cream batches should be one of the first quality standards you strive for. A clean batch is one that has no flavor characteristics from the previous batch. It will be easier to maintain clean batches if you make it a practice to add most of the bulk ingredients (fruits, chocolate chips, nuts, cookie pieces and so on) to the tubs as the finished ice cream is being extracted from the batch freezer. For an even distribution of bulk ingredients throughout the tub, add them to the ice cream a little at a time as you extrude the finished product from the batch freezer.

Most experienced operators use this method because the finished product is so much better in quality than that of one in which all the ingredients, wet and dry, are poured directly into the batch freezer. If you add the ingredients directly into the batch freezer during the freezing process, the blades, or dashers, will break them up into a pureed, mashed or granulated mass. Adding bulk ingredients during extrusion is more difficult to master, but it will help you to produce clean batches as well as bring positive reactions from your customers who will enjoy, for example, biting into a large piece of chocolate or almond.

An alternative to adding bulk ingredients directly into the freezer or during extrusion is to add them at the very end of the batch, just *before* you extrude the finished product. However, sometimes the distribution will be uneven. You'll need to have mastered the batch freezer before expecting good results with this method.

One of the easiest ways to maintain a hands-on approach to quality control is constant tasting of your products. During the batch process, slowly open the extrusion door or place a spatula into the hopper to pick up some of the product. Under no circumstances should your hands touch the hopper opening or extrusion door during the batch process. The blades are sharp and you don't want to contaminate the product. Use clean spatulas at all times. You should know what your ingredients taste like before you use them, and you should know what the product tastes like when it comes out of the batch freezer. Tasting should continue through all stages of freezing and storage. When you don't taste, you have no idea if your product is good or bad.

STANDARDIZED RECIPES AND PROCEDURES

When testing batches of product, it is a good idea to record the exact ingredients and procedures as you go along. Then you will be able to make a consistent product simply by referring to your recipes. You'll find it relatively easy to produce an excellent product one time, but repeating it again and again is another matter entirely.

The texture and body composition of ice cream is determined by the quality and age of the mix. To be assured of using a fresh ice cream mix, note the following:

- Check the dates on the mix containers. Use a first-in, first-out rotation for them. Ice cream mix has a shelf life of approximately 21 days. Like milk, the longer it sits in the refrigerator, the worse it tastes. Keep the mix properly refrigerated.

- Shake the container to thoroughly mix the contents before pouring the mix into the batch freezer.

Most ice cream production equipment will make an excellent product if you know how to use it. Improper use of the batch freezer will create defects that produce icy, sandy or fluffy finished products. When too much air is whipped into the product, the excessive overrun creates fluffy ice cream. This problem occurs because of the high speed of the dasher and the length of time the product remains in the chamber. In most cases, a fluffy product results from firm ice cream left in the batch freezer for 10 minutes or longer with the dasher still on. Drawing ice cream out of the batch freezer takes time to learn, but the end result is better quality, higher yields and improved profit margins.

Most customers are aware of how a product should taste and expect the same taste with each purchase. Therefore, ingredients and flavoring agents should not be altered from any basic recipe. While taste is certainly important, color and appearance of the finished product are also important. Customers know that too much color usually means that artificial flavors or colors have been used. In creating a high-quality product, the color should be characteristic of the flavor. Intense flavor and color done properly with a high butterfat ice cream mix is a desired characteristic of an upscale operation. Using only natural or high-quality artificial ingredients and following recipes closely will set the standards of quality and excellence that should be the benchmarks of your operation.

2

PRODUCTION ROOM:
Major Equipment Needed

Buying equipment for your production room is not an easy task, especially when it comes to buying a batch freezer. So no matter what I am going to say, every batch freezer manufacturer mentioned below is going to be mad at me. But that's my job, to offer you honest and realistic advice.

In addition to choosing a location, deciding on a batch freezer is probably the most important decision you will have to make. There are four major batch freezer manufacturers in the U.S. Each has its advantages and disadvantages, but the most important question you must answer is, "What kind of ice cream or gelato do I want to make?"

So let me give you some free advice. First of all, I am asked over and over again by people wanting to start an ice cream business if I know where to find a used batch freezer. Well, I will be honest with you, it's not a very smart idea and doing so can be costly. While there is a large market for used batch freezers, knowing the following is critical when deciding whether to buy used or new:

- What is the cost of the used batch freezer versus the cost of buying a new one? If the difference is no more than $5,000, forget buying used. Why spend $200,000 to build your store and take a chance on having your used machine break down on a hot summer day?

- How old is the batch freezer? Never purchase a batch freezer manufactured before 1995. That is the year soft metal was outlawed and stainless steel had to be used for any metal parts on a batch freezer.

- What kind of freon is used? Freon that is not in use today is costly to replace.

- What is the condition of the barrel and blades? This can make the purchase of a used batch freezer costly. It is almost impossible for anyone to know prior to use if the dasher assembly is twisted. Always test batch a batch prior to purchasing a used batch freezer. If the batch time is longer than 10 minutes, you know you have a problem.

My advice to you is simply to purchase your first batch freezer new. When and if you add a second batch freezer, that decision will be easier to make because then you will know how a batch freezer works, you will have a good refrigeration person on hand to advise you and correct any deficiencies a used freezer might have, and frankly, by this time, your confidence level will enable you to make the right decision.

So when you are just starting your business, try not to let pricing be the determining factor in your choice of equipment suppliers. It's important to initiate relationships with manufacturers, and being informed about them and their equipment helps cultivate good relationships. A good supplier is interested in seeing you succeed and will help you answer any questions you have. Your suppliers can share ideas for improving your operation and they can let you know about new equipment on the market. Take advantage of this help during your learning phase.

Most importantly, being on good terms with suppliers can improve the service you get from them. That improved service is worth a lot of money over time, but is especially critical in the beginning stages of your operation.

COSTS OF OPERATING A PRODUCTION PLANT

To construct a batch freezer production facility requires between 300 and 800 square feet of space. Here is what you will need and approximate costs:

Batch freezer 20-quart freezer used to produce the product	$18,000
Hardening cabinet (blast freezer) Used to blast freeze the product after production	$ 5,500
Freezer storage cabinet Used to store product blast frozen 24 hours after production	$ 3,200
Refrigerator Used to store ice cream mix & other ingredients	$ 2,500
3-compartment sink For overall cleaning of equipment, tubs, etc.	$ 750
Hand sink Used for washing hands	$ 300
Tables Useful to have two stainless steel, 6-foot long tables	$ 1,000
Shelving For storing ingredient flavorings, tubs, etc.	$ 1,000
Blender and food processor For pureeing fruit, nuts, etc.	$ 1,000
Plastic or cardboard tubs 2½- or 3-gallon tubs & lids (150)	$ 600
Hot water boiler With enough hot water for overall cleaning	$ 800
Hose water connection To be placed behind batch freezer	$ 500
Scale To weigh ingredients	$ 350
Timer To time a batch of ice cream during production	$ 25
Miscellaneous equipment Spatulas, measuring bowls, etc.	$ 1,500
Ingredients Needed to start ice cream production	$ 4,000
Floor drain and grease trap For water dispersing & grease removal	$ 5,000
TOTAL	**$46,025**

ICE CREAM MANUFACTURING EQUIPMENT

There are three types of freezers used in the production of ice cream: batch freezers, blast freezers and walk-in freezers.

Batch Freezers

The original batch freezer, a vertical freezer using rock salt and ice to create a brine solution as a source of cold refrigeration, was in many ways similar to the ice cream freezers used at home today. Modern commercial batch freezers are horizontal and have copper tubing with cold freon surrounding the cylindrical chamber for refrigeration. The original freezers had wooden paddles for scraping the walls of the chamber. The stainless steel blades of today's freezers do the same job. But even with all the improvements made since the 1950s, the main body of the batch freezer has remained basically the same. It is still the reliable workhorse of the industry.

The batch freezer is a relatively compact unit performing all the functions necessary to produce a quality product. It is used to make one batch at a time, hence the name. The process begins with pouring ice cream mix into the chamber at approximately 40 degrees Fahrenheit and ends 8–10 minutes later with a semifrozen product. The length of time depends on the water and butterfat content of the mix. Ice cream mix varies between 10–16 percent butterfat with the lower percentage mixes taking longer to freeze because of the higher water content. The temperature in the semifrozen state is usually 24–25 degrees Fahrenheit, which permits extrusion of product into tubs for hardening.

The process itself is simple and the batch freezer is a simple machine to operate. You fill the freezing chamber with mix and flavoring ingredients and set the time for freezing; it doesn't matter whether you're making butter pecan or strawberry ice cream. The machine takes the ingredients that are fed into it and freezes them to the consistency you want for extruding into a tub.

A typical batch freezer is a large machine. Depending on the manufacturer and model, it is at least 24 inches wide, 37 inches deep and 51 inches high. Most batch freezers are belt driven and have a 3-horsepower compressor and an agitator motor that turns the dasher or beater inside the freezing chamber. Some come with wheels or have them as an option (something that I highly recommend). Electrical requirements are usually single- or three-phase electrical current, 60-cycle, 220 power. When reading equipment literature, you might see the number "3/60/220" or "3/60/208/230" to specify the electrical requirements. Most batch freezers are water cooled, but air-cooled units are available and are found particularly in areas where the use of water is restricted.

The main parts of a batch freezer are as follows:

Dasher A unit consisting of the scraper blades and beater that fits into the freezing chamber. It mixes the ingredients prior to freezing, agitates the ice cream mix during the freezing process and constantly scrapes the mix off the sides of the chamber. After freezing, it helps to extrude the product from the freezing chamber. Dasher blades should be sharpened and aligned by the manufacturer at least once before the spring season begins. The blades are the most important part of the machine and also the part most subject to possible damage. The blades can be bent by resting the dasher on them on the edge of a sink or table; dropping the dasher to the floor; having foreign matter, such as peach pits, hit them; trying to help the discharge of product by sticking a spoon in the discharge gate; starting the dasher against a frozen mass. If the product is over-processed, which means it is "too stiff, " the compressor will turn off (the dasher will stop). Should this happen, wait for the product to thaw before turning the dasher back on. Many batch freezers are available today with two settings—high and low—to control the speed of the dasher, which in turn controls the overrun of the finished product.

Freezing chamber The barrel or drum-shaped container surrounded by refrigerant. The ingredients are poured into the chamber for initial freezing.

Hopper The stainless steel chute attached to the outside walls of the batch freezer through which the ingredients are poured. The hopper has a cover (a requirement of many local health departments) that prevents unwanted outside particles from entering the chamber. A large hopper is recommended for ease when adding large pieces of ingredients.

Handle A lever or arm that controls the extrusion of the product from the freezing chamber.

Spout A tube or lip that projects from the freezing chamber through which the product is extruded.

Switches On/off controls for the dasher and refrigeration. The batch freezer cannot be operated without first turning on the dasher switch. While in operation, turning off the dasher switch automatically turns off the refrigeration. The refrigeration switch can be turned on only after the dasher is in operation.

Choosing a Batch Freezer

Today, there are many choices in batch freezers, manufactured both in the United States and abroad. Each has its advantages and disadvantages, but the most important question you must answer for yourself is, "What kind of ice cream do I want to make?" As I mentioned in the previous chapter, buying a used freezer is not a smart idea for many reasons. My advice is that you purchase your first batch freezer new. You can always decide to purchase a used freezer for a second machine when you are more qualified to make a good decision based on knowledge, experience and con-fidence.

Batch Freezer Manufacturers

CARPIGIANI

Carpigiani is the world leader in the manufacture of batch freezers. If you are interested in making only a gelato-type or low-overrun ice cream product, your choice should be one of the following models. All their batch freezers deliver a finished product with a

55–65 percent overrun, which is far denser than most commercial economy-grade ice creams, with a 100 percent overrun.

Models

- LB-500 and LB-1002 batch freezers make a 75–90% overrun-type ice cream product.
- LB-502G and LB-1002G make a 35–45% overrun superpremium-type gelato or ice cream product.

Features

- Built-in faucet hose that makes cleaning up fast and easy
- Preset timer that can be set for a specific batch time once the dasher and refrigeration are turned on
- Minimal waste of finished product left in the barrel
- Batch time that is less then nine minutes
- Wire safeguards on both the ingredient hopper and the extrusion opening for safety. (Note, however, that the guards make it difficult to use pieces of fruit, chocolate chunks or nuts as part of the actual ice cream making.)
- Very fast freezing time

CATTABRIGA

Cattabriga machines are used all over the world including at the most important workshops of the Italian master ice cream makers. This is because everything at the workshops is selected according to strict criteria in order to make ice cream with a mark of excellence. Excellence goes hand in hand with Cattabriga machines.

This batch freezer is considered the workhorse of all Italian batch freezers. I particularly like the ease of operation and the fact that there are no real frills that many of the other Italian batch freezers have. I also like the Cattabriga dasher assembly and blades that give a clean swipe to the mix in the freezing mode, resulting in a very smooth finished product.

EMERY THOMPSON

Emery Thompson is the oldest manufacturer of batch freezers in the United States, and manufactures different models that are chosen to produce specific frozen desserts.

There are both single and IOC (Infinite Overrun Capability) batch freezers for making either a high or low overrun ice cream, Italian water ice, gelato or sorbet product. If you are concentrating on American-style ice cream products, Italian ice and sorbet, then there is no question that Emery Thompson batch freezers are a wonderful choice.

The Emery Thompson 20- and 40-quart single-speed batch freezers can make up to a 100-percent overrun-type ice cream product. The 20-quart two-speed batch freezer can go as low as a 45-percent overrun superpremium-type gelato or ice cream product on low speed and up to a 100-percent overrun ice cream product on high speed. The two-speed batch freezer also has 2–3 horsepower drive motors for either low or high overrun production.

Features

- Stainless steel construction

- Combination metal and plastic dasher blades

- Easy access ingredient hopper

- Extrusion opening that allows finished product to flow out easily

- Excellent repair record and parts that are easy to obtain

- Resale value that is very high

- Manufactured in the United States

The newest Emery Thompson freezer, CB350 Countertop Infinite Overrun Control Batch Freezer, will produce any overrun air content of hard ice cream, Artisan Gelato, Sorbet, Granita, Frozen Lemonade, Sherbet *and* Italian ices.

Features of Emery Thompson Model CB 350

- In the freezing process you can inject whole cookies, nuts, candies, fruits and chocolate right into the oversized opening while you are making your frozen desserts.

- Made of a stainless steel front door that will discharge the finished product in less than 30 seconds.

- Precision made German transmission coupled with a 1 horsepower motor

- Refrigeration system that is an ultra-quiet air-cooled 1 horsepower condensing unit

TECHNOGEL

Technogel is an Italian-style batch freezer imported from Italy. This top-of-the line batch freezer produces a superior gelato product.

It features a microcomputer that ensures the best-quality product relating to texture and overrun, and a new patented three scraping-blade stainless steel beater shaft.

Features

- Automatic touchpad operation using a computer-type panel with an audible alarm signal that goes off when the product is ready to be extracted

- Built-in faucet hose that makes cleaning fast and easy

- Minimal waste of finished product left in the barrel

- Clam door latch that provides for quick interior access

- Batch time that is less then 9 minutes

- Easy access for removing back panel for any type of repair

- Wire safeguards on both the ingredient hopper and extrusion opening for safety. These guards, however, make it difficult to use fruit, chocolate chunks or nuts as part of the ice cream making.

- Very fast-freezing production time. When you are producing water ice and sorbet, be careful not to overprocess the product being extruded from the barrel chamber.

TAYLOR COMPANY

Taylor has recently introduced a new gelato batch freezer imported from Italy under the Frigomat name. While the Taylor Company is known for its soft-serve machines, now it also makes and distributes four batch freezers: one countertop unit producing low overrun ice cream; two floor-model units producing high overrun ice cream and low overrun gelato; and its newest addition from Frigomat.

Features

- Excellent service support

- Minimal waste of finished product left in the barrel

- Clam door latch that provides for quick interior access

- Batch time that is less then 9 minutes

- Easy access for removing back panel for any type of repair

- Wire safeguards on both the ingredient hopper and extrusion opening for safety. (However, the guards make it difficult to use pieces of fruit, chocolate chunks or nuts as part of the actual ice cream making.)

- Very fast-freezing production time. (Be careful when you are producing water ice and sorbet that you do not overprocess the product being extruded from the barrel chamber.)

Stainless Steel Tables for Batch Freezers

Trying to add partulates and variegates to a product coming out of your batch freezer can be a difficult procedure due to lack of space for a shelf attached to your batch freezer.

Having a stainless steel table flush against the batch freezer really makes it easier to fill the tubs or pans. The additional space has proven to be useful partially eliminating the need for having a second person to help you. The stainless steel table measures 24 inches high, 24 inches deep and 26 inches wide. The table can be made by any stain-less steel fabricating shop.

Blast Freezers

Once the product has been extruded from the batch freezer, it needs to be hardened. That is, the extruded product is at 24-25 degrees Fahrenheit and must be chilled quickly, within 8–10 hours, to between -15 and -30 degrees Fahrenheit. Hardening must be done quickly to prevent ice crystals from forming on the finished product. Ice crystals are the result of melting and exposure to air.

A blast freezer, or hardening freezer, accomplishes this final step of production. The desired temperature inside a blast freezer is between -25 and -45 degrees Fahrenheit. (Note that the temperature inside a holding freezer will be 0 to -25 degrees Fahrenheit.) A well-cared for, uncrowded unit will harden ice cream in 8–12 hours.

To facilitate hardening, fill the freezer from the bottom up because the coldest air will be at the bottom. Whenever possible, avoid stacking the containers on top of one another because the cold air won't be able to circulate properly. Having wire racks inside a hardening room or blast freezer is highly recommended to allow for air circulation and faster hardening.

Always check the doors to make sure they are closed tightly. Make this a habit for everyone in your establishment. A door left open or ajar will keep the ice cream from hardening or cause a meltdown. In addition, the refrigeration will not work properly if the compressor vents are dirty and clogged or if the temperature in the room around the freezer is too high.

Blast Freezer Manufacturers

These freezers are similar to storage freezers in construction and capacity, but they are designed to hold temperatures down to -45 degrees Fahrenheit. Models are available with either one or two doors. Traulsen, Kelvinator, Master-Bilt and Irinox are excellent blast freezers. Traulsen freezers are noted for their heavy-duty construction and durability. The Kelvinator freezer features interior doors that give added insulation for keeping cold air inside the unit. All four manufacturers are recommended because of their many years of experience in making quality freezers.

TRAULSEN

Traulsen blast chillers will not only take your food safely through the Danger Zone—from 135 degrees Fahrenheit to below 41 degrees in approximately 90 minutes—but they will automatically document the process with HACCP compliant records. Traulsen freezers are known for their heavy-duty construction and durability.

Models

- RIF 1-34HUT-BF: 1 door, 208/60/3, 2 hp (48½" x 36 15/16" x 89½")
- RIF 1-34HUT-BF: 2 door, 208/60/3, 2 hp (78" x 36 15/16" x 89½")

KELVINATOR

They are back in business! The Kelvinator freezer features interior doors that give added insulation for keeping cold air inside the unit.

Models

- VHC26: 1 door, 115/60/1, ½ hp (38/18" x 38 3/8" x 84 7/16")
- VHC48: 2 door, 115/230/1, 1½ hp (57" x 38 3/8" x 85")

MASTER-BILT

The Master-Bilt blast freezer features interior doors that give added insulation for keeping cold air inside the unit. Units are available in either one- or two-door models.

Models

- IHC-27: 1 door, 115/230/1, 1 hp (31" x 35¾" x 82")
- IHC-48: 2 door, 115/230/1, 1 1/2 hp (52" x 35¾" x 82")

IRINOX

Irinox from Italy manufactures the fastest hardening cabinets in the industry. Both the countertop (HCM 51.20) and floor models (HCM 141L) are highly recommended.

While their freezers are considerably more expensive than ones from other manufacturers, the fast blast freeze time might just be worth it.

HCM 51.20

What makes the Irinox blast freezers so unique is the way they bring down the temperature of the finished product. When ice cream comes out of the mixer, it is at a temperature of approximately 16–19 degrees Fahrenheit. At this point, about 30 percent of free water is still present in the ice cream, which is directly responsible for early aging and tasteless crystals. With the Irinox, only tiny ice crystals (not large ones) will form shock freezing to 0 degrees Fahrenheit within a short period of time, so the initial quality is kept at its best for a long time.

Models

- HCM 51.20 Countertop: 208v, 60hz (28" x 27¾" x 33½")
- HCM 141L Floor Model: 208v, 60hz (33¼" x 40¼" x 75¾")

Walk-In Freezers

If you have the space and money, build a walk-in freezer and refrigerator into your next store and/or new production facility. It's the most efficient and economical way to go. A walk-in freezer can be custom made to fit any temperature-sensitive situation; for example, convenience store owners prefer walk-ins because of the versatility, features and temperature-recovery qualities. Food service companies appreciate walk-ins for the self-closing doors and cooler/freezer combination options. Food processors enjoy the durability of walk-in panel construction in their refrigerated warehouses. Walk-ins also fit a wide variety of applications in facilities such as hospitals, data storage, scientific testing chambers and telecommunications housing.

From a minimum 36-square foot size to the more elaborate 10,000-square foot warehouses, walk-in freezers can be customized to provide the right amount of temperature-controlled space. Basic modular panel sizes and heights, as well as countless options, offer the right flexibility to fulfill any design requirement. Combine this versatility with the choices of low- and medium-temperature refrigeration systems and practically any-thing can be achieved.

With a wide range of options, you can, in effect, make your walk-in freezer an extension of your business personality. Numerous interior and exterior finish options adapt to existing store layouts or plans. Refrigeration can be configured to achieve any desired temperature requirement. In addition, countless door accessories and add-on features make your walk-in convenient and easy to use.

HELPFUL HINTS FOR THE PRODUCTION ROOM

It's the simple ideas that can make ice cream producing more enjoyable. The following hints about using the batch freezer will help you produce quality, uniform products day in and day out. Adopting some of these ideas can make a world of difference in your work day.

- Enlarge the shelf around your batch freezer with a stainless steel table measuring 24-inches high x 24-inches deep x 24-inches wide. This shelf is especially valuable if you work by yourself. It will enable you to move a full tub to the side while filling up a new tub without stopping the extrusion of your finished product.

- Invest in a filter for your water. It will dramatically improve the flavor of any sorbet or Italian water ice you produce.

- A long-handled plastic spatula is your best working tool for extruding ice cream out of a batch freezer.

- 36 DE corn syrup is the secret ingredient for producing a smooth outstanding sorbet or Italian water ice. It's simply a replacement for sugar on a 2 to 1 basis up to 50-percent replacement; i.e., for every part of sugar removed, replace with 2 parts of 36 DE. If you cannot find 36 DE, you can use 42 DE at the same usage levels.

- Sharpening metal dasher blades at least once a year will improve your pro-duction time as well as the quality of your ice cream. You will know that your blades are dull when production time exceeds 13 minutes per batch of ice cream—no ifs, ands or buts about it!

- The batch freezer must be sanitized at the beginning of each day.

- At the end of each day, the batch freezer must be cleaned thoroughly but *not* sanitized.

- Have a manual 60-minute timer sitting on top of your batch freezer, and time set each batch; this will eliminate guessing whether or not a product is frozen and ready to be extruded.

- Use preset measuring containers (plastic) to measure out your ingredients (extracts, chips, nuts, fruits and so on). If you are interested in uniformity, this is a must.

- Keep the area around your batch freezer clean during production. Cleanliness makes the production process more organized with a greater amount of product produced each day. Use clean cloth towels, paper towels or pre-wet wipes.

- A hot- and cold-water connection with a 12-foot hose will be very useful when you are cleaning your batch freezer and the areas around it.

- A floor drain in front of the batch freezer will enable you to clean your floor easily as well as allow water to drain while you clean the freezer.

- Place a rubber floor mat in front of your batch freezer to eliminate slipping due to spills from dairy products and ingredients.

- Plan in advance what you are going to produce each day. Being organized will enable you to produce better products faster.

- Immediately place all produced products into a blast freezer after extrusion from the batch freezer. The less contrast in temperature between an extruded product and the temperature of the blast freezer will reduce both iciness in the product and freezing time for producing a finished product.

- A digital scale for weighing ingredients is a must-have in all production rooms. It will save you money day in and day out. It is incredible how much money is wasted on guessing. Make sure the digital scale you purchase has a conversion to grams.

- Using a funnel is a simple way to pour ice cream mix into the hopper of a batch freezer without making a mess by spilling the mix all over the place. And you can probably purchase one for less than $10.

REFERENCES

Robbins, Carol T. and Herbert Wolff. *The Very Best Ice Cream and Where to Find It.* New York: Warner Books, 1985.

Stogo, Malcolm. *Ice Cream and Frozen Desserts: A Commercial Guide to Production and Marketing.* New York: John Wiley & Sons, Inc., 1998.

Sullivan, Robert L. "Batch Freezers—Making Your Own Ice Cream with a Batch Freezer, " *The National Dipper*, vol. 4, no. 9, March 1989, pp. 34–35.

Vance, David. "Batch Freezers, " *The National Dipper*, vol. 5, no. 1, April 1989, pp. 32–37.

3

USING THE BATCH FREEZER

To a novice ice cream maker, the size of the batch freezer might seem intimidating. In actuality, it is a very easy and efficient machine to operate. But before using the batch freezer, you should make sure that you understand the mechanics of operating it. Even more importantly, you should take a seminar on how to operate a batch freezer, or spend time at the distributor showroom learning how the machine operates before making a purchase. It is important to read the operating manual and ask questions of the manufacturer's representative.

Once you understand how to work the freezer and have it installed in your production facility, the next thing to do is make sure that the barrel or freezing chamber is spotlessly clean before you use it to make a frozen dessert product for sale. Pour a gallon of warm water with a minimal amount of liquid detergent into the machine, run the dasher for 30 seconds and empty the water. Examining the water will show if any particles are left in the machine or if it is clean. Repeat the warm water rinse until the water comes out clean. Next, pour a cold water chlorine-based sanitizing solution (2 capfuls of bleach to 3 gallons of water, or follow the manufacturer's recommendations for a similar solution) into the machine and run the dasher again for 30 seconds. Empty the solution and pour in a gallon of cold water for a final rinse. Smell the rinse water for any trace of chlorine and continue rinsing as necessary. After you've emptied the machine for the last time, you're ready to start the production run. (At the end of the day, you will take the machine apart for cleaning, so this preliminary cleaning will turn up any leaks from not reassembling the parts properly the previous day.)

MAKING YOUR OWN ICE CREAM BASE OR MIX

When it comes to producing your own ice cream or gelato, you have choices: you can make your own dairy ice cream or gelato base, or you can purchase one from a dairy. Here are the advantages and disadvantages of both.

Advantages of Making Your Own

- Mix made daily has a fresh dairy taste.
- You can create your own mix recipes by changing the fat and sugar content.
- Depending on the location of your operation, the availability of choices in buying an ice cream mix might be limited.

Disadvantages of Making Your Own

- Making your own mix is not cheaper than buying a similar dairy mix from a dairy.

- Dairy mix produced daily should be used within 48 hours.

- Producing your own mix is labor intensive.

- Equipment needed to produce your own mix is expensive.

- There are regulatory considerations when selling a finished product to someone who is going to sell it to a third party.

- Like any other dairy product, ice cream mix loses its freshness in storage. It has a shelf life of no more than 21 days, after which time it deteriorates and curdles. Curdled mix has a sour taste and any attempt to salvage the mix will result in unhealthy and poor-quality products.

When pouring the mix into a batch freezer, be sure to remove all liquid from the container. Shake the container before opening it because sweeteners tend to settle to the bottom; otherwise the quality of the mix will be compromised because the finished product will have an uneven sweetness. It is also a good idea to drain one container into another to get every drop of mix. By doing so, you can save nearly half a gallon of mix during an average day's production.

During the summer season, you should have on hand at least a 3-day supply of mix to cover any contingencies. At the beginning of each week, the plant manager should determine how much mix is required for your batch freezer production for the coming week; then, based on your current inventory of mix on hand, order accordingly.

Storing Ice Cream Mix

Ice cream mix should be stored as follows:

- It should be clearly marked showing the date received.

- It should immediately be placed in a refrigerator or walk-in freezer.

- It should be stored at 36–38 degrees Fahrenheit.

- If you are purchasing mix to be stored in a refrigerator, never have more than a 10-day supply of mix on hand at any one time.

- Any mix taken out of refrigeration for use in production but not used that day should immediately be put back into refrigeration at the end of the day.

If mix is purchased in a frozen state, follow these procedures to ensure good sanitation and proper rotation of mix used:

- Mix should be marked clearly showing the date received.

- Place all mix into the freezer on a first-in, first-out rotation basis.

- At the beginning of each week, determine how much is needed for that week and place that amount in the refrigerator. Ice cream mix needs at least 3 days in the refrigerator to defrost properly before use.

PLANNING A DAY'S PRODUCTION RUN

Never begin a day's production run without a list of the flavors to be produced that day. Being organized with a list will save time and money because you will avoid duplication and be able to operate in an efficient manner. Also, you will be able to make sure that you have all ingredients needed for the day's production, that frozen ingredients have been properly defrosted and that the marinating process has been completed for the flavors requiring it. If anything is missing or if emergencies arise, you'll be able to make changes in the list and still operate efficiently.

The list should be arranged so that you can produce flavors in a sequence that will require little cleaning of the batch freezer during the day's run, except when switching from producing fruit flavors to nut or candy flavors, and from liquor to nonliquor flavors. (The rule of thumb is to avoid mixing one ingredient with another that might result in an objectionable taste; a possible allergic reaction to an ingredient, especially peanuts; or a liquor taste and residue that might be consumed by children.) You can minimize the cleaning required between batches by starting the day's run with vanilla-based flavors, then coffee, and finish with the chocolates. When extruding each flavor, be sure to remove as much of the product as possible as long as it is frozen and firm. Doing so will keep the flavors pure and prevent tastes from being interfered with.

After you've run through the vanilla, coffee and chocolate flavors, you must clean the machine. Drain and discard the excess product left in the chamber. Then run 30-second warm- and cold-water rinses. When the water coming out of the chamber is clear, you can start the next batch. Once you've done this interim cleaning several times, you will understand the value of running flavors in sequence. It takes a lot of experience in operating the batch freezer to learn to run flavor sequences without much interruption for cleaning. The amount of time saved in a small and busy operation is invaluable.

After the interim cleaning, you're ready to run the nut and candy flavors as a group. Then it is necessary to clean the freezer again. Finally, you are ready to run the fruit flavors as a group. Remember, any flavors made with liquor or mint requires a separate cleaning after each batch because of the strong flavors.

OVERRUN

Overrun is the increase in the volume of finished ice cream over the volume of mix used. It results from the amount of air whipped into the product during the freezing process by the action of the dasher. Overrun, which is measured in percentages, can be controlled in a batch freezer operation in these ways:

- It can be lowered by filling the freezer chamber to more than half its volume capacity.

- It can be lowered by letting the refrigerant run slightly longer than the 8–10 minutes usually required for running a batch.

- It can be lowered or raised by changing the speed of the dasher. A low speed will produce overrun of 20–49 percent, while a high speed will produce 50–100 percent overrun. Anything higher than 50 percent is considered high overrun; anything lower is low overrun.

Too much air will dissipate flavor and produce a product that is both fluffy in texture and light in weight. However, the flavor can be enhanced. Most commercial ice cream made for ice cream parlors, restaurants, hotels and foodservice facilities will have an overrun of 75–100 percent because the high yield from the weight of the tub allows the purchase to have a higher profit margin.

A low-overrun batch can be dense and heavy, resulting in a more expensive product. Superpremium ice cream from dairies is a low-overrun product, as are pints, quarts and novelties packed directly from the batch freezer. Low-overrun ice cream requires less flavoring and has a creamy texture. Fruit and nut flavors require a low overrun to allow the flavors to stand out. You need to be careful when producing nut flavors in particular. Because of the oil content, they can overprocess easily in a low-overrun cycle. Oil breaks down the cream, thus forcing out the air that has been pumped into the product during the freezing cycle. Nuts should be added in the middle or at the end of the batch cycle to prevent coagulation, a curdling or clotting process that occurs when nuts absorb moisture. The result is a dense, chalky taste. We recommend using roasted nuts whenever possible because they are less apt to absorb moisture.

Ice Cream Overrun Scale

The Detecto Model PT-2C toploading dial scale comes with a pint measuring cup that is great for checking ice cream overruns. Ideal for overall portions within fixed weight limits, the PT-2C maximizes your profits while ensuring that your customers receive the best value. Sturdy construction, stability, convenient viewing angle, temperature compensation for dependable accuracy in environments with fluctuating temperatures and easy readability make these the petite toploaders of choice.

COST OF MAKING A BATCH OF ICE CREAM

By totaling the ingredient and labor costs of producing your own ice cream and comparing those costs to the selling price of the product, you can establish a food-cost percentage. A single ice cream cone selling for $2.50 will have a cost of 46 cents based on a final cost of $7.05 per gallon to produce the ice cream (see example on the next page), or an 18–21 percent food cost for the retailer. If the ice cream is purchased from a distributor and not produced by the retailer, the cost increases to 28–30 percent. The 8–10 percent difference is due to the distributor's profit markup and delivery charges. That difference is considerable and is magnified with increased volume; for example, on a business grossing $400,000, the food cost of producing your own product is approximately $80,000 as compared with about $120,000 for purchasing a finished product. When you consider the depreciation (four-year amortization of equipment) of the production equipment, the profits on making your own become even larger.

The fact is, a high-quality ice cream can be produced at the same cost as purchasing a finished product of lower quality. In terms of butterfat, a 16-percent butterfat ice cream can be produced for the same cost as buying a finished product with 12-percent butterfat.

The cost of a single batch of 5 gallons of finished product at 100-percent overrun can be figured as follows:

INGREDIENTS	COST PER OZ/LB	TOTAL COST
360 oz (2½ gal) ice cream mix	$ 6.92 per gal	$17.30
4 oz two-fold vanilla extract	$ 2.31 per oz	$ 9.25
TOTAL		**$26.55**

364 oz—5% loss factor—346 oz

Yield: Two 2½-gal tubs, 100% overrun
Weight of tub: 11.4 lb (184 oz)

EACH TUB
Each tub weighs 182 oz
5% loss factor:	174 oz
Cost per tub:	$13.28
Cost per serving:	.076 cents per oz
4½ oz serving:	34 cents
Cone & napkin:	6 cents
Total cost per serving:	40 cents (39 servings per tub)

Cost per tub:	$13.28
Cone & napkin:	$ 2.34
Total food cost:	$15.62

BREAKDOWN OF COSTS BASED ON SALES PER TUB:

4.5 oz scoop = 39 servings

Sale per scoop:	$ 2.25	$2.50	$2.75	$3.00
Total retail:	$ 87.75	$97.50	$107.25	$117.00
Per scoop cost:	$ .40	$ .40	$ .40	$ .40
Cost:	$15.62	$15.62	$15.62	$ 15.62
Food cost %:	17.8%	16%	14.6%	13.3%

Running a Batch

Whether you are making ice cream professionally or at home, a batch is defined the same way—the amount of ingredients measured by weight or volume used to produce any kind of frozen dessert product. For a 20-quart batch freezer, you'll pour in 2½ gallons of ice cream mix (5 gallons for a 40-quart freezer). Before discarding the empty containers, let the excess drip into the next container of mix to be used. Then follow your recipe closely, pouring the other initial ingredients into the chamber. Then turn on the dasher to run for a minute or so to completely blend all the ingredients, after which you turn on the refrigeration and continue with the batch per the recipe you are using. Learning and understanding the recipes is not difficult when you work with them daily; the hard part is always remembering the little things that have to be done.

To make it easier to operate the batch freezer, I have devised a coding system for the recipes presented in this book to allow you to work efficiently and produce a quality product. This is especially helpful for beginners who are unsure about when to add specific ingredients to the batch. The codes have been designed to enable you to follow the recipes in an exact sequence at a glance.

B: Beginning of the batch: designates ingredients to be poured or measured directly into the batch freezer at the very start of the batch, before the refrigeration is turned on.

M: Middle of the batch: designates ingredients to be added to the freezer after about 3 minutes of running the batch.

E: End of the batch: designates ingredients to be added to the freezer after about 8 minutes of running the batch.

O: Out of the batch: designates ingredients poured into the tubs or, with the help of a second person, into the tubs and the freezer while extruding the finished product, the most difficult part of the entire operation.

Extrusion

When the batch reaches the desired consistency after the 8–10 minutes running time, extrude the finished ice cream as soon as possible. It should not take longer than 3–5 minutes to empty the freezer chamber. First, turn off the refrigerant switch to prevent the product from freezing as a solid block inside the chamber. Most batch freezers have an automatic refrigerant shut-off if you accidentally turn off the dasher before the refrigerant. But be careful. If you shut off the refrigerant too soon, the finished ice cream will not harden properly, ice crystals will form in the tubs, and proper overrun will not be achieved. If the refrigerant remains on too long, overprocessed ice cream will result. It is the worst ice cream you can produce because it is too dense and unscoopable and with no air in the finished product, it will be coarse.

Be organized for the extrusion or it can end up taking 10 minutes or more to perform, and the results could be watery or overprocessed. Sometimes it is advisable to keep the refrigerant on slightly longer than usual to keep the overrun within the desired range, but you must be careful when doing so.

Have your out-of-batch ingredients on hand and, if necessary, another person to help pour them into the freezer and/or the tubs. Make sure the tubs and pans are dry and cool before using them because any water mixed with the ice cream will form ice crystals. With a piece of masking tape, mark the tubs with the name of the flavor and the date.

Years ago, almost all dairy manufacturers of ice cream used either stainless steel tubs or paperboard cartons. Since the 1970s, plastic containers have become the preference of independent ice cream operators. Stainless steel containers corrode and get bent out of shape. They are hard to find now, are expensive, and look unappealing when worn out. The Ropak Corporation produces an excellent line of plastic containers, the Quality-Pak. These containers are made of freezer-grade resins specifically formulated for the dairy industry in general and for frozen dessert products in particular. They come with snap-on lids to inhibit crystallization and oxidation and maintain freshness and quality. Paperboard containers are difficult to handle. They are not reusable, cause refuse problems, and are difficult to scrape because of the thinness of the paperboard. Constant scooping and scraping makes cuts in the paperboard. On the other hand, the smooth walls and bottoms of the Ropak container eliminate waste and increase the number of scoops per container. These containers fit all major dipping cabinets and come in 1½-, 2½- and 3-gallon sizes.

If you have a space problem and still want to offer as many flavors as possible, the Negus Square Pak container is an excellent choice. If you are going to pack pints or novelties for individual sale, do so only after the batch freezer has been emptied and all of the finished product has been put into the blast freezer. If you don't want to pack your pints manually, Sawvel's and Tindall Packaging's Model 890 semiautomatic filling machine are very versatile alternatives. These machines can pack units up to ½ gallon. Many operators make the mistake of letting their finished product sit on the counter to melt while they move on to loading pints or making novelties, or trying to decide what to do next. Don't jeopardize the quality of your finished product by being disorganized.

Storing the Product

Ice particles and icing result for the most part from slow hardening or poor storage of the finished product. Poor storage practices include having too much product in the hardening cabinets, which prevents cold air from circulating properly, and not properly caring for the cabinets themselves. If the compressors aren't working properly, this will result in a warmer temperature inside the cabinets.

Ice is formed by water, warm temperatures, and exposure to air. Failure to store the product immediately after it has been removed from the batch freezer will result in melting that promotes icing during hardening. There is less chance of ice forming in products made with a high butterfat mix because of the increased percentages of fat, sugar, and other solids.

Ice crystals will also form in the product as it sits in the dipping case, where there is a strong possibility for temperature changes throughout the day. Also, once in the case, it is exposed to air and loses some of its creaminess and flavor. Be sure to examine the product periodically for texture, color, and appearance. Look for meltdowns along the edges of the tubs that occur when the product has been removed from the dipping case or if there has been a drastic change in temperature.

Ice cream with a sandy or gritty texture is caused by improper freezing in the blast or hardening cabinets at temperatures above -15 degrees Fahrenheit. Ice cream stored for long periods of time in either a storage freezer or dipping case will also tend to become sandy. So be sure to rotate your products, particularly in the storage freezers. But try not to move them back and forth between the dipping case and storage freezer because the subsequent softening and rehardening will break down the product and allow ice crystals and bacteria to form.

Using Inventories

Keeping track of inventory is an essential part of any operation, large or small. You cannot prepare an accurate profit and loss statement without conducting an inventory first. The task can be made easier by using forms. Taking monthly or more frequent inventories will help you figure product costs and keep tabs on what is being used, as well as provide a psychological deterrent to pilferage by employees.

4

KEEPING IT SANITARY

For the most part, batch freezer ice cream production takes place in the back room of a retail frozen dessert shop or in a separate manufacturing facility. Whichever facility is used, the room or area must be treated according to the highest sanitary standards. While it is virtually impossible to produce bacteria-free products in such environments, products can be safe for consumption if they have a low enough bacteria count, achieved only through rigorous and continual sanitary practices.

PROCEDURES FOR CLEANING EQUIPMENT

Proper daily maintenance can involve a wide variety of procedures and products. Overall, the procedures fall into three categories: cleaning, milkstone removal and sanitizing.

Cleaning

Cleaning involves draining mix from the freezer barrel, rinsing the machine with water and then running a cleaner through the machine. To remove fat deposits and protein soils normally encountered in an ice cream freezer, we recommend using a product such as HC-10 Chlorinated Kleer-Mor from Ecolab; this product is used both for cleaning and sanitizing. After cleaning, disassemble the machine and place removable parts in the sink for cleaning. Then, disassemble the machine and wash all removable parts at the sink.

How to Use the Cleaner

When the freezing operations are completed, rinse the freezer several times with cold tap water (until the drain water is mostly clear), rinse once with hot water (110–120 degrees Fahrenheit), then put 3 gallons (for a 5-gallon freezer) of very hot water (120–125 degrees Fahrenheit) into the freezer. Add the powdered HC-10 cleaner at the rate of 1 ounce per gallon. Run the dasher (beater) for about 1 minute and let the freezer set for about 1 minute, then run the beater occasionally for 15 seconds during the next 3–5 minutes. While this is happening, remove a small amount of the wash water from the freezer for cleaning both the mix inlet of the batch freezer and the outside of the equipment, as well as any utensils you have been using. After the allotted time, drain the solution from the freezer and rinse with warm water enough times to remove all the cleaner. The hot, soapy water can be used for general utensil cleaning, as well as for floors and/or walls. After the rinse has been completed, open the freezer and remove the beater assembly. Place the beater in a clean, dry area to air dry. Remove the beater shaft and hand wash this part and any other freezer parts that may have been missed with the general cleaning. Make sure that the freezing chamber is very clean.

Milkstone Removal

Milkstone is a white-gray film that forms on equipment and utensils when they come in contact with dairy products. This film will accumulate slowly on surfaces because of ineffective cleaning, use of hard water or both. Milkstone is usually a porous deposit, which will harbor microbial contaminants and eventually defy sanitizing efforts.

Once milkstone has formed, it is very difficult to remove. Without using the correct product and procedure, it is nearly impossible to remove a thick layer of it. (Note that general purpose cleaners do *not* remove milkstone.) Milkstone can lead to high bacteria counts and a food safety dilemma. It is best to control milkstone on a daily basis before it becomes a significant food safety problem.

In addition to compromising food safety, milkstone can cause premature wear to machine parts, resulting in additional costs for replacements. If worn machine parts are not replaced once they have become excessively worn, repairs may be even more expensive.

Since most cleaners are not able to remove milkstone, a delimer may become necessary. Although this may not be needed on a daily basis, the use of a delimer will usually follow the cleaning procedure. The delimer solution must soak in the machine for at least 1 hour. Individual machine parts should also be soaked in a deliming solution for about the same length of time.

Sanitizing

After the machine has been cleaned and contains no milkstone, it can be reassembled. Then you must run an FDA-approved sanitizing solution through the machine to kill bacteria. The machine is now ready for food preparation.

Cleaning Ice Cream Tubs and Utensils

A three-compartment sink is required for batch-freezing production to completely wash, rinse and dry tubs and utensils. A well-designed sink will have the following components:

- Drainboard for soiled utensils
- Prerinse hose
- Detergent dispenser
- Drainboard for clean utensils
- Storage rack (separate equipment) above sink for clean utensils and tubs

The following procedure is recommended for using the three sinks:

Sink 1: Wash and scrub, using a stiff-bristled brush, all tubs and utensils in hot (115–120 degrees Fahrenheit) water and use a cleaning agent, not soap, to remove milk remnants.

Sink 2: Fill sink with warm water for rinsing all tubs and utensils.

Sink 3: Fill sink with a sanitizing solution. Follow manufacturer's recommended usage level for sanitizer used. Rinse all tubs and utensils in this solution, then let tubs and utensils air dry on sink countertop.

Cleaning the Batch Freezer

After the day's production run is complete, each of the following procedures should be carried out to ensure that the batch freezer is thoroughly cleaned and sanitized.

- At the beginning of each day, insert the dasher into the barrel. Clean first with sanitizing solution and then with cold water.
- At the end of each day, rinse the chamber with lukewarm water until all the excess ingredients are cleaned out.
- Open the chamber, remove the entire dasher assembly and clean all the parts using a sanitized sponge with the same kind of chlorine-based sanitizing solution that was used for the preuse cleaning procedure.
- Pour a cold sanitizing solution into the chamber as the last function before the cleaning is complete. This is done by a modified rinse method. Prepare a sterile rinse solution following manufacturer's recommendations in 100-milliliter quantities per 9.46 liter capacity of the batch freezer barrel (fill at least half of the barrel with solution). With the outlet valve of the barrel closed, pour sterile rinse into the inlet. Operate the scraper for 2 minutes and collect a sample through the outlet valve in a sterile bottle.
- Wipe all other parts of the batch freezer with liquid dishwashing detergent and rinse thoroughly with a hot water chlorine-based sanitizing solution. Make sure there are no film marks left on the batch freezer from the detergent.
- Use a sanitizing kit to check for any bacteria in the freezer chamber.
- Place a sanitary lubricant (Haynes or Petro Gel) on all the movable parts.

Weekly Cleaning Procedures

At the end of the week, the following areas should be cleaned to ensure proper sanitary conditions:

- Take all containers off the shelves, and clean the shelves thoroughly using a disposable sponge with a sanitizing solution.
- Wipe down all walls with an abrasive cleaner.
- Clean all floor drains with an abrasive cleaner.

- Clean and then remove all equipment from the tables; then clean the tables with a sanitizing solution.

- Clean the floors with a Clorox-based cleaner, and then repeat with clean hot water.

- Soak the mop in a Clorox-based solution overnight to remove any odors.

- Wash all trash containers with a cleaning agent on the last day of the week.

Monthly Cleaning Procedures

Quarterly, but preferably monthly, you should conduct a major thorough cleaning of the production plant.

- Remove all tubs from the blast freezers, and clean the freezer thoroughly by removing all the shelves and cleaning them and the walls of the freezer with both a sanitizing solution and clean hot water.

- Take all ingredient containers out of the walk-in refrigerator and clean the floors and walls thoroughly with a sanitizing solution and clean hot water.

- Sweep all floors in both the walk-in refrigerator and freezer.

PRODUCTS FOR CLEANING AND SANITIZING

Whether you clean manually or have a CIP (Clean In Place) unit, having and using the correct cleaning and sanitizing agent is important in maintaining a clean working environment.

A sanitizer is an agent, usually chemical, that is applied in a separate step after washing. Sanitizers destroy both disease-causing and harmless bacteria. The effectiveness of the sanitizer weakens as it contacts more and more dish and equipment surfaces, so the solution should be changed whenever it falls below the required strength. Use of a sanitizing kit with color codes lets you know if the solution is still effective. For mixing with a chemical, a water temperature of at least 75 degrees Fahrenheit is needed.

Do not use cleaning agents containing soap; they will leave a surface film that is difficult to rinse away. Certain alkalis, such as sodium hydroxide, should not be used because they cause corrosion of metallic surfaces.

Make sure the water you use does *not* contain any appreciable amount of calcium or magnesium. Water containing these substances is classified as hard water, which will leave a deposit of milkstone on the surface of the equipment. If the source of your water is classified this way, you can alter it by adding a water-softening agent, such as pyrophosphate or metasilicate, to the washing compound.

Sanitizing agents work best under strict temperature and time controls. Heat penetrates and facilitates drying of equipment. Low temperatures and short times do not adequately sanitize or dry equipment. Chemical agents work effectively as a sanitizing agent only when equipment surfaces are completely clean and in contact with chemical agents for the required time, and when the active chemical that is used is sufficiently concentrated. For adequate sanitizing with chemical agents, volatile chemical sanitizers must be used and stored at lower temperatures. When used at 110 degrees Fahrenheit or higher, there is a rapid loss of concentration. There are many advantages to using sanitizing agents at lower temperatures:

- Low-temperature sanitizing permits sanitizing just before using equipment.

- Equipment undergoes less strain due to expansion and contraction as with high-temperature sanitizing. This is very important when cleaning freezers and pumps.

- Low-temperature sanitizing encourages the flushing out of equipment just before use.

- Low-temperature sanitizing removes any dust that may have entered the equipment.

The disadvantage to lower-level temperature sanitizing is that it seldom leaves equipment dry, thereby encouraging corrosion.

Only four types of sanitizing agents have pleasing odors; all others produce objectionable aromas in dairy products:

1. **Hypochlorides (sodium hypochloride)** work fast, but quickly lose strength and are slightly corrosive. The solution should contain no less than 50 parts available chlorine per million parts solution in contact with surface a minimum of 15 seconds.

2. **Chloramines** are less rapid in action, lose strength less quickly and are less corrosive than hypochlorides. The solution should contain no less than 50 parts available chlorine per million parts solution in contact with surface a minimum of 1 minute.

3. **Quaternary ammonium compounds** are odorless, nontoxic, noncorrosive but less effective sanitizers. They are extremely effective on clean surfaces and are less influenced by water type, i.e., hard or soft.

4. **Soaps, calcium and magnesium** are less effective than any of the above. When correctly formulated, these compounds work at 220 parts per million or more, at pH levels of 5.0 or higher and at 75 degrees Fahrenheit or higher in contact with the surface at least 30 seconds.

For sanitizing your batch freezer or soft-serve machine, we recommend Stera-Sheen Green label sanitizer, either in a bulk package or in individual portion-control packets.

We also recommend use of rubber floor mats near the sinks and batch freezer to help avoid accidents. In most states, grease traps and floor drains are required in food-production areas. The grease trap is usually positioned directly below the three-compartment sink, while one floor drain should be placed near the batch freezer and the other under the sink to allow for proper water drainage. The drains also help make cleanup easier. To prevent food particles from falling into or getting embedded in any areas behind or alongside the equipment, be sure that there are no rough edges or crevices anywhere.

The room or area should be properly ventilated either with windows, air conditioning or an exhaust system to remove the hot air resulting from the refrigeration units that are constantly running. Consider air conditioning for cooling in the summer. Without proper ventilation, sanitary conditions will be difficult to maintain because the buildup of hot air from the ambient temperature as well as from refrigeration compressors in the production area will be conducive to roach or rodent problems.

Sanitation Controls for Finished Products

From time to time, it is important to check a completed product's bacteriological characteristics regarding compliance to Health Department standards. This would be done after all steps in the process have been completed, meaning production, freezing and storing.

Weekly examinations should be made for bacteria count, flavor, body and texture, color and appearance. Packages should be clean, neat and properly labeled. Any products not meeting company and Health Department standards should be discarded. To measure for bacteria in a dairy product, contact your dairy supplier or specialists who deal with measuring bacteria such as 3M or Nelson Jameson.

REFERENCES

Arbuckle, W.S. *Ice Cream*, 4th edition. Westport, Conn: AVI, 1986.

Birchfield, John C. *Design & Layout of Foodservice Facilities*. New York: Van Nostrand Reinhold, 1988.

Blumenthal, Michael M. and Robert F. Stier, Robert F. "Plant Self Inspection," *Dairy, Food and Environmental Sanitation*, September 1993, pp. 549–553.

Flickinger, Bruce. "Defining and Designing the Modern QC Laboratory," *Food Quality Magazine*, September 1995, pp. 33–38.

Gorski, Donna. "Efficient Labs," *Dairy Foods Magazine* (June 1996), pp. H–K.

IAMFES. *Pocket Guide to Dairy Sanitation*, Des Moines, Iowa.

Marshall, Robert T. *Standard Methods for the Examination of Dairy Products*, 16th edition. Washington, D.C.: American Public Health Association, 1992.

Pennsylvania State University. *Ice Cream Manufacture, Plant Sanitation*. Course 102, Lesson 12, 1990.

Stogo, Malcolm. *Ice Cream and Frozen Desserts: A Commercial Guide to Production and Marketing*. New York: John Wiley & Sons, Inc., 1998.

Stogo, Malcolm. *How to Succeed in the Incredible Ice Cream Business*. New York, 2001.

5

USING FLAVOR INGREDIENTS

The only way to make a high-quality frozen dessert product is by using high-quality ingredients. And it will not matter to your business what ingredients you use if the flavors you produce are not what the buying public wants.

Listen to your customers, read everything that is available on current trends in the industry and watch people's eating habits. The popularity in the late 1990s of lowfat products was unanticipated by many in the business who were left behind in the marketplace because of their lack of awareness. We are now going through a similar life cycle with gelato, sorbet, mix-in ice cream concepts, low-carb products and nonfat soy-based products. Only those dairies that are consumer oriented are going to benefit from the surge of demand that is now taking place for premium-based frozen dessert products.

Today's consumers are sensitive to nutrition and how it affects their health. Everyone is looking for sugar and fat substitutes. To be successful, the products you market should focus on what the consumer is looking for (and by extension will buy).

CHOOSING AN INGREDIENT SUPPLIER

The kind and quality of the ingredients themselves are important as well as the care taken in their manufacture and shipping. Choose only those suppliers with reputations for an overall concern for their products. Likewise, ingredient suppliers like Guittard Chocolate of Burlingame, California; Limpert Brothers of Vineland, New Jersey; Oringer of Brockton, Massachusetts; Star Kay White of Congers, New York; Nielsen-Massey Vanillas of Waukegan, Illinois; Lochhead Vanillas of Denver, Colorado; Edgar Weber of Chicago, Illinois; and The Fabbri Company of Bologna, Italy, have standards of quality in conducting their businesses that make them leaders in their respective fields.

Controlled purchasing is the most important preproduction function of any ice cream production operation. It takes a lot of energy and planning, but without it you could soon run into financial trouble, end up producing poor-quality products and potentially go out of business. Likewise you'll find that taking the time to learn about suppliers and their products will help foster good relationships with them. Such relationships are invaluable because suppliers can teach you about how to use certain ingredients and advise you of trends in the industry.

Today's trends include using fresh, natural ingredients in large pieces so consumers can see what they are getting. In general, don't keep excessive inventory of ingredients on hand. The longer a product sits in storage and the more it is handled, the more its flavor and freshness will dissipate. It will also lose its basic pro-perties that affect the texture and appearance of the finished product.

Dealing with an established ingredient manufacturer will give you a choice of ingred-ients for a particular flavor. As much as possible, buy direct from a manufacturer to obtain the best prices. Many manufacturers do not require large-quantity purchases, particularly if they are located in your vicinity. Freight costs are a major factor in pricing, so you should educate yourself on what is available locally. You might be able to pur-chase high-quality ingredients locally for the same price as a lesser grade from elsewhere. Also, buying direct will usually get you a fresher product than buying from a distributor.

Use a distributor only when your storage is limited or price minimums make it imposs-ible to buy direct. Keep in mind that a distributor does provide the advantage of being able to choose from a variety of ingredients from different manufacturers, and working with a distributor knowledgeable in the industry can be a valuable asset.

Whether you buy direct or from a distributor, be sure to ask for samples with a range of quality and price for each ingredient. Then you can choose the quality and price you prefer. Taste the samples and run small batches of product to see how they compare to the manufacturer's claims. You will also get an inkling of how your own sense of taste compares to the manufacturer's rating of its own products. You'll quickly learn to rely on common sense and your own taste buds. The sampling and experimenting will give you a good understanding of the ingredients and help determine your own standards of quality.

EVALUATING PURCHASING NEEDS

At the beginning of each season, evaluate your needs and order accordingly. Keep an adequate supply of ingredients you use constantly such as vanilla extract, cocoa, chocolate chips, different varieties of nuts and processed fruits. Then you won't run out of product at the height of the season. If you don't produce your own ice cream mix, then you should keep a five-day inventory on hand because dairies run out of mix at least once during every season due to heavy demand.

Buying in advance and in quantity gives you leverage for volume discounts. It may not always be possible to purchase this way, but it's worth trying because the extra 10 percent discount is bottom-line profit.

Ordering

Don't pick up the telephone to order supplies until you know exactly what you want. Having preprinted order sheets for each supplier will make ordering easier and more efficient. The sheets should list every item you could possibly need so that all you have to do is check off the items needed.

Don't let suppliers substitute items unless you are told about it and approve in advance. Suppliers will frequently use the excuse that they didn't want you to run out of an item, so they substituted a different quality or manufacturer. Tell them that doing so is unacceptable to you so that they know they can't take advantage of you. If you use substitutes, you'll end up with an inconsistent product and a potential loss of business.

Receiving and Storing

Plan orders with each supplier so that delivery times are set in advance (because everyone wants morning deliveries). If you know that your ice cream mix delivery is going to arrive on a Monday afternoon, make sure your Friday order includes extra cases of mix to allow you to start production on Monday morning.

When your order arrives, be sure to check the invoice before the delivery person leaves:

- Check the amount received against what is recorded on the invoice and on your purchase order.

- Always check for weight, quantity, freshness and overall condition of the package. In particular, ice cream mix should be checked for expiration dates, usually marked on the top of the container.

- If there is a shortage, note it on the invoice and have the delivery person acknowledge the shortage in writing. Complaining about a shortage after the delivery person has left is not a good business practice because most suppliers are reluctant to give a credit after the fact.

- Make sure that prices on the invoice are correct. Mistakes, honest or otherwise, do occur. Careless, unorganized operators won't notice them at all and will have only themselves to blame either for the extra effort involved in correcting the errors or for potential losses.

If you fail to store your purchases properly in refrigerated or ventilated dry storage areas, you've defeated the purpose of buying high-quality ingredients. An organized storage system should be considered during the design of your establishment because inadequate storage leads to a dirty environment and wasted ingredients. Date all containers the day you receive them. All frozen or refrigerated items must be stored immediately. In particular, be sure to store ice cream mix in proper rotation according to expiration dates so that you use the oldest containers first.

FLAVORINGS

Among the characteristics by which consumers will judge your frozen dessert products, taste will be a major factor. Eating one of your products will elicit an impulse reaction, either good or bad. How your products taste is influenced not only by their butterfat content, but also by the flavorings you use. When aiming for a particular quality, you'll need to seriously consider the use of artificial versus natural flavorings, as well as their price and availability; for example, using a 14-percent mix with all natural flavorings will produce a superior product to one made from a 16-percent mix with artificial ingredients.

Flavoring ingredients are divided into three categories:

Category I: Pure or natural extracts; used for premium and superpremium products
Category II: Pure extracts combined with artificial flavoring; used for premium and economy products
Category III: Completely artificial flavoring; used for most economy products

An *extract* must contain at least 35 percent alcohol by volume; anything containing less is called a *flavor*. The alcohol used for extracting and holding the flavoring matter in suspension permits a higher concentration of flavoring matter in an extract than in a flavor.

Modern technology has made artificial flavors available in virtually unlimited quantities at low cost. They are used mainly in fruit, liquor, liqueur and candy-flavored products. If not used properly, artificial flavorings can result in poor-quality products. Their overuse can result in products that taste harsh, overpowering and objectionable. They are especially used by companies wanting to create an intense flavor profile that sometimes can be very difficult to accomplish with a natural flavor. Peach is an example of an artificial flavor that can bring out the true essence of the fruit.

Natural flavors and extracts, although costly and limited in supply, are preferred by today's consumers for almost all food products. The use of natural vanilla is especially popular. In most cases, the delicate, mild flavors imparted by natural flavoring materials assure little danger of overflavoring even at high concentrations. Thus the use of natural flavorings and extracts can be unrestricted and dictated by your own preference.

Most of the frozen dessert industry uses category II ingredients because of price considerations. Those in the business of producing premium or superpremium products will use category I ingredients, and will use more of them per product than other operators.

Vanilla

Vanilla is America's favorite ice cream flavor, evoking feelings of warmth and comfort. Even infants seem soothed by its flavor and aroma. Just taking a whiff from a bottle of pure vanilla extract can send the olfactory system into euphoria. The Aztecs and the Europeans once considered the vanilla bean to be a powerful aphrodisiac. More than 75 percent of all ice cream produced contains vanilla flavoring in some form, derived from either the vanilla bean or the extract from the bean. Vanilla is the single most important flavoring ingredient used in the production of ice cream. Just as wine grapes vary by region and harvest, vanilla beans vary by strain, climate, soil, time of harvest and curing practices. Vanilla originated in Mexico and comes from vanilla pods, the fruit of the Tlilxochitl vine, the orchid *Vanilla fragrans*. This plant is now also grown in the Bourbon Islands (of which Madagascar is one), Indonesia and Tahiti. The Mexican and Bourbon vanilla beans are superior in flavor to the Tahitian beans; however, the supply from Mexico is limited because of labor costs and the use of most land for oil fields.

The finest of the Bourbon vanilla beans come from Madagascar, the fourth-largest island in the world. Bourbon growers vine ripen their beans to yield higher levels of betaglucosidase, gluco vanillin and other flavor precursors. Compared to the Bourbon and Mexican vanilla, the flavor of the Indonesian bean is a little weaker, with a slightly woody, smoky taste. Indonesian growers pick their beans prematurely. Instead of slow-curing in the sun as practiced in Madagascar and Mexico (a 3–4 month process that draws the maximum flavor from each bean), Indonesians often cure beans in a few weeks over wood or kerosene fires. Early harvesting and fire-curing create a vanilla bean with flavor and aroma characteristics that are sharp, smoky and woody, a far cry from the smooth unassuming flavor of a Bourbon vanilla bean. Tahitian beans produce an extract that has a more aromatic flavor than Bourbon and Mexican vanilla, with a bit of harshness to it.

Classifications

Vanilla extracts are described by the term *fold*, which refers to the amount of concentrated vanilla in the extract. As established by the U.S. Food and Drug Administration, 13.35 ounces of vanilla beans are used to make 1 gallon of one-fold vanilla extract, while 26.7 ounces of beans are used for 1 gallon of two-fold vanilla. The advantage of using two-fold pure vanilla over a single fold is a concentration of flavor that, if used properly, results in less expense in the long run. All the recipes in this book use two-fold pure vanilla extract, sometimes called double-strength.

The categories of vanilla flavorings are (I) pure vanilla, (II) vanilla-vanillin blend and (III) imitation vanilla. Pure vanilla (I) is derived from an extraction process involving the vanilla beans and alcohol. Imitation vanilla (III) is composed primarily of USP vanillin (an artificial version of the principal flavoring component of vanilla) and/or ethyl vanillin. Many other ingredients, synthetic and natural from substances other than vanilla beans, can be used to make imitation vanilla. Many flavoring essences make up the well-rounded pure vanilla flavor; scientists and flavor chemists have not yet been able to truly duplicate the flavor. Imitation vanilla is not recommended in the production of ice cream because if used improperly, it results in a harsh unnatural flavor easily detected in the finished product.

A vanilla-vanillin blend (II) is the combination of pure vanilla and vanillin, with not less than half the flavor derived from vanilla beans. Artificial vanillin is made from lignin contained in sulfite waste pulp liquor, a by-product of papermaking, derived from coniferous trees. Adding 1 ounce of vanillin to a fold of pure vanilla produces a two-fold vanilla-vanillin blend, which is less expensive to make and use than pure vanilla. The categories of vanilla flavoring ingredients are reflected on ice cream cartons as "Vanilla Ice Cream" when flavored with pure vanilla, "Vanilla-Flavored Ice Cream" when flavored with a vanilla-vanillin blend and "Artificially Flavored" when imitation vanilla is used. The use of vanilla-vanillin blends provides a way to economize on vanilla costs. To do so, add between 2–8 ounces of vanillin to 1 gallon of extract.

Using Vanilla

To bring out the full flavor of the components of ice cream, some dairies use vanilla beans to make their own vanilla, but most use extracts. The amount of vanilla used depends to a large extent on the butterfat and sugar content of the ice cream mix. The lower the butterfat and sugar content, the more vanilla will be needed. With 10%–14% butterfat content, a Madagascar Bourbon works very well. At the 14%–16% fat level, the fat tends to mask the vanilla flavor, so a blend of Bourbon/Indonesian is more effective. This blend delivers an initial impact of vanilla at the front of the mouth, followed by the Bourbon at the back of the mouth.

For use in the production of fruit-flavored frozen yogurts, a combination of Madagascar Bourbon and Tahitian pure vanilla is recommended. Each flavor component in this special blend has its individual attributes. To appreciate the synergy created by the two, it's important to look at each separately. Pure Madagascar vanilla is described as a sweet, creamy, woody and mellow flavor. Tahitian pure vanilla is described as floral, sweet and fruity. The Madagascar Bourbon vanilla smooths and mellows the acidic bite of the yogurt, while the Tahitian vanilla component lifts and enhances the fruit flavor. When combined, the resulting vanilla extract has a sweet, fruity and creamy flavor.

In general, you have to use 50% more vanilla flavor in low- or nonfat systems in order to produce the best-tasting products. When alternative sweeteners are used, you must alter the type of vanilla used in the formulation. This is especially true in a sugarfree ice cream mix versus a sucrose-based mix. You need to evaluate the sugarfree base independently.

Vanilla as a Flavor Enhancer

If you had a product with and without vanilla, people would perceive the one with vanilla as sweeter.

- **Chocolate** The marriage of vanilla and chocolate has been a successful one dating back to the 1500s when Montezuma welcomed Cortes to Mexico with a vanilla-cocoa beverage. Vanilla softens or rounds out harsh, bitter notes in most chocolate ice cream applications.

- **Fruit Flavors** Vanilla is often used to enhance fruit ice cream flavors. It is used as a background flavor to round out the fruit flavor and take off some of the tart edges.

Chocolate

Chocolate ice cream is second only to vanilla in popularity. Its demand has increased since the mid-1980s when consumers developed a passion for everything chocolate.

Origins

Chocolate originates from the fruit of the cocoa tree, the cacao bean, which undergoes much processing before it can be used. Cocoa trees, *Theobroma cacao,* grow in Central America and other tropical regions such as the East Indies and the African Gold Coast. The young plants need the ample shade provided by the tropical forests. Most trees bear fruit within 4 years of planting and continue to yield cocoa beans for an average of 40 years.

The two basic varieties of cocoa are Criollo and Forastero, with the latter being the major source of the world's cocoa. The Criollo variety is found mainly in Ecuador and Venezuela. Criollo trees tend to produce a smaller yield, only about 10 percent of the world's crop, and ripen later than other varieties. The seeds are of a finer quality and have a mild aroma. They are used in the production of high-quality chocolate or for blending with other varieties.

Usage

For flavoring ice cream, cocoa is considered a more concentrated ingredient than chocolate liquor. Cocoa contains a larger percentage of real chocolate flavor and less of the tasteless fat than does the liquor.

Cocoa used in ice cream production typically comes in two ways:

- **22–24% fat** A very high-fat cocoa that adds excellent body to the finished ice cream; used mainly for the production of premium to superpremium ice cream.

- **10–12% fat** A lower-fat cocoa that is used to flavor 10-, 12- and 14-percent butterfat chocolate ice creams. This cocoa is richer in flavor but lacks the full body texture of the 22–24 percent cocoa.

In most cases, because there is at least 15 percent sugar in the ice cream mix, it is not necessary to add sugar to the cocoa mixture for use in either a continuous freezing operation or batch freezer. Industry standards and many recipes in other books call for additional sugar, but if a bittersweet chocolate ice cream is preferred, don't add any sugar. If you desire a less bittersweet flavor in your chocolate ice cream, add sugar at the ratio of 4 ounces sugar to each pound of cocoa. Consider consumer preferences when deciding whether or not to add sugar.

All chocolate recipes in this book, unless otherwise stated, use a Dutch-process 22–24% fat cocoa. For dairies using continuous freezing ice cream equipment, the cocoa is blended into the mix operation before actual ice cream production takes place. For batch freezer operations, approximately 2 pounds of cocoa are used with 2½ gallons of ice cream mix. Remember that when cocoa is mixed with water, the water has to be nearly boiling in order to create a loose paste or syrup. Always mix cocoa paste or syrup with at least 1 gallon of ice cream mix in the batch freezer for at least 10 minutes to properly dissolve the cocoa mixture. The reason we recommend using a Dutch-process cocoa is because it provides an excellent flavor and a dark brown color for your ice cream. All chocolate ice cream recipes in this book were tested using a 22–24% cocoa from Guittard Chocolate of Burlingame, California, but there are other manufacturers in the United States that make excellent cocoa for use in ice cream production. For a strong chocolate flavor, Forbes 289 chocolate flavor base (Double Dark) is also highly recommended.

Chocolate Chips

The chocolate chips or flakes you use can make the difference between simply good ice cream and great ice cream. These products come in different sizes and varieties, so sampling them before you start production is essential. Chips and flakes are either cocoa-based or a blend of cocoa and chocolate liquor. They are available in liquid and solid form. The liquid version is added to the ice cream during the freezing process to form irregularly sized pieces. Over the last few years the "soft chip" has become very popular as a flavor using a chocolate chip. Because soft chunks have a lower melting point, they stay soft in ice cream and melt instantly in your mouth, releasing a full rich chocolate flavor.

CANDY-BASED INCLUSIONS

While vanilla and chocolate remain the most popular flavors, ice cream varieties containing various candy-based inclusions now make up a sizable portion of the market. This growth has enabled product designers to flex their creativity by developing varieties that taste almost like eating Heath®, Milky Way®, Almond Joy®, and Snickers® candy bars. Most of the credit for this idea belongs to the small independent ice cream operators of the 1970s and 1980s.

A number of factors come into play when working with candy-based inclusions. Foremost is defining the target market and deciding what contribution the inclusion gives to the final product. This is no different from designing any flavor. The question to ask is, how should the product look and taste? Because ice cream with candy-based inclusions promotes a value-added image, most inclusions should appear in high con-trast to the ice cream itself. With chunk-type pieces, this often means that "bigger is better." Ideally, the consumer should find a piece in every bite or at least several per scoop.

Most manufacturers of these candies have now caught up with the craze. But some, such as Leaf, Inc. of Lake Forrest, Illinois, have actually been promoting the use of their candy bars (Heath Bar) in ice cream production. You can purchase broken or bite-size pieces in bulk form from most manufacturers.

As part of the new candy inclusion technology sweeping the ice cream industry, one company, Gertrude Hawk in Dunmore, Pennsylvania, has created what it calls mini-melt technology that it uses to produce candy ice cream cones and cups with an outer chocolate shell and an inner fruit or chocolate inclusion.

The following manufacturers make candy products that you should consider using in your ice cream (*See* Appendix for addresses):

- M&M® Mars: M&Ms (plain and peanut), Milky Way bars, Snickers
- Hershey Chocolate USA: Reese's Pieces®, Almond Joy and Mounds® bars
- Nabisco: Oreo® cookies, Graham Crackers, Ginger Snaps, Chips Ahoy®, Nutter Butter® peanut butter cookie pieces
- Nestle: Raisinets, Butterfinger®, Rainbow Morsels, Nestles Buncha Crunch, Goobers® peanuts, Nestle Crunch bars, Chunky pieces, Alpine White pieces
- Pecan Deluxe: Pecan Pralines, Milky Way pieces (Candy Bar Blend), Chocolate Truffles

These and other products can be purchased directly from the manufacturers and/or wholesalers.

NUTS

Many popular flavors of ice cream contain nuts and, of course, they can be used as wet or dry toppings as well. Because of their popularity and versatility, the nut industry caters to the ice cream industry by coming up with new flavors and ideas and by providing nut products in different sizes. In particular, the peanut, pecan, and walnut marketing board associations promote new nut flavors on a fairly regular basis through their newsletters. (*See* Appendix)

Nuts contain protein and fat. Their flavor is derived from the oils in them. The most popular nuts used in the ice cream industry are pecans, almonds, walnuts and peanuts. They are used primarily as nutmeats, pastes or extracts, all of which should be refrigerated or stored in a cool, dry place to prevent them from becoming rancid. Pistachios, almonds and hazelnuts should be purchased already blanched with the outer skins removed. Nuts added to ice cream need to be coated with some kind of barrier or they become soggy or rancid. This can be done by oil roasting the nuts or using an actual coating of chocolate or praline. Most operators purchase their nutmeats already roasted, with little or no salt added. I prefer the latter because I believe that salt hinders the production freezing process as well as the melting effect in the display case. For a strong visual appeal to the customer, use large pieces of nutmeats, both in the product and as a garnish or topping.

Most nut flavors of ice cream are prepared using a nut flavor-base in liquid, as an extract, or paste form. A combination of the base and nutmeats during the freezing process creates the final flavor of the ice cream. Nuts can also be added to the fruit feeder in a continuous freezing operation or into the batch freezer directly during processing or added by hand to the tubs during extrusion. Since you'll get different results with each method, you should use different sizes of nut products depending on the method chosen. In a batch freezer operation, add the nuts to the freezer during processing, and use only halves or large pieces because the dasher blades will cut them apart. Use syruper, a specific small-size category, when adding nuts by hand as you extrude the finished product. Small pieces added during processing will be granulated by the dasher blades.

Walnuts

Walnuts are rich in food value. They are a good source of several vitamins, including thiamine, vitamin B and folacin. They are naturally low in sodium and contribute substantial amounts of dietary fiber. They contain no cholesterol and are high in unsaturated fats.

Walnuts are harvested from late August to early November. After harvesting, they are hulled, washed, mechanically dehydrated, sized and separated by size and color. Once purchased, they should be kept in refrigerated storage (32–38 degrees Fahrenheit and 65 percent relative humidity) to maintain their freshness. As an ingredient for ice cream, most operators prefer large, light-colored halves and pieces or regular small syruper pieces. Either of these forms can also be used for toppings.

Walnuts add a slightly bitter taste that contrasts well with the sweetness of ice cream. If sandiness appears, soak or boil walnuts in a simple syrup solution and drain them prior to use for optimal appearance in ice cream products. Ten pounds of sugar to 1 gallon of water makes an excellent syrup solution. Raw walnuts can be roasted at 375 degrees Fahrenheit for approximately 10 minutes. Usage level in ice cream production is about 7 percent.

Walnuts are popular in a number of different ice cream flavors around the world. Spumoni, an Italian ice cream with candied fruit and chopped walnuts, Kulfi Ruh Giulab, an Indian ice cream with rose essence and walnuts, and Azuuki Bean and Walnut ice cream are just a few examples.

Walnuts make excellent ice cream toppings. Alone or part of a topping such as maple walnut fudge, walnuts add the body and mouthfeel consumers look for in upscale, premium ice creams. Walnuts also make an excellent coating for ice cream bars. Just dip the bars in chocolate and coat them with walnuts, either granulated or small pieces, for a unique crunch.

Peanuts

Americans have had a long love affair with the peanut in all its forms. According to the Georgia Peanut Commission in Tifton, Georgia, more than 4 million pounds are consumed daily, with children literally growing up on peanut butter sandwiches. India and China produce over half of the world's peanut supply, so it is safe to assume that any flavor made with peanuts in that part of the world is very popular.

Providing "nutrition in a nutshell" (Georgia Peanut Commission), a peanut contains 26 grams of protein along with many of the essential B vitamins and polyunsaturated fats. Peanuts are also low in sodium and are cholesterol free.

Pecans

With more than 80 percent of the world's pecan crop being produced in the United States, it's no wonder they are so popular here. You can drive through the South and find pecans for sale in all varieties and shapes at every roadside restaurant and gift shop. Hundreds of varieties are harvested during the season, from October to March.

Pecans contain mostly unsaturated fatty acids, are low in sodium and contain no cholesterol. Their full flavor is easily brought out in almost any ice cream flavor produced. Pecan praline and butter pecan ice cream rank high on the consumer's list of favorites.

Pecans come finely granulated and in halves as well as pieces. To ensure freshness, you should store below 41 degrees Fahrenheit. In storage, they should be protected from moisture, light, heat and oxygen to preserve freshness. Because they absorb other odors easily, they should also be stored separately, when possible, or with nonodorous products. Once opened, vacuum-packed nuts should be used as quickly as possible and stored under refrigeration.

To ensure a nice show of pecans in your finished product, you should use fancy large pecan halves for either continuous or batch freezer operations.

Almonds

Almonds are low in fat and come in varieties ranging from raw, blanched and roasted to chocolate covered. They have become increasingly popular since the introduction of such flavors of ice cream as Vanilla Chocolate Almond and Chocolate Chocolate Almond by the Haagen-Dazs Company. You might choose to use roasted slivers or chopped (diced) pieces for making regular almond flavored ice cream, and large pieces to provide the full nut taste when using chocolate-coated almonds.

Pralines

Pralines have become increasingly popular since the late 1980s. Originally popular only in the southern parts of the United States, their popularity has now been extended all over the country, as well as internationally in the Middle East. A praline is a nut coated in sugar and applied to an oil-roasted nut. Because pralines are sugar coated, the sugar from the nut will dissolve in the ice cream over an extended period of time. The most widely used praline nut is the pecan, while almonds and cashews also make a terrific praline product.

Other Nuts

Other nuts such as hazelnuts, pistachios and macadamias provide a special appeal in superpremium ice cream products that attract consumers willing to spend more. Because these nuts are so expensive, care should be taken in their handling, storage and precise usage in recipes. In particular, hazelnut paste from Fabbri in Bologna, Italy, is an outstanding product to use for a flavor base in gelato and ice cream production.

FRUITS

There is no question that particularly in summer any ice cream flavor made with fruit, especially fresh fruit, will sell. Americans love fruit, always have and always will. Fruit flavors as a category is the largest one that you will produce. Strawberry ice cream has always ranked third in popularity after Vanilla and Chocolate. Because of the availability of fresh fruit during the summer, other popular flavors include Banana (although good bananas are available year round), Raspberry, Cherry and Peach.

Fruit flavorings come in four forms: the fruit itself, puree, variegates and extracts. Extracts can be natural or artificial. Fruit is available fresh, frozen and processed.

Fresh Fruit

For the best-quality frozen dessert, fresh is preferable, but it is expensive when not in season and time consuming to prepare for the production run. However, anything fresh appeals to the buying public, so the use of fresh fruit (uncooked) whenever possible is worth considering.

Fresh fruit can be used in an ice cream mix only after the fruit has been washed, peeled and pitted when necessary, cut up, and marinated with sugar to produce a fruit syrup. Marinating the fruit takes at least 8–12 hours, so you'll have to prepare the fruit for production use a day in advance. The syrup imparts the full flavor of the fruit to the ice cream more effectively than does the fruit by itself. It also breaks down the fruit so that icing doesn't occur during the production run. Depending on the fruit used, either citric acid or lemon juice solutions can be used at the rate of 5 ounces of solution to each 100 pounds of the batch to bring out both a more balanced fruit flavor and smooth out any excess sweetness that sometimes camouflages the flavor.

For the marinating process, mix 2–7 pounds of fruit with 1 pound of sugar, depending on the natural sweetness of the fruit being used. Some suggested ratios for fruit to sugar are as follows:

Apples	7:1
Strawberries	3:1
Raspberries	4:1
Peaches	2½:1
Cherries	3:1

The ratio will also vary depending on the percentage of butterfat in your ice cream mix; for example, a 16% butterfat mix will require less sugar in the fruit syrup than a lower butterfat mix. Remember, too, that sweetening is a matter of taste, so adjust your recipes according to customer feedback. The fruit-sugar ratio is essential because without an adequate amount of sugar in the fruit mixture, the pieces of fruit in the ice cream will impart an icy texture that consumers find objectionable.

Frozen Fruit

Frozen fruits, like fresh fruits, require marinating, but remember that most frozen fruits already contain 10 percent sugar (unless they are IQF, individually quick frozen). These fruits are cheaper and easier to use than fresh, but the taste of a fresh fruit is far superior to anything frozen. The best mixture for marinating all fruits, fresh or frozen, is 1 part puree and 1 part pieces.

The total weight of the marinated fruit mixture used should not exceed 25 percent of the weight of the finished product; for example, if you use 3 pounds of strawberries and 1 pound of sugar, you'll have 4 pounds of marinated fruit. That quantity must be used with 12 pounds of ice cream mix to result in 16 pounds of product; that is, 4 is 25% of 16, and 12 is the remaining 75%.

Lastly, remember that most superpremium fruit-flavored frozen desserts are slightly overflavored because that's what consumers want, given the success of the category.

When frozen fruit is used, you will get the best results by considering the following:

- To best preserve flavor and texture, defrost slowly.

- Defrost in a refrigerator or walk-in box.

- Defrosting may take 24–30 hours for a 30-pound box or 5-gallon pail.

- Most properly thawed fruits will return to their original freshness.

- Never refreeze thawed fruit.

- To accelerate thawing of syrup packs only, thaw at room temperature or run cool water over the container or plastic bag.

- Thawed fruit should immediately be used within 2 hours if stored at room temperature, or immediately place in refrigerator to maintain sanitary health conditions.

- Cover thawed fruit tightly to preserve its color and flavor.

- Once thawed fruit is refrigerated, make sure to use it within 2 days.

Processed Fruit

Fruit that is cooked, or pasteurized, is used more and more by ice cream producers worldwide because of health concerns regarding bacteria in fruit not being handled properly during the harvesting, picking and washing process prior to shipment to dairy processors. Processed fruit comes three ways: whole, sliced or pureed. It is packed in either #10 cans, 5- or 55-gallon pails or totes. Whole or sliced fruit is processed and packed either solid or dry pack. The solid pack is designed for those ice cream formulations requiring some juice and syrup for additional flavor (approximate ratio of fruit to juice is 36 parts fruit, 14 parts juice). The dry pack is designed for those ice cream formulations requiring only fruit.

Kinds of Fruit

Strawberry

The strawberry, the fruit of the plants of the genus *Fragaria,* has a particular and unique structure. The seeds, which unlike those of other fruits, are on the outside, are the true fruits of the plant. The inside of the fruit has a fleshy "berry" fiber to it. The fiber, or flesh, is particularly flavorful and bodied so that when used for ice cream production, it is easy to get the true flavor of the strawberry in the finished hardened product.

There are now hundreds of varieties of strawberries. They exhibit great diversity of size and flavor; but one thing is certain, strawberries are best used when fully ripe. Strawberries from Washington and Oregon have the best overall flavor of any U.S. strawberry. Their fiber content is excellent; the only negative is the off color of less red; they are more purple and blue. Strawberries from California have excellent color, but they have more water content, less fiber and are not as flavorful as the berries from Washington and Oregon.

Fresh or unsugared frozen strawberries should be purchased and used whole. They do not have to be mashed, sliced or heated to enhance their flavor during marinating. Using a 3:1 ratio of fruit to sugar will give a balance of sweet and tart flavor that can be adjusted based on the butterfat of the ice cream mix. Use less sugar with higher butterfat percentages.

If frozen strawberries are used, they should be fully defrosted. Once defrosted, combine with sugar (4 parts fruit to 1 part sugar) and let them sit for 6–8 hours to allow the marinating to take full effect. If you plan on using the fruit within 4 hours, add an additional 4 ounces of sugar to each pound of strawberries used. Then drain off the juice. Some of the juice—25% of what is left—can be used for flavoring the batch, but be careful not to use more because juice is water and you do not want to create ice, or crystallization, in your finished product.

Because of improved flavor technology, many ice cream producers are using processed strawberries. Given a batch of ice cream calling for 2½ gallons of ice cream mix, use about 3 quarts of processed strawberries to produce an excellent-tasting product.

Raspberry

The raspberry, *Rubus ideas* and other *Rubus* species, grows wild in cooler regions of the northern hemisphere, as well as in some southern parts. The first people known to have cultivated raspberries were the ancient Greeks, who are said to have called the fruit "idaeus" because it grew thickly on the slopes of Mount Ida, as it still does. Raspberries can be either red or black. Both are excellent for use in ice cream production.

For at least 6 months of the year, the high cost of fresh raspberries limits their use by many large operators. Raspberries have a strong, full-bodied flavor, but must be pureed to remove all or at least 85 percent of the seeds. Because raspberries contain water, more sugar is used than for other fruits to inhibit icing. Frozen raspberries are readily available and less expensive than fresh, and they are very acceptable for use in frozen dessert production. Processed raspberries tend to be too sweet and should be used only when mixed with either fresh or frozen fruit to improve the flavor.

Peach

The freestone peach, *Prunus Persica,* is one of the world's favorite fruits. With early origins in Asia Minor or Persia, this peach is a descendant of the wild almond which still grows in that region.

Successfully producing a peach-flavored ice cream is difficult. Only fully ripened yellow peaches have any flavor, and because peaches are a water-based fruit, icing occurs easily. Proper flavoring can be achieved by using a natural peach extract in conjunction with the marinated (for a minimum of 12 hours) peach pulp mixture. The skins should not be removed because they increase flavor substantially.

Frozen peaches are now being used more and more by ice cream manufacturers and they are in demand year round. They are usually shipped IQF. Frozen peaches come either in halves, sliced, diced or irregular cuts.

Cherry

The Montmorency cherry is considered the best fresh cherry for ice cream production. A 3:1 ratio of fruit to sugar and a natural extract will produce a good flavor. The cherries need not be mashed or pureed because of their good body structure. During either a continuous or batch freezer operation, the cherries will maintain their integral character throughout the freezing process. Since fresh cherries are considered mildly flavored, you'll need to use more of them. Cherries in a frozen state are available as wholes, halves, slices and mixed diced.

Banana

Bananas are a wonderful summer addition for any type of ice cream or sorbet production. It is a remarkable fruit. More bananas are consumed than perhaps any other kind of fruit in the world.

The banana plant, of the genus *Musa,* is a strange growth that looks like a palm tree but is not a tree at all. It is a perennial herb that grows a new trunk every year, and dies back to its roots after it has flowered and fruited. Bananas are basically an easy fruit to use in ice cream production if one major consideration is controlled, that being the ripening process. A banana totally yellow, almost rotten, is the best banana to use. The riper the banana, the more flavor in the fruit. The ripening process involves a chemical change in which starch is converted to sugar, made up of sucrose 66%, fructose 14% and glucose

20%. Protopectin is also converted to soluble pectin. As bananas ripen, they give off ethylene gas. Most fruits do this during ripening, but bananas produce an exceptionally large amount. Ethylene causes ripening and development of color, as well as being produced by it, so one fruit can help another to ripen.

Fresh bananas can be pureed and dispersed directly into the flavor tank in a continuous freezing operation or poured directly into the batch freezer. The blades of the batch freezer will puree them instantly.

Processed bananas are available from a number of manufacturers such as Chiquita Brands in Cincinnati, Ohio. Their banana puree comes in cans, pails and drums with no sugar added.

Blueberry

Blueberries in the past were a neglected fruit in ice cream production; however, today that status is rapidly changing. The reason is that there has been a major commercial cultivation of the fruit since the mid-1990s, taking the fruit from the wild into the commercial world in many areas of food production.

It is a small bluish fruit of various scrubby (lowbush) and bushy (high bush) plants of the genus *Vaccinium*. Wild blueberries are found wherever suitable conditions, specifically acid soil and enough moisture in all seasons, exist. Most commercially cultivated blueberries are grown in North America and Canada.

Blueberries have a sweet tart flavor that, when balanced properly in ice cream production, creates a very smooth creamy delicious texture in the finished product.

Other Fruit

Fresh or frozen pineapple, kiwi, cranberries, mangoes, dates and apricots can all be used successfully in ice cream production. They are full-bodied and have bulk and texture characteristics for proper freezing with ice cream mix.

When it comes to tropical fruits, the mango is a rising star. In sorbet production, mango, kiwi, passion fruit and guava are all getting a lot of attention from sorbet manufacturers because they are perceived as being both refreshing and healthy. The combination of exotic tropical flavors with more familiar flavors such as strawberry-kiwi has become an effective strategy for broadening their appeal.

PUREE FLAVOR BASES & VARIEGATING SAUCES

Puree Flavor Bases

A flavor base is a concentrated amount of whole fruit that is pureed. Sugar or corn syrup is then added to bring out the flavor of the fruit. For a product designer, a puree's primary function is to add fruit solids (creating fruit body texture to the ice cream mix) to the ice cream flavor being produced. Purees do not add as much flavor as an extract or concentrated flavor base, but they help make the flavor well-rounded. When using a puree, make sure it is agitated properly with the ice cream mix in the flavor tank, prior to production. Each flavor has its own particular usage level, so it is important to sample some of the combined flavor before production begins.

Variegating Sauces

A variegating sauce is thick syrup that is used to create a marble pattern in the hardened ice cream. Variegates are often used instead of and/or in addition to pieces of fruit or candy. In the finished ice cream, variegates appear as ribbon. Caramels, marshmallows, chocolate, fudge and butterscotch are commonly used as variegating sauces. From both a textural and shelf-life standpoint, the percent in solids needs to be higher than a fruit prep. The correct viscosity to deposit successfully through a variegating pump to display the correct textural attributes in the finished product falls approximately in the 80,000 to 100,000 centipose range. Since all variegates are cooked preps, the longer a variegate is cooked, the thicker it will become.

Variegates are added to the semisoft ice cream in a continuous freezing operation through the variegator (ripple pump). In a batch freezer operation, they are hand swirled into the tubs as the ice cream is being extruded. Do not add a variegate into the hopper of the batch freezer because the resulting action will be too much of a blending of the variegate with the ice cream being frozen, causing changed color and flavor. If you line the tubs with the variegating sauce before the extrusion step, you can create a very nice marble pattern as the product is being extruded. This is done by using a spatula to swirl the variegate off the walls of the tubs as the ice cream is being extruded.

Bakery Mix-Ins

Like candy-based ice cream products, bakery mix-ins now play a very similar role in the development of new ice cream flavors. This flavor ingredient category is becoming enormously popular with ice crream manufacturers. Bakery mix-in ingredients are shipped frozen and must be kept frozen until use.

REFERENCES

Arbuckle, W. S. *Ice Cream.* 4th edition. Westport, Conn.: AVI, 1986.

Brandt, Laura. "The Creation and Use of Vanilla," *Food Product Design,* March 1996, pp. 70–87.

Davidson, Alan. *Fruit, A Connoisseur's Guide and Cookbook.* New York: Simon & Schuster, 1991.

Hegenbart, Scott. "Harvesting the Benefits of Fruit-containing Ingredients," *Food Product Design,* December 1994, pp. 25–46.

Ingredient Technology Application. "Two Desserts in One," *Dairy Foods Magazine,* January 1996, p. 50.

Kuhn, Mary Ellen. "Flavor Forecast: Anything Goes!" *Food Processing*, Aug. 1995, p. 30.

Kuntz, Lynn. "Ice Cream Inclusions: Deep Freeze Delights," *Food Product Design*, July 1994, pp. 50–64.

Lind, Peter. "Ben & Jerry's: Beyond Specifications and Price," *Dairy Foods Magazine*, May 1993, p. 54.

McWard, Christine. "Going Nuts," *Baking Buyer*, September 1995, p. 23.

Soronson, Bryan. "How to 'Taste' Ice Cream," *The National Dipper*, vol. 3, no. 7, March 1988, pp. 32–34.

Stogo, Malcolm. *Ice Cream and Frozen Desserts: A Commercial Guide to Production and Marketing.* New York: John Wiley & Sons, Inc., 1998

Stogo, Malcolm. *How to Succeed in the Incredible Ice Cream Business.* New York, 2001.

Vanderpool, Ray. "Finding a Flavor Supplier," *The National Dipper*, vol. 4, no. 2, May 1988, pp. 16–17.

Webb, Judy. "Flavoring Trends for '88 & '89," *The National Dipper*, vol. 4, no.2, May 1988, p. 18.

6

HOME ICE CREAM JUNKIES
MAKING IT LIKE THE PROS

There is nothing better than running your fingers around the sides of an ice cream freezing bowl and tasting the ice cream—could it taste any fresher? While much in the preceding chapters is not aimed at the casual home ice cream maker who is more interested in having fun without the hassle, there are a few lessons that can be learned from the professional operation:

- Always measure your ingredients.

- Freeze or refrigerate the freezing bowl prior to use.

- Cover the finished product tightly before putting it in the freezer to harden.

- Always use half-and-half when making the base for the cream because it is both pasteurized and homogenized, while heavy cream is pasteurized only.

Is there anything more fun than making ice cream at home, and then eating it immediately out of the ice cream maker? Ice cream is a universal treat; travel just about anywhere around the world, as I have done, and you will see this phenomenon. It's served at birthday parties, beach parties and dinner parties, from the simplest to the most sophisticated flavors and presentations. Whether it's topped with hot fudge, just scooped into a cone or cup or used in an elaborate ice cream bombe, ice cream is a tasty, refreshing dessert that brings a smile to everyone. There are many inexpensive and user-friendly ice cream makers for home use and it's easy to see why your home kitchen can be a first-class ice cream shop and the home cook, an ice cream professional!

Freshly made ice cream and gelato is refreshing and has a wonderfully creamy texture. Both can be made in a great variety of flavors, from old favorites such as chocolate and strawberry (using strawberries picked from your garden or frozen strawberries purchased at the store) to new and exciting flavors such as pistachio, hazelnut, dulce de leche, cake batter or cookie dough. During the summer you can use whatever fruit is in season such as watermelon, cantaloupe, blueberry and mango and make the most incredible fruit ice cream and other frozen desserts.

Sorbet is very popular and currently being served regularly as a dinner dessert; at one time it was primarily used as a refresher between courses. Sorbet has become popular because it is simple to prepare, uses few ingredients (fruit, water, sugar and lemon) and has none of the fat of more traditional desserts. Sorbet is not limited to everyday fruit such as lemon and strawberries; almost any fruit in season can be used. So if you want to satisfy your sweet tooth but not be too self-indulgent, why not try an ice cream or sorbet—you can make it as simple or as exotic as you wish.

ICE CREAM MACHINES

White Mountain Electric and Manual　　**Cuisinart**　　**Musso Ice Cream 4080**

Rock Salt and Ice for Making Ice Cream

Some 35 years ago I made my first ice cream in a White Mountain ice cream maker that used the rock salt and ice method of freezing. We were clueless in trying to make it, but it certainly was a lot of fun. Sometimes called a bucket freezer that many of us remember from childhood, this ice cream maker has a large bucket with a small canister that fits into it. Today most machines come with a plastic or fiberglass bucket. The canister, made of stainless steel, has a removable lid. Inside is a stationary paddle called a dasher with blades usually made of plastic and positioned so that they gently scrape inside the canister as it turns. The canister is continuously rotated by an electric motor (which replaced a hand crank used years ago), while an equal mixture of crushed ice and rock salt is placed between the outside bucket and inside canister. This mixture freezes the ice cream. You can find this type of freezer today for about $50–$150.

The texture of the finished ice cream depends on how fast it is processed. The slower the freezer process, the smoother the texture. You can control the rate of freezing by varying the amount of salt you use with the ice. Use about three-quarters of a standard 26-ounce box of rock salt for relatively fast freezing and excellent across-the-board results. Using a whole box of salt shortens the freezing time and results in an icier texture; using half a box lengthens the freezing time and gives a finer, smoother texture. Because little air is incorporated during the churning process, the ice cream from this machine becomes very hard when stored. While this method of making ice cream is still used, it has been mostly replaced by freezers with self-contained refrigeration for use at home.

Freezer with Self-Contained Refrigeration

Cuisinart ICE-50BC Supreme Commercial-Quality Ice Cream Maker

Freezing coils are wrapped around the canister, and a motorized dasher mixes the ice cream as it freezes. This is a very easy machine to use. Just pour in the ice cream mixture and turn on the freezer. Because of the constant beating of the dasher, this type of machine makes ice cream with a very smooth texture. Its chief drawbacks are its high price—$100 to $400—and the amount of counter space it takes up.

Other Equipment for Making Ice Cream

Ice cream preparation does not require much equipment. The bowls, spoons and saucepans you use for everyday cooking can certainly be used for ice cream. The items listed here are helpful but not mandatory for making ice cream and other frozen desserts. However, the one indispensable tool is a rubber spatula for scraping ice cream from around the canister as well as smoothing icing and toppings over the finished product.

- **Scale** (preferably digital) To measure all ingredients.

- **Rubber Spatula** An indispensable tool; you should have at least three.

- **Blender or Food Processor** Either can be used to puree fruit for ice cream and sorbet.

- **Candy Thermometer** Using a candy thermometer is the best way to keep track of the changes sugar goes through as it is heated. Small instant-read thermometers sold in cookware and hardware stores also serve this purpose, in addition to being useful for baking and roasting. Be sure to get one that measures up to 2600 degrees Fahrenheit.

- **Ice Cream Spades and Scoops** Spades and scoops are usually made from a solid casting of sturdy aluminum to eliminate the possibility of handles getting bent. Nonstick scoops contain fluid antifreeze to ensure easy release of the ice cream. It is helpful to dip scoops without coolant into warm water between servings. Mechanical ice cream scoops have an arc-shaped blade that sweeps across the interior of the bowl to release the ice cream. The numbers imprinted on the handles of many scoops indicate how many scoops of that size can be removed from 1 quart of ice cream.

- **Handheld or Countertop Mixer** This is useful for combining egg yolks and sugar, as well as for blending other commonly used ingredients.

MAKING ICE CREAM

There are a number of important concepts that you, the home ice cream maker, should be aware of to improve both the overall product *and* your popularity rating!

Basic Ingredients

For ice cream to have a smooth, creamy texture, both the water molecules and fat globules in the mixture must be suspended evenly so that very small ice crystals are formed during freezing. The basic ice cream ingredients help this to happen and also add flavor. Many commercial ice cream manufacturers use emulsifiers and stabilizers to improve the texture of their products, to mask or compensate for inferior ingredients and/or to achieve an extended shelf life. Such artificial ingredients are never needed in ice cream made at home in small quantities with fresh, wholesome ingredients. The butterfat in cream is primarily responsible for providing the rich, smooth texture of the ice cream. Typically, the higher the proportion of butterfat, the richer and smoother the ice cream. As a general rule, do not exceed a ratio of 50 percent cream to 25 percent milk.

Precooling

It is important to cool an ice cream mixture thoroughly before churning it. It may be cooled slowly in the refrigerator or rapidly over an ice-water bath. If the mixture is warmer than 100 degrees Fahrenheit when the freezing process begins, the required increased churning time is likely to produce flecks of butter, especially in those recipes that call for a high proportion of cream to milk. Butter flecks are harmless but are unpleasant and will ruin the fine texture of homemade ice cream. If butter forms in a batch of ice cream, allow the ice cream to melt in the refrigerator. When the mixture is liquid, strain it through a fine sieve to remove the butter and then refreeze.

Expansion During Freezing

When filling an ice cream machine with the ice cream mixture, stop at least 2 inches below the top of the canister. As ice cream freezes, it expands slightly. Even more importantly, the churning action incorporates air. This aeration, called overrun, improves the texture of the finished ice cream and helps to prevent it from becoming a solid block of ice. If the freezing canister is filled two-thirds full and the finished ice cream reaches the top, the overrun is approximately 50 percent. If the canister is filled three-quarters full and the ice cream reaches the top, the overrun is approximately 30 percent. High-quality ice cream has 20 to 50 percent overrun. (Baskin Robbins and Carvel are examples of high overrun; Haagen-Dazs low overrun.)

Storing and Serving Temperatures

Ice cream and other frozen desserts should be stored at low temperatures to prolong their shelf life and protect their texture and flavor. The ideal temperature is between 0 degrees and 10 degrees Fahrenheit (-18 to -23 degrees Celcius). Ice cream should be allowed to warm slightly before serving; about 30 degrees Fahrenheit is an ideal serving temperature. If a container of ice cream is frozen firmly, transfer it from the freezer to the refrigerator for 20–30 minutes before serving or leave it at room temperature for 10–15 minutes. Be careful not to let ice cream thaw too much; repeated thawing and refreezing will destroy its texture.

Ripening and Eating

Ice cream custard bases can be made in advance, up to 48 hours before the ice cream is to be frozen and left to "ripen" in the freezer for several hours before serving. This improves the texture and allows time for the flavors to blend. Most homemade ice cream should be kept frozen for no more than a day or two. Ice cream stored longer develops ice crystals on top and takes on a heavy, undesirable texture. Fortunately, homemade ice cream is so delicious few cooks ever encounter this problem!

Using Fruit

Most fruit used to flavor ice cream contain naturally occurring pectin and a certain amount of fiber. Both substances help to keep milk fat and water molecules in an even suspension as they freeze. Milk fat forms small globules in the ice cream mix-ture that help to keep the water molecules dispersed.

The principles discussed above are used in making ice cream, gelato, sorbet and ices. Beginning in Chapter 7, you will find many recipes that you can make at home. Simply look for this symbol:

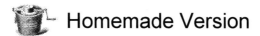 Homemade Version

REFERENCE

Gandara, Lonnie. *Ice Cream & Frozen Desserts*. The California Culinary Academy series. San Ramon, CA: Ortho Books, 1988.

7

ICE CREAM RECIPES

INTRODUCTION TO THE RECIPES IN THIS BOOK

The recipes in this book are for both commercial and home use. For those people working in gelaterias, ice cream stores and restaurants who want to prepare product at various quart capacities, the recipes include 10-quart, 20-quart and 40-quart sizes. Recipes for the home assume home-use equipment such as a Cuisinart Ice Cream Machine with a 1½ quart capacity. The recipes are a compilation of 32+ years of experience making ice cream, gelato and sorbets. All recipes have been made and tested by Malcolm Stogo (as well as by many of the hundreds of students he has worked with over the years). They include a wide range of Vanilla-based, Chocolate-based, Nut-based and Fruit-based frozen desserts.

Many of the recipes have been converted for home use. A supplier section for ingredients is included in the Appendix; if you can't find ingredients that you need, just send an email to malcolm@icecreamuniversity.org. We'll be pleased to provide the information you are looking for.

We have created a code system to help you follow the recipes in an exact sequence at a glance so that you know when to put in specific ingredients (beginning, middle, end or out of the batch):

B (**B**eginning of batch): Designates ingredients to be poured or measured directly into the batch freezer at the very start of the batch, before the refrigeration is turned on.

M (**M**iddle of batch): Designates ingredients to be added to the batch freezer after about three minutes of running the batch.

E (**E**nd of batch): Designates ingredients to be added to the batch freezer after about eight minutes of running the batch.

O (**O**ut of batch): Designates ingredients to be poured into the tubs (or into the tubs and freezer if you are working with another person) while extruding the finished product, the most difficult part of the entire operation.

Most importantly, these recipes will bring joy and pleasure to everyone who experiences them—so have fun and step back to enjoy the results!

VANILLA-BASED ICE CREAM FLAVORS

Vanilla is considered the "gold" standard of ice cream flavors. The old adage that you will always be judged by the quality of your Vanilla ice cream is as true today as it was then. It is very important that your Vanilla ice cream be the highest quality—whether French Vanilla or without egg yolks. Also, make sure you use the highest quality pure vanilla extract in your vanilla flavors. This is definitely not a flavor you want to skimp on. There is also no doubt that this will be among your best-selling flavors overall.

French Vanilla Ice Cream

This is the ultimate Vanilla ice cream recipe—and the benchmark by which others will judge the quality of your products. French Vanilla contains egg-yolk solids that enhance flavor and texture.

INGREDIENTS

10-Qt Batch	20-Qt Batch	40-Qt Batch	
1¼ gal	2½ gal	5 gal	Ice cream mix (B)
2 oz	4 oz	8 oz	Two-fold vanilla extract (B)
½ Tbsp	1 Tbsp	2 Tbsp	Vanilla specks (optional) (B)
6½ oz	13 oz	26 oz	Pasteurized eggs* (B)

*You can substitute egg base for pasteurized eggs. If you do so, use 12 ounces of egg base for a 20-quart batch and adjust accordingly for other size batches.

PREPARATION   Batch time: 8–10 minutes**

Pour all ingredients into batch freezer. Turn on the dasher, set timer to 8 minutes, turn on the refrigeration and begin the batch. When the batch is complete, turn off the refrigeration and extrude the finished product.

**If this is the first batch of the day, batch time is 9–11 minutes. When extruding the finished product from the batch freezer, make sure the product is firm.

MALCOLM SAYS: If you want to make a great Vanilla ice cream, be sure to use egg yolks.

 ## Homemade Version

Crank up your ice cream maker and treat yourself to the best Vanilla ice cream you've ever had!

INGREDIENTS

8	Egg yolks
8 oz	Sugar
16 oz	Milk
16 oz	Heavy cream
1 Tbsp	Vanilla extract

PREPARATION

Use a double boiler to create a custard base. Pour the egg yolks, sugar and milk into the pot. Heat the mixture slowly but do *not* bring to a boil. When a film forms over the back of your spoon, remove custard base from heat and place the pot into a larger pot filled with cold water to cool. Add in heavy cream and place in refrigerator until cold (at least 2 hours). Then stir in vanilla extract and transfer to an ice cream maker. Freeze according to manufacturer's instructions. Turn off refrigeration and extrude the finished product. Yield: 1½ quarts of ice cream

Philadelphia Vanilla Ice Cream (1)

Philadelphia Vanilla is made without egg yolks, strictly cream and vanilla extract. The finished product is much whiter-looking than French Vanilla.

INGREDIENTS

10-Qt Batch	20-Qt Batch	40-Qt Batch	
1¼ gal	2½ gal	5 gal	Ice cream mix (B)
2 oz	4 oz	8 oz	Two-fold vanilla extract (B)
½ Tbsp	1 Tbsp	2 Tbsp	Vanilla specks (optional) (B)

PREPARATION   Batch time: 8–10 minutes

Pour all ingredients into batch freezer. Turn on the dasher, set timer to 8 minutes, turn on the refrigeration and begin the batch. When the batch is complete, turn off refrigeration and extrude the finished product.

MALCOLM SAYS: You can also make great ice cream with an ice cream mix that has no egg yolks. In fact, a majority of all ice cream produced in independent ice cream shops is made this way.

 Homemade Version

Some people like egg yolks in their ice cream; others don't. This is a great Vanilla ice cream made without eggs.

INGREDIENTS

7 oz	Sugar
16 oz	Milk
16 oz	Heavy cream
1 Tbsp	Vanilla extract

PREPARATION

Use a double boiler to create a custard base. Pour the egg yolks, sugar and milk into the pot. Heat the mixture slowly but do *not* bring to a boil. When a film forms over the back of your spoon, remove custard base from heat and place the pot into a larger pot filled with cold water to cool. Add in heavy cream and place in refrigerator until cold (at least 2 hours). Then stir in vanilla extract and transfer to an ice cream maker. Freeze according to manufacturer's instructions. Turn off the refrigeration and extrude the finished product. Yield: 1½ quarts of ice cream

Philadelphia Vanilla Ice Cream (2)

This is a fabulous Vanilla ice cream recipe from The Grateful Bean Café in Oklahoma City. The café won "Best of Oklahoma City" for its great ice cream, and this flavor defines what the café is all about: excellence. The Irish cream extract is used to create color and add a subtle taste to the overall flavor. This ice cream is made without egg yolks.

INGREDIENTS

10-Qt Batch	20-Qt Batch	40-Qt Batch	
1¼ gal	2½ gal	5 gal	Ice cream mix (B)
1 oz	2 oz	4 oz	Two-fold Tahitian vanilla extract* (B)
2 oz	4 oz	8 oz	Indonesian vanilla extract* (B)
2 oz	4 oz	8 oz	Madagascar Bourbon vanilla (B)
¼ tsp	½ tsp	1 tsp	Irish cream extract* (B)
2 oz	4 oz	8 oz	Malted milk powder (B)

*The general rule for using extracts is 1 ounce of extract per gallon of ice cream mix. But you may prefer to adjust to your own taste.

PREPARATION   Batch time: 8–10 minutes

Pour all ingredients into batch freezer. Turn on the dasher, set timer to 8 minutes, turn on the refrigeration and begin the batch. When the batch is complete, turn off refrigeration and extrude the finished product.

Honey Vanilla Ice Cream

There was a time in the late 1960s and early '70s when honey-based ice creams were all the rage. Even Haagen-Dazs produced a Honey ice cream that sold like hot cakes. With the popularity of organic foods today, it is very possible that Honey Vanilla ice cream will make a comeback.

INGREDIENTS

10-Qt Batch	20-Qt Batch	40-Qt Batch	
1¼ gal	2½ gal	5 gal	Ice cream mix (B)
1½ oz	3 oz	6 oz	Madagascar Bourbon vanilla (B)
16 oz	32 oz	64 oz	Dark blossom honey (E)

PREPARATION   Batch time: 8–10 minutes

Pour ice cream mix and vanilla into the batch freezer. Turn on the dasher, set the timer to 8 minutes, turn on refrigeration and begin the batch. When the batch is complete, add in the honey, turn off refrigeration and extrude the finished product.

Biscotti Ice Cream

My clients Tony and Marc Boccaccio of Fresco Desserts, Holbrook, NY, spoil me. They're always giving me their amazing biscotti. So the natural thing for me to do was create ice cream with biscotti!

INGREDIENTS

10-Qt Batch	20-Qt Batch	40-Qt Batch	
1 lb	2 lb	4 lb	Tempered chocolate (candy melts) (B)
1½ lb	3 lb	6 lb	Almond or hazelnut biscotti: ½ (B), ½ (E)
1¼ gal	2½ gal	5 gal	Ice cream mix (B)
2 oz	4 oz	8 oz	Two-fold vanilla extract (B)
½ oz	1 oz	2 oz	Almond or hazelnut extract (B)

PREPARATION   Batch time: 8–10 minutes

Melt tempered chocolate in a double boiler. Dip biscotti in the chocolate and harden in refrigerator before cutting them into small pieces. Pour ice cream mix, vanilla and almond extracts and ½ of the biscotti cookie pieces into the batch freezer. Turn on dasher, set timer to 8 minutes, turn on refrigeration and begin the batch. When the batch is complete, add in the rest of the biscotti pieces, turn off the refrigeration and extrude the finished product.

MALCOLM SAYS: The reason to dip the biscotti cookies in the chocolate is to prevent the cookies from becoming mealy in the finished product.

 ## Homemade Version

You don't have to be Italian to enjoy making Biscotti Cookie ice cream for your family!

INGREDIENTS

8	Egg yolks	1 Tbsp	Vanilla, almond or hazelnut extract
8 oz	Sugar	4 oz	Tempered chocolate
16 oz	Milk	6 oz	Almond or hazelnut biscotti
16 oz	Heavy cream		

PREPARATION

Use a double boiler to create a custard base. Pour the egg yolks, sugar and milk into the pot. Heat the mixture slowly but do *not* bring to a boil. When a film forms over the back of your spoon, remove the custard base from heat and place the pot into a larger pot filled with cold water to cool. Add in heavy cream and place in refrigerator until cold (at least 2 hours). Then stir in vanilla extract and transfer to an ice cream maker. Freeze according to manufacturer's instructions. Melt tempered chocolate in a double boiler. Dip biscotti in the chocolate and harden in the refrigerator before cutting into small pieces. Add biscotti pieces to the ice cream, turn off refrigeration and extrude the finished product. Yield: 1½ quarts of ice cream

Biscuit Tortoni Ice Cream

Sweet sherry and almond cookies make this flavor a hit in restaurants and upscale ice cream shops.

INGREDIENTS

10-Qt Batch	20-Qt Batch	40-Qt Batch	
1¼ gal	2½ gal	5 gal	Ice cream mix (B)
1 oz	2 oz	4 oz	Two-fold vanilla extract (B)
¾ oz	1½ oz	3 oz	Almond extract (B)
5 oz	10 oz	20 oz	Sweet sherry or sherry extract (M)
12 oz	24 oz	48 oz	Almond cookies, crushed (E)
			Almond cookie pieces and sliced almonds (O)

PREPARATION   Batch time: 8–10 minutes

Pour all ingredients except the almond and sherry extracts and almond cookies into the batch freezer. Turn on the dasher, set timer to 8 minutes, turn on refrigeration and begin the batch. Midway through the batch, add in the sweet sherry or sherry extract. When the batch is complete, add in the crushed almond cookies, turn off refrigeration and extrude the finished product. Decorate tops of tubs with cookie pieces and sliced almonds.

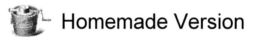 ## Homemade Version

This is a wonderful flavor to make during the winter holiday season.

INGREDIENTS

8	Egg yolks	1 tsp	Almond extract
8 oz	Sugar	2 oz	Sliced almonds
16 oz	Milk	2 oz	Sweet sherry
16 oz	Heavy cream	4 oz	Crushed almond cookies
1 Tbsp	Vanilla extract		

PREPARATION

Use a double boiler to create a custard base. Pour the egg yolks, sugar and milk into the pot. Heat the mixture slowly but do *not* bring to a boil. When a film forms over the back of your spoon, remove custard base from heat and place the pot into a larger pot filled with cold water to cool. Add in heavy cream and place in refrigerator until cold (at least 2 hours). Then stir in vanilla and almond extracts and transfer to an ice cream maker. Freeze according to manufacturer's instructions. Add in the sliced almonds, sweet sherry and crushed almond cookies, turn off the refrigeration and extrude the finished product. Yield: 1½ quarts of ice cream

Vanilla Chocolate Chip Ice Cream

This is an old-fashioned flavor popular with children. It's similar to French Vanilla with chocolate chips added, or use large chocolate chunks so you can see them and get the "taste" of chocolate.

INGREDIENTS

10-Qt Batch	20-Qt Batch	40-Qt Batch	
1¼ gal	2½ gal	5 gal	Ice cream mix (B)
2 oz	4 oz	8 oz	Two-fold vanilla extract (B)
1¼ lb	2½ lb	5 lb	Chocolate chips or chunks: ½ (B), ½ (E)
4 oz	8 oz	16 oz	Liquid chocolate* (E)

PREPARATION   Batch time: 8–10 minutes

Pour ice cream mix, vanilla extract and ½ of the chocolate chips or chunks into the batch freezer. Turn on dasher, set timer to 8 minutes, turn on refrigeration and begin the batch. When the batch is complete, add in remainder of chocolate chips and liquid chocolate, turn off refrigeration and extrude finished product. Decorate tops of tubs with chocolate chips and liquid chocolate.

MALCOLM SAYS: Why I like and use liquid chocolate so much is because it creates a dimension that makes it different from most chocolate chip ice creams—and customers love it!

 Homemade Version

INGREDIENTS

8	Egg yolks	1 Tbsp	Vanilla extract
8 oz	Sugar	5 oz	Chocolate chips or chunks
16 oz	Milk	2 oz	Liquid chocolate*
16 oz	Heavy Cream		

PREPARATION

Use a double boiler to create a custard base. Pour the egg yolks, sugar and milk into the pot. Heat the mixture slowly but do *not* bring to a boil. When a film forms over the back of your spoon, remove custard base from heat and place the pot into a larger pot filled with cold water to cool. Add in heavy cream and place in refrigerator until cold (at least 2 hours). Then stir in vanilla extract and transfer to an ice cream maker. Freeze according to manufacturer's instructions. Add in the chocolate chips and liquid chocolate, turn off refrigeration and extrude the finished product. Yield: 1½ quarts of ice cream

*To make the liquid chocolate, melt in a double boiler 5 parts chocolate (any flavor chocolate bar) to 1 part vegetable oil by weight. Mix thoroughly with a spatula, then pour into a measuring container.

Chocolate Chunk Mint Ice Cream

If you want the flavor to look green, add a bit of green food coloring to the ice cream base. However, with the emphasis today on natural products, you just might want to leave out the coloring.

INGREDIENTS

10-Qt Batch	20-Qt Batch	40-Qt Batch	
1¼ gal	2½ gal	5 gal	Ice cream mix (B)
1¼ oz	2½ oz	5 oz	Two-fold vanilla extract (B)
8 oz	16 oz	32 oz	Menta flavoring (B)
1½ lb	3 lb	6 lb	Soft chocolate chips or chunks: ⅓ (B), ⅔ (E)
6 oz	12 oz	24 oz	Liquid chocolate* (E)

PREPARATION   Batch time: 8–10 minutes

Pour ice cream mix, vanilla extract, menta flavoring and ⅓ of the chocolate chips or chunks into the batch freezer, set timer to 8 minutes, turn on refrigeration and begin the batch. When the batch is complete, add in remainder of chocolate chunks and the liquid chocolate, turn off the refrigeration and extrude the finished product. Decorate tops of tubs with chocolate chunks and liquid chocolate.

MALCOLM SAYS: **I prefer menta flavoring for its overall flavor profile.**

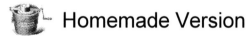 ## Homemade Version

Everyone loves mint, so here's a chance to be as minty as you want! But keep in mind that too much will spoil the taste.

INGREDIENTS

8	Egg yolks	1 Tbsp	Vanilla extract
8 oz	Sugar	1 tsp	Mint or peppermint extract
16 oz	Milk	5 oz	Chocolate chips
16 oz	Heavy cream	2 oz	Liquid chocolate*

PREPARATION

Use a double boiler to create a custard base. Pour the egg yolks, sugar and milk into the pot. Heat the mixture slowly but do *not* bring to a boil. When a film forms over the back of your spoon, remove base from heat and place the pot into a larger pot filled with cold water to cool. Add in heavy cream and place in refrigerator until cold (at least 2 hours). Then stir in vanilla extract and transfer to an ice cream maker. Freeze according to manufacturer's instructions. Then add chocolate chips and liquid chocolate, turn off refrigeration and extrude the finished product. Yield: 1½ quarts of ice cream

*To make liquid chocolate, melt in a double boiler 5 parts chocolate (any flavor chocolate bar) to 1 part vegetable oil by weight.

Cinnamon Bun Ice Cream

If you like cinnamon buns for breakfast, then you will surely love this ice cream flavor for dessert. This flavor was originally developed by Star Kay White, but I later enhanced it to what you see here.

INGREDIENTS

10-Qt Batch	20-Qt Batch	40-Qt Batch	
1¼ gal	2½ gal	5 gal	Ice cream mix (B)
1 oz	2 oz	4 oz	Two-fold vanilla extract (B)
10 oz	20 oz	40 oz	Caramel base emulsion (B)
12 oz	24 oz	48 oz	Raisin fruit (E)
8 oz	16 oz	32 oz	Pecan pieces, dark roasted (E)
2¼ lb	4½ lb	9 lb	Caramel cinnamon variegate (O)

PREPARATION   Batch time: 8–10 minutes

Pour ice cream mix, vanilla extract and caramel base emulsion into the batch freezer. Turn on the dasher, set timer to 8 minutes, turn on refrigeration and begin the batch. When the batch is complete, add in the raisin fruit and pecan pieces. Turn off the refrigeration and slowly swirl the caramel cinnamon variegate into the tubs and extrude the finished product. Decorate tops of tubs with raisin fruit, pecan pieces and caramel cinnamon variegate.

 Homemade Version

If you like to eat messy but delicious cinnamon buns that are sold at airports and malls, then you will really enjoy making this delicious ice cream at home.

INGREDIENTS

8	Egg yolks	1 Tbsp	Vanilla extract
8 oz	Sugar	¼ tsp	Dry cinnamon
16 oz	Milk	2	Cinnamon buns, crumbled
16 oz	Heavy cream		

PREPARATION

Use a double boiler to create a custard base. Pour egg yolks, sugar and milk into the pot. Heat the mixture slowly but do *not* bring to a boil. When a film forms over the back of your spoon, remove custard base from heat and place the pot into a larger pot filled with cold water to cool. Add in heavy cream and place in refrigerator until cold (at least 2 hours). Then stir in vanilla extract and dry cinnamon and transfer to an ice cream maker. Freeze according to manufacturer's instructions. Add in the crumbled cinnamon buns, turn off refrigeration and extrude the finished product. Yield: 1½ quarts of ice cream

Coconut Almond Joy Ice Cream

Tastes just like the candy bar!

INGREDIENTS

10-Qt Batch	20-Qt Batch	40-Qt Batch	
1¼ gal	2½ gal	5 gal	Ice cream mix (B)
2 oz	4 oz	8 oz	Two-fold vanilla extract (B)
1 qt	2 qt	4 qt	Coconut fruit base (B)
¾ qt	1½ qt	3 qt	Fudge (O)
4 oz	8 oz	16 oz	Shredded coconut (M)
4 oz	8 oz	16 oz	Chocolate chips (M)
1 lb	2 lb	4 lb	Almonds (M)

PREPARATION   Batch time: 8–10 minutes

Pour the ice cream mix, vanilla extract and coconut fruit base into the batch freezer. Turn on dasher, set timer to 8 minutes, turn on refrigeration and begin the batch. While batch is running, heat fudge in a food warmer or keep at room temperature until loosened up and creamy. Spread inner lining of tubs with the fudge. When the batch is almost complete, add in the shredded coconut, chocolate chips and almonds and continue freezing for 2–3 minutes. Turn off refrigeration and slowly swirl the fudge into the tubs as you extrude the finished product. Decorate tops of tubs with coconut, chocolate chips, fudge and almonds.

 Homemade Version

INGREDIENTS

8	Egg yolks	1 Tbsp	Vanilla extract
8 oz	Sugar	6	Almond Joy candy bar pieces
16 oz	Milk	½ oz	Shredded coconut
16 oz	Heavy cream		

PREPARATION

Use a double boiler to create a custard base. Pour the egg yolks, sugar and milk into the pot. Heat the mixture slowly but do *not* bring to a boil. When a film forms over the back of your spoon, remove custard base from heat and place the pot into a larger pot filled with cold water to cool. Add in heavy cream and place in refrigerator until cold (at least 2 hours). Then stir in vanilla extract and transfer to an ice cream maker. Freeze according to manufacturer's instructions. Add in the candy bar pieces and shredded coconut, turn off the refrigeration and extrude the finished product. Yield:1½ quarts of ice cream

MALCOLM SAYS: Freeze the candy bars *first* so they are easier to cut into small pieces.

Cookie Dough Ice Cream

INGREDIENTS

10-Qt Batch	20-Qt Batch	40-Qt Batch	
1¼ gal	2½ gal	5 gal	Ice cream mix (B)
1 oz	2 oz	4 oz	Two-fold vanilla extract (B)
2 lb	4 lb	8 lb	Cookie dough pieces: ½ (B), ½ (E)
5 oz	10 oz	20 oz	Chocolate chips (E)
½ qt	1 qt	2 qt	Fudge (E)
½ lb	1 lb	2 lb	Chocolate chip cookies (E)

PREPARATION   Batch time: 8–10 minutes

Pour ice cream mix, vanilla extract and ½ of the cookie dough pieces into the batch freezer. Turn on dasher, set timer to 8 minutes, turn on refrigeration and begin the batch. While the batch is running, heat fudge in a food warmer or keep at room temperature until loosened up and creamy. Spread inner lining of tubs with fudge. When the batch is complete, turn off the refrigeration, slowly swirl the fudge into the tubs and add the rest of the cookie dough pieces, chocolate chips and chocolate chip cookies as you extrude the finished product. Decorate tops of tubs with cookie dough pieces.

 Homemade Version

You must make this ice cream with your kids. Why? Because it's their favorite flavor!

INGREDIENTS

8	Egg yolks	1 Tbsp	Vanilla extract
8 oz	Sugar	4 oz	Cookie dough
16 oz	Milk	5 oz	Chocolate chips
16 oz	Heavy cream		

PREPARATION

Use a double boiler to create a custard base. Pour egg yolks, sugar and milk into the pot. Heat the mixture slowly but do *not* bring to a boil. When a film forms over the back of your spoon, remove custard base from heat and place the pot into a larger pot filled with cold water to cool. Add in heavy cream and place in refrigerator until cold (at least 2 hours). Then stir in vanilla extract and transfer to an ice cream maker. Freeze according to manufacturer's instructions. Freeze the cookie dough for about 1 hour, remove from freezer, cut into small pieces and add them along with the chocolate chips into ice cream. Turn off the refrigeration and extrude the finished product. Yield:1½ quarts of ice cream

MALCOLM SAYS: Since this flavor is a major hit with kids, you will probably have lots of demand to make it. Freeze the cookie dough *first* so that it will be easier to cut into small pieces.

Cookie Galore Ice Cream

Cookies & Cream is probably one of the top-selling ice cream flavors ever invented, but, honestly, everyone offers it. To be really different, try this recipe. It will be a great addition to your ice cream menu.

INGREDIENTS

10-Qt Batch	20-Qt Batch	40-Qt Batch	
1¼ gal	2½ gal	5 gal	Ice cream mix (B)
2 oz	4 oz	8 oz	Two-fold vanilla extract (B)
16 oz	32 oz	64 oz	Oreo cookies, broken: ¼ (B), ¾ (O)
16 oz	2 lb	4 lb	Chocolate chip cookies: ¼ (B), ¾ (O)
½ qt	1 qt	2 qt	Hot fudge (O)

PREPARATION   Batch time: 8–10 minutes

Pour ice cream mix, vanilla extract and ¼ of the Oreo and chocolate chip cookies into the batch freezer. Turn on dasher, set timer to 8 minutes, turn on refrigeration and begin the batch. While batch is running, spread inner lining of tubs with hot fudge. When the batch is complete, turn off refrigeration and add in the remaining Oreo and chocolate chip cookies. Then slowly swirl the hot fudge into the tubs as you extrude the finished product. Decorate tops of tubs with the cookies.

MALCOLM SAYS: If you want your finished ice cream to look white with lots of big cookie pieces, hand feed the cookies into the tubs at the end of the batch.

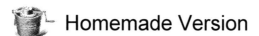 ## Homemade Version

It's an eating-dessert frenzy, just for kids!

INGREDIENTS

8	Egg yolks	1 Tbsp	Vanilla extract
8 oz	Sugar	12 oz	Oreo cookies in pieces
16 oz	Milk	12 oz	Chocolate chip cookie pieces
16 oz	Heavy cream	12 oz	Hot fudge

PREPARATION

Use a double boiler to create a custard base. Pour the egg yolks, sugar and milk into the pot. Heat the mixture slowly but do *not* bring to a boil. When a film forms over the back of your spoon, remove custard base from heat and place the pot into a larger pot filled with cold water to cool. Add in heavy cream and place in refrigerator until cold (at least 2 hours). Stir in vanilla extract and transfer to an ice cream maker. Freeze according to manufacturer's instructions. Add all the cookie pieces into the ice cream maker and continue freezing for 1 minute. Turn off the refrigeration and extrude finished product while layering the fudge into the ice cream in the container. Yield: 1½ quarts of ice cream

Crème Caramel Ice Cream

This is clearly one of the best-selling flavors at Longford's Ice Cream of Port Chester, New York. I particularly love the succulent creamy mouth feel after each delicious bite.

INGREDIENTS

10-Qt Batch	20-Qt Batch	40-Qt Batch	
1¼ gal	2½ gal	5 gal	Ice cream mix (B)
2 oz	4 oz	8 oz	Two-fold vanilla extract (B)
6 oz	12 oz	24 oz	Caramel base (B)
24 oz	48 oz	96 oz	Caramel fudge (O)

PREPARATION   Batch time: 8–10 minutes

Pour ice cream mix, vanilla extract and caramel base into the batch freezer. Turn on dasher, set timer for 8 minutes, turn on refrigeration and begin batch. When batch is complete, turn off refrigeration and slowly swirl the caramel fudge into the tubs with a pastry bag* as you extrude finished product. Decorate tops of tubs with caramel.

*Longford's uses a pastry bag to swirl the caramel into the tubs. It gives an even, con-trollable distribution of caramel.

Dulce de Leche (Caramel) Ice Cream

Originally introduced by Haagen-Dazs in South America, it is among the top-selling flavors. The name in English means "caramelized sweet milk."

INGREDIENTS

10-Qt Batch	20-Qt Batch	40-Qt Batch	
1¼ gal	2½ gal	5 gal	Ice cream mix (B)
1 oz	2 oz	4 oz	Two-fold vanilla extract (B)
1¼ lb	2½ lb	5 lb	Caramel base (Star Kay White-8951) (B)
2¼ lb	4½ lb	9 lb	Caramel Kremia variegate (Star Kay White 1PE) (O)

PREPARATION   Batch time: 8–10 minutes

Pour all ingredients except the Caramel Kremia variegate into the batch freezer. Turn on the dasher and run for 1 minute, set timer to 8 minutes, turn on refrigeration and begin the batch. When the batch is complete, turn off refrigeration and slowly swirl the Caramel Kremia variegate into the tubs as you extrude the finished product. Decorate tops of tubs with Caramel Kremia variegate.

VARIATION

DULCE DE LECHE EXTRAVAGANZA: For a 20-quart batch, add 1 pound each of choc-olate chips and pecan pralines at the end of the batch. Adjust accordingly for other size batches.

Gianduja (Chocolate & Hazelnut) Ice Cream

INGREDIENTS

10-Qt Batch	20-Qt Batch	40-Qt Batch	
1¼ gal	2½ gal	5 gal	Ice cream mix (B)
1¼ oz	2½ oz	5 oz	Two-fold pure vanilla extract (B)
1¼ lb	2½ lb	5 lb	Gianduja paste* (B)
¾ lb	1½ lb	3 lb	Hazelnut pieces, chopped, dry roasted, without salt: ½ (B), ½ (E)
8 oz	16 oz	32 oz	Chocolate chunks (E)

*Substitute for gianduja paste:

10-Qt Batch	20-Qt Batch	40-Qt Batch	
¾ lb	1½ lb	3 lb	Cocoa (B)
1¼ lb	2½ lb	5 lb	Filbert paste (B)

PREPARATION
Batch time: 8–10 minutes

Pour the ice cream mix, vanilla extract, gianduja paste, and ½ of the hazelnut pieces into batch freezer. Turn on dasher, set timer to 8 minutes, turn on refrigeration and begin the batch. When the batch is complete, add in the remaining hazelnut pieces and chocolate chunks, turn off refrigeration and extrude the finished product.

MALCOLM SAYS: If the name "Gianduja" is unfamiliar to your customers, simply call it "Chocolate Hazelnut."

Fresh Ginger Ice Cream

This is a favorite of Maraline Olson of Screamin' Mimi's in Sebastopol, California, who says, "I cannot keep it in stock." Need I say more?

INGREDIENTS

10-Qt Batch	20-Qt Batch	40-Qt Batch	
1 lb	2 lb	4 lb	Fresh ginger root (yield: 8 oz juice) (B)
1¼ gal	2½ gal	5 gal	Ice cream mix (B)
1 oz	2 oz	4 oz	Two-fold Tahitian vanilla extract (B)
1¼ lb	2½ lb	5 lb	Candied ginger pieces (E)

PREPARATION
Batch time: 8–10 minutes

Use a fruit juicer to juice the ginger root. (You may need more than what is called for to obtain 8 ounces of juice.) Pour the ice cream mix, vanilla extract and ginger juice into the batch freezer, turn on the dasher and blend for 1 minute. Then set the timer to 8 minutes, turn on refrigeration and begin the batch. When the batch is complete, add in ginger pieces, turn off refrigeration and extrude finished product. Decorate tops of tubs with ginger pieces.

MALCOLM SAYS: There are many variations with ginger; I like it with mango.

Green Mint Chip Ice Cream

Here is another terrific recipe from Denise's Ice Cream in Columbus, Ohio. What Stan Zafran likes best about this flavor is that it doesn't taste like toothpaste! It has a very subtle mint flavor and is made with organic peppermint leaves and semisweet chocolate flakes.

INGREDIENTS

10-Qt Batch	20-Qt Batch	40-Qt Batch	
1½ lb	3 lb	6 lb	Semisweet chocolate flakes: (E)
1¼ gal	2½ gal	5 gal	Ice cream mix (B)
1¼ oz	2½ oz	5 oz	Two-fold vanilla extract (B)
½ oz	1 oz	2 oz	Organic peppermint leaves in powder form* (B)
½ oz	1 oz	2 oz	Pure peppermint extract (B)

*Use a food processor to grind down peppermint leaves into powder form.

PREPARATION
Batch time: 8–10 minutes

Freeze the semisweet chocolate flakes. Pour the rest of the ingredients into the batch freezer. Turn on the dasher, set timer to 8 minutes, turn on refrigeration and begin the batch. When batch is complete, add in the chocolate flakes, turn off refrigeration and extrude the finished product. Decorate tops of tubs with chocolate flakes.

MALCOLM SAYS: It's entrepreneurs like Stan Zafran who have lots of passion and are always looking for out-of-the-box ways to make flavors. This one is a prime example. It tastes great!

Honey Almond Brickle Ice Cream

The addition of praline almonds to this honey-based ice cream results in an very delicious flavor.

INGREDIENTS

10-Qt Batch	20-Qt Batch	40-Qt Batch	
1¼ gal	2½ gal	5 gal	Ice cream mix (B)
1½ oz	3 oz	6 oz	Madagascar Bourbon vanilla (B)
16 oz	32 oz	64 oz	Dark blossom honey (E)
8 oz	16 oz	32 oz	Praline almonds (E)

PREPARATION
Batch time: 8–10 minutes

Pour the ice cream mix and vanilla into the batch freezer. Turn on the dasher, set timer to 8 minutes, turn on refrigeration and begin the batch. When the batch is complete, add in the honey and praline almonds, turn off refrigeration and extrude the finished product.

Kulfi Ice Cream

Kulfi is the traditional Indian ice cream and has a strong cooked-milk flavor and a dense texture.

INGREDIENTS

10-Qt Batch	20-Qt Batch	40-Qt Batch	
1¼ gal	2½ gal	5 gal	Ice cream mix (B)
3½ oz	7 oz	14 oz	Rosewater (B)
1 oz	2 oz	4 oz	Ground cardamom (B)
1 lb	2 lb	4 lb	Pistachios, finely granulated (B)

PREPARATION   Batch time: 8–10 minutes

Pour all ingredients into the batch freezer. Turn on dasher, set timer to 8 minutes, turn on refrigeration and begin the batch. When the batch is complete, turn off the refrigeration and extrude the finished product. Decorate with pistachio pieces.

MALCOLM SAYS: In India, Kulfi is served in cone-shaped, lidded metal containers that are rubbed between the hands to warm and release the flavor of the ice cream. It is a very time-consuming flavor to prepare and I am not sure it is suited to an American palate. The overall taste is interesting and makes a terrific dessert after an Indian curry meal. Make sure the pistachios are finely granulated to create a feeling of nut flavor without actually seeing or eating the pistachio nut itself.

 ## Homemade Version

If you are preparing a festive Indian dinner, then making this ice cream flavor is a must!

INGREDIENTS

8	Egg yolks	1 Tbsp	Vanilla extract
8 oz	Sugar	½ tsp	Cardamom
16 oz	Milk	2 oz	Rosewater
16 oz	Heavy cream	4 oz	Pistachios, unsalted, roasted, finely granulated

PREPARATION

Use a double boiler to create a custard base. Pour the egg yolks, sugar and milk into the pot. Heat the mixture slowly but do *not* bring to a boil. When a film forms over the back of your spoon, remove custard base from heat and place the pot into a larger pot filled with cold water to cool. Add in heavy cream and place in refrigerator until cold (at least 2 hours). Then stir in vanilla extract, cardamom, rosewater and pistachios and transfer to an ice cream maker. Freeze according to manufacturer's instructions. Turn off the refrigeration and extrude the finished product. Yield: 1½ quarts of ice cream

MALCOLM SAYS: To make this flavor truly unique, add in candied fruit pieces at the end.

Lemon Custard Ice Cream

If you follow this recipe to a T, you'll make a wonderful lemon ice cream. If you recall the taste of the lemon filling in a lemon meringue pie, you'll be able to duplicate it by making your own lemon curd.

INGREDIENTS

10-Qt Batch	20-Qt Batch	40-Qt Batch	
1¼ gal	2½ gal	5 gal	Ice cream mix (B)
2 oz	4 oz	8 oz	Two-fold vanilla extract (B)
12 oz	24 oz	48 oz	Lemon curd* (B)
24 oz	48 oz	96 oz	Lemon curd for variegating (O)

PREPARATION   Batch time: 8–10 minutes

Pour ice cream mix, vanilla extract and lemon curd into the batch freezer. Turn on dasher, set timer to 8 minutes, turn on refrigeration and begin the batch. When the batch is complete, turn off the refrigeration and slowly swirl the lemon curd for variegating into the tubs as you extrude the finished product.

 Homemade Version

INGREDIENTS

8	Egg yolks	1 Tbsp	Vanilla extract
6 oz	Sugar	12 oz	Lemon curd*
16 oz	Milk	8 oz	Lemon juice
16 oz	Heavy cream		

*You can either purchase lemon curd at a food specialty store or make it yourself. If you choose the latter, simply adapt the recipe shown below.

PREPARATION

Use a double boiler to create a custard base. Pour egg yolks, sugar and milk into the pot. Heat the mixture slowly but do *not* bring to a boil. When a film forms over the back of your spoon, remove custard base from heat and place the pot into a larger pot filled with cold water to cool. Add in heavy cream and place in refrigerator until cold (at least 2 hours). Then stir in vanilla extract, lemon curd and lemon juice, and transfer to an ice cream maker. Freeze according to manufacturer's instructions. Turn off refrigeration and extrude finished product. Yield: 1½ quarts of ice cream

*To Make Lemon Curd for a 20-Qt Batch:

24 oz	Fresh lemon juice	30	Whole eggs
7 lb	Sugar, granulated	½ lb	Egg yolks
2¾ oz	Gelatin	4½ lb	Sweet butter

Heat lemon juice. Add in sugar, gelatin, whole eggs and egg yolks. When hot, add butter and cook until thick, then strain into a container and cool. To use lemon curd later, warm it slightly in a double boiler and whip in a mixer. Freeze unused portion.

Mint Pattie Ice Cream

I have tasted mint from many companies, but nothing compares to the taste of Fabbri's mint paste.

INGREDIENTS

10-Qt Batch	20-Qt Batch	40-Qt Batch	
1¼ gal	2½ gal	5 gal	Ice cream mix (B)
1¼ oz	2½ oz	5 oz	Two-fold vanilla extract (B)
8 oz	16 oz	32 oz	Menta paste (B)
8 oz	1 lb	2 lb	Soft chocolate chunks: ⅓ (B), ⅔ (E)
1 lb	2 lb	4 lb	Peppermint Mint Patties (E)

PREPARATION   Batch time: 8–10 minutes

Pour ice cream mix, vanilla extract, menta paste and ⅓ of the chocolate chunks into the batch freezer. Turn on dasher, set timer to 8 minutes, turn on refrigeration and begin batch. When the batch is complete, turn off the refrigeration, add in Peppermint Mint Patties and remainder of chocolate chunks and extrude finished product. Decorate tops of tubs with Peppermint Mint Patties and chocolate chunks.

 Homemade Version

This is a fun flavor, especially when you add the Peppermint Patties!

INGREDIENTS

8	Egg yolks	1 tsp	Mint or peppermint extract
8 oz	Sugar	5 oz	Chocolate chips
16 oz	Milk	2 oz	Liquid chocolate*
16 oz	Heavy cream	4 oz	Peppermint Mint Patties
1 Tbsp	Vanilla extract		

PREPARATION

Use a double boiler to create a custard base. Pour egg yolks, sugar and milk into the pot. Heat the mixture slowly but do *not* bring to a boil. When a film forms over the back of your spoon, remove custard base from heat and place the pot into a larger pot filled with cold water to cool. Add in heavy cream and place in refrigerator until cold (at least 2 hours). Then stir in vanilla extract and mint extract and transfer to an ice cream maker. Freeze according to manufacturer's instructions. Then add in chocolate chips, liquid chocolate and Peppermint Mint Patties. Turn off the refrigeration and extrude the finished product. Yield: 1½ quarts of ice cream

*To make liquid chocolate, melt in a double boiler 5 parts chocolate (any flavor chocolate bar) to 1 part vegetable oil by weight.

Oreo Ice Cream

From Denise's Ice Cream of Columbus, Ohio are Denise and Stan Zafran's own creation! It's like eating cookies and cream, not just Oreo cookies in Vanilla ice cream.

INGREDIENTS

10-Qt Batch	20-Qt Batch	40-Qt Batch	
1½ lb	2½ lb	5 lb	Oreo cookie pieces (E)
1¼ gal	2½ gal	5 gal	Ice cream mix (B)
1¼ oz	2½ oz	5 oz	Two-fold vanilla extract (B)
2¼ oz	4½ oz	9 oz	Heavy cream* (B)

*If you want to beef up the butterfat of your ice cream mix, add 7½ ounces of heavy cream to a 14% ice cream mix or 4½ ounces to a 16% mix.

PREPARATION   Batch time: 8–10 minutes

Freeze the Oreo cookie pieces prior to the start of production. Pour the ice cream mix, vanilla extract and heavy cream into the batch freezer. Turn on the dasher, set timer to 8 minutes, turn on the refrigeration and begin the batch. When the batch is complete, add in the cookie pieces, turn off refrigeration and extrude the finished product. Decorate tops of tubs with cookie pieces.

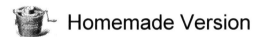 ## Homemade Version

This is every kid's favorite flavor, make no bones about it!

INGREDIENTS

8	Egg yolks	16 oz	Heavy cream
8 oz	Sugar	1 Tbsp	Vanilla extract
16 oz	Milk	1 lb	Oreo cookie pieces

PREPARATION

Use a double boiler to create a custard base. Pour egg yolks, sugar and milk into the pot. Heat the mixture slowly but do *not* bring to a boil. When a film forms over the back of your spoon, remove custard base from heat and place the pot into a larger pot filled with cold water to cool. Add in heavy cream and place in refrigerator until cold (at least 2 hours). Then stir in vanilla extract and transfer to an ice cream maker. Freeze according to manufacturer's instructions. Add in the Oreo cookie pieces and continue freezing for 1 minute, turn off the refrigeration and extrude the finished product. Yield: 1½ quarts of ice cream

Rice Pudding Ice Cream

Simply put, I love rice pudding. When I invented this flavor, I served it to a large group and it was a major success. The following year, I perfected it even more with input from instructors and students at one of my ice cream seminars. It's possible that someone, like Ben & Jerry's, will produce this flavor someday and say they invented it. You'll know better. Remember this date: April, 1998!

INGREDIENTS

10-Qt Batch	20-Qt Batch	40-Qt Batch	
1¼ gal	2½ gal	5 gal	Ice cream mix (B)
2 oz	4 oz	8 oz	Two-fold vanilla extract (B)
3 lb	6 lb	12 lb	Rice/raisin mixture* ½ (B), ½ (E)
1½ oz	3 oz	6 oz	Cinnamon (B)

*To Make the Rice/Raisin Mixture for a 20-Qt Batch
Rice Mixture

2 lb	Superfino Arborio rice (Italian rice used for risotto)
3 qt	Water
¾ lb	Sugar

Prepare rice using a 3:1 ratio of 3 parts water/1 part rice. Boil water, then add rice and sugar. Turn heat to simmer until done. Let cooked rice sit covered for ½ hour.

Raisin Mixture

2 lb	Golden raisins
2¼ lb	Sugar
1 qt	Water
1 oz	Cinnamon

Put all ingredients into a pot and bring to a boil. Simmer for 15 minutes. Drain off the water thoroughly and add cooked rice to the mixture. Refrigerate for 2 hours.

PREPARATION   Batch time: 8–10 minutes

Pour ice cream mix, vanilla extract, rice mixture and cinnamon into the batch freezer. Turn on the dasher, set timer to 8 minutes, turn on refrigeration and begin the batch. When the batch is almost complete, add in the remaining rice mixture, turn off the refrigeration and extrude the finished product while sprinkling tubs with cinnamon.

MALCOLM SAYS: If you want to use baked rice pudding, cook rice, add raisin mixture without water and bake at 400° F for ½ hour. Remove from oven, cool and add to ice cream mix.

Vanilla Fudge Ice Cream

This is a favorite among traditional ice cream lovers but difficult to produce without proper planning because swirling the fudge into tubs is messy. Our secret is lining the sides of the tubs with fudge first.

INGREDIENTS

10-Qt Batch	20-Qt Batch	40-Qt Batch	
1¼ gal	2½ gal	5 gal	Ice cream mix (B)
2 oz	4 oz	8 oz	Two-fold vanilla extract (B)
1¼ qt	2½ qt	5 qt	Hot fudge (O)

PREPARATION   Batch time: 8–10 minutes

Pour ice cream mix and vanilla extract into batch freezer. Turn on dasher, set timer to 8 minutes, turn on refrigeration and begin batch. While batch is running, use a spatula to spread inner lining of tubs with hot fudge. When the batch is complete, turn off refrigeration and, as you extrude the finished product, slowly swirl fudge into tubs. Decorate tops of tubs with fudge.

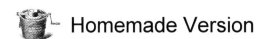 Homemade Version

INGREDIENTS

8	Egg yolks	16 oz	Heavy cream
8 oz	Sugar	1 Tbsp	Vanilla extract
16 oz	Milk	24 oz	Hot fudge sauce*

*To Make Hot Fudge Sauce:

1¼ lb	Bittersweet or semisweet chocolate	11 oz	Sugar
½ lb	Unsweetened chocolate	11 oz	Light corn syrup
6 oz	Unsalted (sweet) butter	1 Tbsp	Vanilla extract
11 oz	Heavy cream		

Use a double boiler to melt both chocolates with butter. Then add the cream, sugar, and light corn syrup and cook on low heat until the sugar is completely dissolved. Remove from heat and add in vanilla extract.

PREPARATION

Use a double boiler to create a custard base. Pour the egg yolks, sugar and milk into the pot. Heat the mixture slowly but do *not* bring to a boil. When a film forms over the back of your spoon, remove custard base from heat and place the pot into a larger pot filled with cold water to cool. Add in heavy cream and place in refrigerator until cold (at least 2 hours). Then stir in vanilla extract and transfer to an ice cream maker. Freeze according to manufacturer's instructions. Turn off the refrigeration and extrude the finished product. As you do so, layer the fudge on top of each layer of ice cream. Yield: 1½ quarts of ice cream

Rum Raisin Ice Cream

Rum Raisin is a very important flavor to offer because there is a built-in clientele that wants it.

INGREDIENTS

10-Qt Batch	20-Qt Batch	40-Qt Batch	
13 oz	26 oz	52 oz	Dark rum (E)
1½ lb	3 lb	6 lb	Golden raisins: ⅓ (B), ⅔ (E)
1¼ gal	2½ gal	5 gal	Ice cream mix (B)
2 oz	4 oz	8 oz	Two-fold vanilla extract (B)

PREPARATION   Batch time: 8–10 minutes

Combine rum and raisins and marinate for 8 hours. Drain off juice and put it aside for later use. Puree ⅓ of the raisins with 1 quart of the ice cream mix in a blender. Then pour all ingredients except ⅔ of the raisins into the batch freezer. Turn on the dasher, set timer to 8 minutes, turn on refrigeration and begin the batch. When the batch is complete, add in the rum juice, turn off refrigeration, add in the remaining raisins and extrude the finished product. Decorate tops of tubs with raisins.

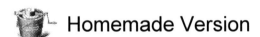 Homemade Version

Crank up your ice cream maker and treat yourself to the best Rum Raisin ice cream ever!

INGREDIENTS

8 oz	Golden raisins
8 oz	Dark rum
8	Egg yolks
8 oz	Sugar
16 oz	Milk
16 oz	Heavy cream
1 Tbsp	Vanilla extract

PREPARATION

Combine and marinate the golden raisins and rum for 24 hours. At the end of the marination process, drain off the liquid rum and set aside for later use. Use a double boiler to create a custard base. Pour the egg yolks, sugar and milk into the pot. Heat the mixture slowly but do *not* bring to a boil. When a film forms over the back of your spoon, remove custard base from heat and place the pot into a larger pot filled with cold water to cool. Add in heavy cream and place in refrigerator until cold (at least 2 hours). Then stir in the vanilla extract and transfer to an ice cream maker. Freeze according to manufacturer's instructions. When the ice cream is semifrozen, add back in the liquid rum and continue freezing for 5 minutes. Turn off the refrigeration and extrude the finished product. Yield: 1½ quarts of ice cream

Eggnog Ice Cream

This flavor is perfect for the Christmas and New Year holiday season. It is excellent for use in restaurants.

INGREDIENTS

10-Qt Batch	20-Qt Batch	40-Qt Batch	
1¼ gal	2½ gal	5 gal	Ice cream mix (B)
1 oz	2 oz	4 oz	Two-fold vanilla extract (B)
1½ qt	3 qt	6 qt	Eggnog base (B)
1 oz	2 oz	4 oz	Nutmeg (B)

PREPARATION   Batch time: 8–10 minutes

Pour all ingredients into batch freezer. Turn on dasher, set timer to 8 minutes, turn on the refrigeration and begin the batch. When the batch is complete, turn off the refrigeration and extrude the finished product. Decorate by sprinkling tops of tubs with nutmeg.

Eggnog Chip Ice Cream

Chocolate chips add a touch of class to this exceptional flavor.

INGREDIENTS

10-Qt Batch	20-Qt Batch	40-Qt Batch	
1¼ gal	2½ gal	5 gal	Ice cream mix (B)
1 oz	2 oz	4 oz	Two-fold vanilla extract (B)
1½ qt	3 qt	6 qt	Eggnog base (B)
1 oz	2 oz	4 oz	Nutmeg (B)
12 oz	24 oz	48 oz	Chocolate chips (B)

PREPARATION   Batch time: 8–10 minutes

Pour all ingredients into the batch freezer. Turn on the dasher, set the timer to 8 minutes, turn on refrigeration and begin the batch. When the batch is complete, turn off the refrigeration and extrude the finished product. Decorate by sprinkling tops of tubs with nutmeg.

White Gold Ice Cream

I found this flavor on the Internet from an ice cream company in the UK called G&D Ice Cream and Café. They say that the idea came from the production crew who was bored making simple traditional flavors. The flavor is Vanilla ice cream with white chocolate chips, butterscotch and cookie dough. The actual recipe is my interpretation. I know it will work, so try it out.

INGREDIENTS

10-Qt Batch	20-Qt Batch	40-Qt Batch	
1¼ gal	2½ gal	5 gal	Ice cream mix (B)
2 oz	4 oz	8 oz	Two-fold vanilla extract (B)
1¼ qt	2½ qt	5 qt	Butterscotch or caramel fudge (E)
2 lb	4 lb	8 lb	White chocolate chunks (O)
2 lb	4 lb	8 lb	Cookie dough pieces (O)

PREPARATION   Batch time: 8–10 minutes

Pour ice cream mix and vanilla extract into the batch freezer. Turn on the dasher, set timer to 8 minutes, turn on the refrigeration and begin the batch. While batch is running, heat butterscotch or caramel fudge in a food warmer or keep at room temperature until loosened up and creamy. Using a spatula, spread the inner lining of tubs with fudge. When the batch is complete, turn off refrigeration and add in white chocolate chunks and cookie dough pieces. As you extrude the finished product, slowly swirl fudge into the tubs. Decorate tops of tubs with fudge and cookie dough.

CHOCOLATE-BASED ICE CREAM FLAVORS

Besides Vanilla, the other flavor your customers will judge you by regarding a "standard" of quality is your basic Chocolate ice cream. There are three basic forms of Chocolate ice cream: milk chocolate, semisweet chocolate and bittersweet chocolate. While most people on the East Coast like a bittersweet-flavored ice cream, the majority of the rest of the country likes a milk chocolate-flavored ice cream. Regardless of the type of Chocolate ice cream you make, be sure that there is no dry cocoa appearing in the finished product.

For a more basic chocolate ice cream, I would recommend using cocoa, water and sugar for creating the chocolate base. (*see* recipe on page 92)

If you want to create a more premium chocolate base, I would recommend using a ratio of 50% cocoa and chocolate plus water and sugar. The more bittersweet you want your base to be depends on the amount of sugar in your recipe. A ratio of 4 parts chocolate and 1 part sugar is the most bitter; a ratio of equal parts chocolate and sugar creates a more milk or semisweet chocolate base.

Chocolate Ice Cream

This recipe for Chocolate ice cream is the standard for all the chocolate recipes in this segment, and over the years has been my standard for chocolate in general. It is dark and not too sweet.

INGREDIENTS

10-Qt Batch	20-Qt Batch	40-Qt Batch	
1¼ lb	2½ lb	5 lb	Cocoa (22–24% fat) (B)
½ lb	1 lb	2 lb	Sugar (B)
1½ pt	3 pt	6 pt	Hot water (B)
1¼ gal	2½ gal	5 gal	Ice cream mix (B)
2 oz	4 oz	8 oz	Two-fold vanilla extract (B)
½ oz	1 oz	2 oz	Chocolate extract (B)

PREPARATION   Batch time: 9–11 minutes

Thoroughly mix cocoa and sugar with extremely hot water in a double boiler to create a smooth, creamy paste. Pour ¼ of the ice cream mix into the batch freezer and turn on the dasher. Add the cocoa paste and let dasher run until ingredients are completely blended. Pour in remaining ice cream mix, vanilla extract and chocolate extract. Set timer to 9 minutes, turn on refrigeration and begin the batch. When the batch is complete, turn off refrigeration and extrude the finished product.

MALCOLM SAYS: Chocolate needs an extra minute to freeze because of the weight of the cocoa and the fat content. Set timer to 9 minutes and check if done. It should be shiny, firm and very wavy. If it's slightly liquidy, continue to freeze for 1–2 minutes.

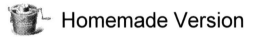 Homemade Version

What's great about making your own Chocolate ice cream is that you can make it as dark and chocolatey as you wish!

INGREDIENTS

8	Egg yolks	6 oz	Cocoa
12 oz	Sugar	16 oz	Heavy cream
16 oz	Milk	1 Tbsp	Vanilla extract

PREPARATION

Mix thoroughly the egg yolks, sugar and milk in a double boiler. As the mixture is being heated, add in the cocoa to create a smooth paste. Continue heating but do *not* bring to a boil. When a film forms over the back of your spoon, remove from heat and place the pot into a larger pot filled with cold water to cool. Add in heavy cream and place in refrigerator until cold (at least 2 hours). Then stir in vanilla extract and transfer to an ice cream maker. Freeze according to manufacturer's instructions. Turn off refrigeration and extrude finished product. Yield: 1½–2 quarts of ice cream

Bittersweet Chocolate Ice Cream

INGREDIENTS

10-Qt Batch	20-Qt Batch	40-Qt Batch	
¾ lb	1½ lb	3 lb	Semisweet chocolate bar (B)
¾ lb	1½ lb	3 lb	Cocoa (22–24% fat) (B)
1¼ lb	2½ lb	5 lb	Sugar (B)
2 pt	4 pt	8 pt	Hot water (B)
1¼ gal	2½ gal	5 gal	Ice cream mix (B)
2 oz	4 oz	8 oz	Two-fold vanilla extract (B)
½ oz	1 oz	2 oz	Pure chocolate extract (B)

PREPARATION
Batch time: 9–11 minutes

Cut chocolate bar into small pieces and melt it down. Thoroughly mix cocoa and sugar with extremely hot water in a double boiler to create a smooth paste, then add in the melted chocolate. Pour all ingredients into the batch freezer, turn on dasher and let it run for 5 minutes until the ingredients are completely blended. Set the timer to 9 minutes, turn on refrigeration and begin the batch. When the batch is complete, turn off refrigeration and extrude finished product.

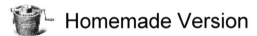 Homemade Version

If you like dark chocolate, then this recipe is a must to make!

INGREDIENTS

8	Egg yolks
12 oz	Sugar
16 oz	Milk
4 oz	Cocoa
4 oz	Semisweet chocolate bar pieces
16 oz	Heavy cream
1 Tbsp	Vanilla extract

PREPARATION
Mix thoroughly the egg yolks, sugar and milk in a double boiler. As the mixture is being heated, add in the cocoa and chocolate-bar pieces to create a smooth, creamy paste. Continue heating but do *not* bring to a boil. When a film forms over the back of your spoon, remove from heat and place the pot into a larger pot filled with cold water to cool. Add in heavy cream and place in refrigerator until cold (at least 2 hours). Then stir in vanilla extract and transfer to an ice cream maker. Freeze according to manufacturer's instructions. Turn off the refrigeration and extrude the finished product. Yield: 1½–2 quarts of ice cream

Milk Chocolate Ice Cream

This is a favorite of my partner, Bill Lambert, who prefers a sweeter, less dark chocolate ice cream.

INGREDIENTS

10-Qt Batch	20-Qt Batch	40-Qt Batch	
¾ lb	1½ lb	3 lb	Cocoa (22–24% fat) (B)
1½ lb	3 lb	6 lb	Sugar (B)
2¼ pt	4½ pt	9 pt	Hot water (B)
1¼ gal	2½ gal	5 gal	Ice cream mix (B)
2 oz	4 oz	8 oz	Two-fold vanilla extract (B)
½ oz	1 oz	2 oz	Chocolate extract (B)

PREPARATION   Batch time: 9–11 minutes

Thoroughly mix cocoa and sugar with very hot water in a double boiler to create a smooth, creamy paste. Pour ¼ of the ice cream mix into the batch freezer and turn on the dasher. Add the cocoa paste and let dasher run until the ingredients are completely blended. Pour in remaining ice cream mix and the vanilla and chocolate extracts, set timer to 9 minutes, turn on refrigeration and begin the batch. When the batch is complete, turn off refrigeration and extrude the finished product.

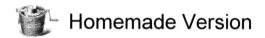 Homemade Version

INGREDIENTS

8	Egg yolks
16 oz	Sugar
16 oz	Milk
3 oz	Cocoa
16 oz	Heavy cream
1 Tbsp	Vanilla extract

PREPARATION

Mix thoroughly the egg yolks, sugar and milk in a double boiler. As the mixture is being heated, add in the cocoa to create a smooth, creamy paste. Continue heating but do *not* bring to a boil. When a film forms over the back of your spoon, remove from heat and place the pot into a larger pot filled with cold water to cool. Add in heavy cream and place in refrigerator until cold (at least 2 hours). Then stir in vanilla extract and transfer to an ice cream maker. Freeze according to manufacturer's instructions. Turn off the refrigeration and extrude the finished product. Yield: 1½–2 quarts of ice cream

White Chocolate Ice Cream

INGREDIENTS

10-Qt Batch	20-Qt Batch	40-Qt Batch	
1¾ lb	3½ lb	7 lb	White chocolate chunks: ½ (B), ½(E)
1¼ gal	2½ gal	5 gal	Ice cream mix (B)
1 oz	2 oz	4 oz	Two-fold vanilla extract (B)

PREPARATION   Batch time: 9–11 minutes

Using a double boiler, melt ½ of the white chocolate chunks with some ice cream mix and heat until smooth and creamy. Watch the chocolate closely and stir often; do *not* allow mixture to boil or chocolate to become dried out. Pour the rest of the ice cream mix and vanilla extract into the batch freezer, turn on the dasher and let it run for 3 minutes as you slowly pour in the white chocolate mixture. Set timer to 9 minutes, turn on refrigeration and begin the batch. When the batch is complete, add in the remaining white chocolate chunks, turn off refrigeration and extrude finished product. Decorate tops of tubs with white chocolate chunks.

Chocolate Chocolate Etc. Ice Cream

INGREDIENTS

10-Qt Batch	20-Qt Batch	40-Qt Batch	
¾ lb	1½ lb	3 lb	Cocoa (22–24% fat) (B)
2 pt	4 pt	8 pt	Hot water (B)
¾ lb	1½ lb	3 lb	Semisweet chocolate bar in pieces (B)
1¼ lb	2½ lb	5 lb	Sugar (B)
1¼ gal	2½ gal	5 gal	Ice cream mix (B)
2 oz	4 oz	8 oz	Two-fold vanilla extract (B)
½ oz	1 oz	2 oz	Pure chocolate extract (B)
1½ oz	3 oz	6 oz	Cinnamon (B)
1¼ lb	2½ lb	5 lb	Chocolate chunks: ½ (B), ½ (E)
8 oz	16 oz	32 oz	Liquid chocolate* (E)

*To make the liquid chocolate, melt in a double boiler 5 parts chocolate (any flavor chocolate bar) to 1 part vegetable oil by weight.

PREPARATION   Batch time: 9–11 minutes

Mix cocoa with very hot water in a double boiler to create a smooth paste, then add in the chocolate-bar pieces. Pour all ingredients except ½ of the chocolate chunks and liquid chocolate into batch freezer, turn on dasher and let it run for 5 minutes to blend ingredients. Set timer to 9 minutes, turn on refrigeration and begin the batch. When batch is almost complete, add in the rest of the chocolate chunks and liquid chocolate, turn off refrigeration and extrude the finished product.

Chocolate Milk Ice Cream

This is as smooth as silk and delightfully delicious.

INGREDIENTS

10-Qt Batch	20-Qt Batch	40-Qt Batch	
6 oz	12 oz	24 oz	Semisweet chocolate bar (B)
6 oz	12 oz	24 oz	Cocoa (22–24% fat) (B)
8 oz	1 lb	2 lb	Sugar (B)
1½ pt	3 pt	6 pt	Hot water (B)
1¼ gal	2½ gal	5 gal	Ice cream mix (B)
2 oz	4 oz	8 oz	Two-fold vanilla extract (B)
½ oz	1 oz	2 oz	Chocolate extract (B)

PREPARATION   **Batch time: 9–11 minutes**

Cut chocolate bar into small pieces and melt it down. Thoroughly mix cocoa and sugar with very hot water in a double boiler to create a smooth paste, then add in melted chocolate. Pour all ingredients into batch freezer, turn on dasher and let it run for 5 minutes to blend ingredients. Set timer to 9 minutes, turn on refrigeration and begin batch. When batch is complete, turn off refrigeration and extrude product.

Chocolate Cream Pie Ice Cream

INGREDIENTS

10-Qt Batch	20-Qt Batch	40-Qt Batch	
12 oz	24 oz	48 oz	Semisweet chocolate bar (B)
12 oz	24 oz	48 oz	Cocoa (22–24% fat) (B)
14 oz	28 oz	56 oz	Sugar (B)
1½ pt	3 pt	6 pt	Hot water (B)
1¼ gal	2½ gal	5 gal	Ice cream mix (B)
2 oz	4 oz	8 oz	Two-fold vanilla extract (B)
¼ oz	½ oz	1 oz	Chocolate extract (B)
¾ lb	1½ lb	3 lb	Oreo cookies, broken: ½ (B), ½ (E)
1 qt	2 qt	4 qt	Marshmallow variegate (O)

PREPARATION   **Batch time: 9–11 minutes**

Melt down chocolate bar. Thoroughly mix cocoa and sugar with extremely hot water to create a smooth paste, then add in melted chocolate. Pour all ingredients except ½ of Oreo cookies and marshmallow variegate into the batch freezer, turn on dasher and let it run for 5 minutes to blend ingredients. Set timer to 9 minutes, turn on refrigeration and begin batch. When batch is complete, add in remaining cookies, turn off refrigeration and swirl marshmallow variegate into the tubs as you extrude finished product. Decorate tops of tubs with cookies and marshmallow variegate.

Chocolate Fudge Brownie Ice Cream

INGREDIENTS

10-Qt Batch	20-Qt Batch	40-Qt Batch	
¾ lb	1½ lb	3 lb	Semisweet chocolate bar (B)
¾ lb	1½ lb	3 lb	Cocoa (22-24% fat) (B)
1¼ lb	2½ lb	5 lb	Sugar (B)
2 pt	4 pt	8 pt	Hot water (B)
1¼ gal	2½ gal	5 gal	Ice cream mix (B)
2 oz	4 oz	8 oz	Two-fold vanilla extract (B)
½ oz	1 oz	2 oz	Pure chocolate extract (B)
1 lb	2 lb	4 lb	Chocolate brownies: ⅓ (B), ⅔ (E)
6 oz	12 oz	24 oz	Large walnut pieces (E)
6 oz	12 oz	24 oz	Chocolate chips (E)
20 oz	1¼ qt	2½ qt	Hot fudge (O)

PREPARATION
Batch time: 9–11 minutes

Cut chocolate bar into small pieces and melt down. Mix cocoa and sugar with extremely hot water in a double boiler to create a smooth paste, then add in the melted chocolate. Pour cocoa paste, ice cream mix, the two extracts and ⅓ of the brownies into the batch freezer. Turn on dasher, let it run for 5 minutes to blend ingredients, set timer to 9 minutes, turn on refrigeration and begin the batch. While it is running, spread inner lining of tubs with fudge. When the batch is complete, add in the rest of the brownies, walnuts and chocolate chips, turn off refrigeration and slowly swirl hot fudge into tubs as you extrude finished product. Decorate tops of tubs with brownies, chips and nuts.

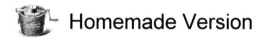 Homemade Version

INGREDIENTS

8	Egg yolks	1 Tbsp	Vanilla extract
12 oz	Sugar	2 oz	Large walnut pieces
4 oz	Cocoa	4 oz	Chocolate brownies
4 oz	Semisweet chocolate pieces	1 oz	Chocolate chips
16 oz	Heavy cream	5 oz	Hot fudge

PREPARATION

Mix together egg yolks, sugar, and milk in a double boiler, heat as you add cocoa and chocolate pieces to create a smooth paste. Continue heating but do *not* bring to a boil. When a film forms over the back of your spoon, remove from heat and place pot into a larger pot filled with cold water. Add in heavy cream and place in refrigerator until cold (at least 2 hours). Stir in vanilla and transfer to an ice cream maker. Freeze according to manufacturer's instructions. Then add nuts, brownies and chips; turn off refrigeration and swirl in fudge as you extrude the finished product. Yield: 1½–2 quarts of ice cream

94

Chocolate Burgundy Wine Ice Cream

INGREDIENTS

10-Qt Batch	20-Qt Batch	40-Qt Batch	
¼ lb	½ lb	1 lb	Semisweet chocolate bar (B)
¼ lb	½ lb	1 lb	Cocoa (22–24% fat) (B)
¾ lb	1½ lb	3 lb	Sugar (B)
1¼ pt	2½ pt	5 pt	Hot water (B)
1¼ gal	2½ gal	5 gal	Ice cream mix (B)
2 oz	4 oz	8 oz	Two-fold vanilla extract (B)
½ oz	1 oz	2 oz	Pure chocolate extract (B)
13 oz	26 oz	52 oz	Burgundy table wine (E)

PREPARATION **Batch time: 9–11 minutes**

Cut chocolate into pieces and melt down. Thoroughly mix cocoa and sugar with extremely hot water in a double boiler to create a smooth paste, then add in the melted chocolate. Pour all ingredients except wine into batch freezer, turn on dasher and let it run for 5 minutes to blend ingredients, set timer to 9 minutes, turn on refrigeration and begin the batch. When the batch is almost complete, add in the wine, continue freezing for 2–3 minutes, then turn off refrigeration and extrude finished product.

Chocolate-Covered Cherry Ice Cream

INGREDIENTS

10-Qt Batch	20-Qt Batch	40-Qt Batch	
1 lb	2 lb	4 lb	Bordeaux cherries (E)
1 lb	2 lb	4 lb	Semisweet chocolate (E)
3 oz	6 oz	12 oz	Vegetable oil (E)
1¼ lb	2½ lb	5 lb	Cocoa (22–24% fat) (B)
½ lb	1 lb	2 lb	Sugar (B)
1½ pt	3 pt	6 pt	Hot water (B)
1¼ gal	2½ gal	5 gal	Ice cream mix (B)
2 oz	4 oz	8 oz	Two-fold vanilla extract (B)

PREPARATION **Batch time: 9–11 minutes**

Drain cherries and lay them on a baker's tray. Melt chocolate and vegetable oil in a double boiler, pour chocolate over cherries and freeze for 15 minutes before chopping them up. Mix cocoa and sugar with very hot water in a double boiler to create a smooth paste. Pour ¼ of ice cream mix into batch freezer and turn on dasher. Add cocoa paste and run dasher a few minutes. Pour in rest of ice cream mix and vanilla extract, set timer to 9 minutes, turn on refrigeration and begin batch. When the batch is complete, add in chocolate cherries, turn off refrigeration and extrude finished product. Decorate tops of tubs with cherries.

Rocky Road Ice Cream

This is always a favorite with kids—and grown-ups too!

INGREDIENTS

10-Qt Batch	20-Qt Batch	40-Qt Batch	
1¼ lb	2½ lb	5 lb	Cocoa (22–24% fat) (B)
½ lb	1 lb	2 lb	Sugar (B)
1½ pt	3 pt	6 pt	Hot water (B)
1¼ gal	2½ gal	5 gal	Ice cream mix (B)
2 oz	4 oz	8 oz	Two-fold vanilla extract (B)
½ oz	1 oz	2 oz	Chocolate extract (B)
½ lb	1 lb	2 lb	Mini marshmallows: ½ (M), ½ (E)
½ lb	1 lb	2 lb	Large walnut pieces (E)

PREPARATION   Batch time: 9–11 minutes

Thoroughly mix cocoa and sugar with extremely hot water in a double boiler to create a creamy paste. Pour ¼ of the ice cream mix into batch freezer and turn on dasher. Add cocoa paste and let dasher run until ingredients are blended. Pour in remaining ice cream mix, vanilla and chocolate extracts, set timer to 9 minutes, turn on refrigeration and begin the batch. Midway through the batch, add in ½ of the marshmallows. When the batch is complete, add in the remaining marshmallows and walnuts, turn off the refrigeration and extrude the finished product. Decorate tops of tubs with marshmallows and walnuts.

 Homemade Version

INGREDIENTS

8	Egg yolks	16 oz	Heavy cream
12 oz	Sugar	1 Tbsp	Vanilla extract
16 oz	Milk	4 oz	Mini marshmallows
3 oz	Cocoa	4 oz	Large walnut pieces

PREPARATION

Mix thoroughly the egg yolks, sugar and milk in a double boiler. As the mixture is being heated, add in the cocoa to create a smooth, creamy paste. Continue heating but do *not* bring to a boil. When a film forms over the back of your spoon, remove from heat and place the pot into a larger pot filled with cold water to cool. Add in heavy cream and place in refrigerator until cold (at least 2 hours). Then stir in vanilla extract and transfer to an ice cream maker. Freeze according to manufacturer's instructions. Add in the mini marshmallows and walnut pieces, turn off refrigeration and extrude the finished product. Yield: 1½–2 quarts of ice cream

Chocolate Macapuno Ice Cream

Combining the flavor of milk chocolate with Macapuno coconut (a popular flavor in the Philippines) creates a creamy, smooth flavor full of the punch of both.

INGREDIENTS

10-Qt Batch	20-Qt Batch	40-Qt Batch	
1½ lb	3 lb	6 lb	Macapuno coconut, defrosted (B)
6 oz	12 oz	24 oz	Sugar (B)
½ lb	1 lb	2 lb	Cocoa (B)
1 lb	2 lb	4 lb	Sugar (B)
1½ pt	3 pt	6 pt	Hot water (B)
1¼ gal	2½ gal	5 gal	Ice cream mix (B)
1 oz	2 oz	4 oz	Two-fold vanilla extract (B)
2 oz	4 oz	8 oz	Shredded sweet coconut (B)

PREPARATION   Batch time: 9–11 minutes

Add sugar to defrosted Macapuno coconut and marinate for 2–3 hours. Thoroughly mix cocoa and sugar with extremely hot water in a double boiler to create a smooth paste. Then pour all ingredients into the batch freezer. Turn on dasher, set timer to 9 minutes, turn on refrigeration and begin the batch. When the batch is complete, turn off refrigeration and extrude the finished product.

Chocolate Raisin Ice Cream

INGREDIENTS

10-Qt Batch	20-Qt Batch	40-Qt Batch	
1 lb	2 lb	4 lb	Cocoa (22–24% fat) (B)
½ lb	1 lb	2 lb	Sugar (B)
3–6 cups	6–8 cups	8–12 cups	Hot water (B)
1¼ gal	2½ gal	5 gal	Ice cream mix (B)
1 oz	2 oz	4 oz	Two-fold vanilla extract (B)
4 oz	8 oz	16 oz	Raisins (B)
¾ lb	1½ lb	3 lb	Chocolate-covered raisins (E)

PREPARATION   Batch time: 9–11 minutes

Thoroughly mix cocoa and sugar with extremely hot water in a double boiler to create a smooth paste. Pour ¼ of the ice cream mix into the batch freezer and turn on dasher. Add the cocoa paste and let the dasher run for 5 minutes to blend these ingredients. Pour in the remaining ingredients except the chocolate-covered raisins, set timer to 9 minutes, turn on refrigeration and begin the batch. When the batch is complete, add in chocolate-covered raisins, turn off refrigeration and extrude finished product. Decorate tops of tubs with chocolate-covered raisins.

Chocolate Coconut Chip Ice Cream

This flavor is a good change of pace when you're thinking of new items to offer your customers.

INGREDIENTS

10-Qt Batch	20-Qt Batch	40-Qt Batch	
1 lb	2 lb	4 lb	Cocoa (22–24%) (B)
4 oz	8 oz	16 oz	Sugar (B)
3–6 cups	6–8 cups	8–12 cups	Hot water (B)
1¼ gal	2½ gal	5 gal	Ice cream mix (B)
1 oz	2 oz	4 oz	Two-fold vanilla extract (B)
½ lb	1 lb	2 lb	Shredded coconut (M)
½ lb	1 lb	2 lb	Chocolate chips (M)

PREPARATION   Batch time: 9–11 minutes

Thoroughly mix cocoa and sugar with extremely hot water in a double boiler to create a smooth paste. Pour ¼ of the ice cream mix into the batch freezer and turn on dasher. Add cocoa paste and let dasher run for 5 minutes to blend ingredients. Add the rest of the ice cream mix and vanilla, set timer to 9 minutes, turn on the refrigeration and begin batch. Midway through the batch, add in shredded coconut and chocolate chips. When the batch is complete, turn off refrigeration and extrude the finished product. Decorate tops of tubs with coconut and chips.

Chocolate Crème Cake Ice Cream

This recipe with Bailey's Irish Cream liqueur produces a rich and flavorful ice cream.

INGREDIENTS

10-Qt Batch	20-Qt Batch	40-Qt Batch	
14 oz	1¾ lb	3½ lb	Cocoa (22–24% fat) (B)
4 oz	8 oz	16 oz	Sugar (B)
3–6 cup	5–7 cup	6–8 cup	Hot water (B)
1¼ gal	2½ gal	5 gal	Ice cream mix (B)
1 oz	2 oz	4 oz	Two-fold vanilla extract (B)
1 lb	2 lb	4 lb	Chocolate cake: ½ (B), ½ (E)
7 oz	13 oz	26 oz	Bailey's Irish Cream liqueur (M)

PREPARATION   Batch time: 9–11 minutes

Thoroughly mix cocoa and sugar with extremely hot water to create a smooth paste. Pour ¼ of the ice cream mix into the batch freezer and turn on dasher. Add the cocoa paste and let dasher run for 5 minutes to blend ingredients. Add in remaining ice cream mix, vanilla and ½ of the chocolate cake. Set timer to 9 minutes, turn on refrigeration and begin batch. Midway through the batch, add in Bailey's Irish Cream. When the batch is complete, add in remaining chocolate cake, turn off refrigeration and extrude the finished product. Decorate tops of tubs with chocolate cake.

"Fudgy Wudgy" Ice Cream
(Chocolate-Covered Almond Fudge)

Chocolate-covered almonds taste great eaten all by themselves. For this decadent chocolate ice cream, we have swirled in a lot of fudge to go along with the almonds. Need I say more?

INGREDIENTS

10-Qt Batch	20-Qt Batch	40-Qt Batch	
12 oz	24 oz	48 oz	Semisweet chocolate bar (B)
12 oz	24 oz	48 oz	Cocoa (22–24% fat) (B)
14 oz	28 oz	56 oz	Sugar (B)
1½ pt	3 pt	6 pt	Hot water (B)
1¼ gal	2½ gal	5 gal	Ice cream mix (B)
2 oz	4 oz	8 oz	Two-fold vanilla extract (B)
¼ oz	½ oz	1 oz	Chocolate extract (B)
¾ lb	1½ lb	3 lb	Chocolate-covered almonds (E)
12 oz	24 oz	48 oz	Hot fudge (O)

PREPARATION
Batch time: 9–11 minutes

Melt down the chocolate bar. Thoroughly mix cocoa and sugar with extremely hot water to create a smooth paste, then add in melted chocolate. Pour all ingredients except the almonds and fudge into the batch freezer, turn on dasher and let it run for 5 minutes to blend the ingredients. Set timer to 9 minutes, turn on refrigeration and begin the batch. While the batch is running, spread inner lining of tubs with fudge. When the batch is complete, add in the almonds, turn off refrigeration and, as you extrude the finished product, slowly swirl fudge into the tubs. Decorate tops of tubs with almonds and fudge.

COFFEE-BASED ICE CREAM FLAVORS

For those people who like coffee, what they particularly like in their Coffee ice cream is a strong coffee essence. There are many ways to produce a coffee-flavored ice cream including using a liquid coffee flavoring, a coffee paste or a coffee flavored from seeping ground coffee up to 130° F for about 3 hours. For most of the coffee flavors included in this book, the use of freeze-dried coffee is recommended. Most importantly, the finished product should have a smooth-tasting flavor with no aftertaste. The use of cocoa is the secret ingredient that makes these coffee flavors taste great. Why? Because it takes away the bitterness that many Coffee ice cream flavors have.

Coffee Ice Cream

This is a basic great-tasting Coffee ice cream.

INGREDIENTS

10-Qt Batch	20-Qt Batch	40-Qt Batch	
2½ oz	5 oz	10 oz	Freeze-dried coffee (B)
2 tsp	4 tsp	6 tsp	Cocoa (22–24% fat) (B)
1 oz	2 oz	4 oz	Hot water (B)
1¼ gal	2½ gal	5 gal	Ice cream mix (B)
2 oz	4 oz	8 oz	Two-fold vanilla extract (B)
½ oz	1 oz	2 oz	Ground espresso beans (E)

PREPARATION
Batch time: 8–10 minutes

Mix freeze-dried coffee with as little hot water as possible. Add cocoa and blend thoroughly until mixture is very smooth with no dry coffee or cocoa visible. Pour ingredients including coffee mixture into the batch freezer. Turn on dasher and run for 2 minutes, set timer to 8 minutes, turn on the refrigeration and begin the batch. When the batch is complete, add ground espresso beans, turn off refrigeration and extrude the finished product.

 # Homemade Version

Coffee ice cream is a favorite flavor for people who like to drink great strong-flavored coffee.

INGREDIENTS

½ oz	Freeze-dried coffee
½ tsp	Cocoa
8	Egg yolks
8 oz	Sugar
16 oz	Milk
16 oz	Heavy cream
1 Tbsp	Vanilla extract

PREPARATION

Mix freeze-dried coffee with as little hot water as possible. Add cocoa and blend thoroughly until mixture is very smooth with no dry coffee or cocoa visible. Use a double boiler to create a custard base. Pour the coffee mixture, egg yolks, sugar and milk into the pot and heat slowly but do *not* bring to a boil. When a film forms over the back of your spoon, remove custard base from heat and place the pot into a larger pot filled with cold water to cool. Add in heavy cream and place in refrigerator until cold (at least 2 hours). Then stir in vanilla extract and transfer to an ice cream maker. Freeze according to manufacturer's instructions. Then turn off the refrigeration and extrude the finished product. Yield: 1½ quarts of ice cream

Cappuccino Rum Ice Cream

INGREDIENTS

10-Qt Batch	20-Qt Batch	40-Qt Batch	
2½ oz	5 oz	10 oz	Freeze-dried coffee (B)
1 oz	2 oz	4 oz	Hot water (B)
2 tsp	4 tsp	8 tsp	Cocoa (22–24% fat) (B)
1¼ gal	2½ gal	5 gal	Ice cream mix (B)
2 oz	4 oz	8 oz	Two-fold vanilla extract (B)
10 oz	20 oz	40 oz	Dark rum (E)
½ oz	1 oz	2 oz	Cinnamon (E)
½ oz	1 oz	2 oz	Ground espresso beans (E)

PREPARATION   Batch time: 8–10 minutes

Mix freeze-dried coffee with as little hot water as possible. Add cocoa and blend until mixture is very smooth with no dry coffee or cocoa visible. Pour the coffee mixture, ice cream mix and vanilla into batch freezer. Turn on dasher and run for 2 minutes, set timer to 8 minutes, turn on refrigeration and begin batch. When it is complete, add in rum, cinnamon and espresso beans, turn off refrigeration and extrude finished product.

Coffee Cake Ice Cream

The cinnamon and sugar-cinnamon crust from the coffee cake add a very nice touch to this flavor.

INGREDIENTS

10-Qt Batch	20-Qt Batch	40-Qt Batch	
2½ oz	5 oz	10 oz	Freeze-dried coffee (B)
1 oz	2 oz	4 oz	Hot water (B)
2 tsp	4 tsp	6 tsp	Cocoa (22–24% fat) (B)
1¼ gal	2½ gal	5 gal	Ice cream mix (B)
2 oz	4 oz	8 oz	Two-fold vanilla extract (B)
½ oz	1 oz	2 oz	Cinnamon (B)
½ lb	1 lb	2 lb	Pecan pieces: ⅓ (B), ⅔ (O)
1¼ lb	2½ lb	5 lb	Cinnamon pecan coffee cake (O)

PREPARATION   Batch time: 8–10 minutes

Mix freeze-dried coffee with as little hot water as possible. Add cocoa and blend thoroughly until mixture is very smooth with no dry coffee or cocoa visible. Pour the coffee mixture, ice cream mix, vanilla extract, cinnamon and ⅓ of the pecan pieces into the batch freezer. Turn on dasher, set timer to 8 minutes, turn on refrigeration and begin the batch. When the batch is almost complete, turn off refrigeration, add in the cinnamon pecan coffee cake and the remaining pecan pieces and extrude the finished product. Decorate tops of tubs with pecan pieces and chunks of coffee cake.

Irish Coffee Ice Cream

Celebrate St. Patrick's Day with this special treat!

INGREDIENTS

10-Qt Batch	20-Qt Batch	40-Qt Batch	
2½ oz	5 oz	10 oz	Freeze-dried coffee (B)
1 oz	2 oz	4 oz	Hot water (B)
2 tsp	4 tsp	8 tsp	Cocoa (22–24% fat) (B)
1¼ gal	2½ gal	5 gal	Ice cream mix (B)
2 oz	4 oz	8 oz	Two-fold vanilla extract (B)
10 oz	20 oz	40 oz	Irish whiskey or brandy (E)

PREPARATION   Batch time: 8–10 minutes

Mix freeze-dried coffee with as little hot water as possible. Add cocoa and blend until mixture is very smooth with no dry coffee or cocoa visible. Pour ¼ of the ice cream mix into batch freezer, then add coffee mixture and vanilla. Turn on the dasher and let it run for a few minutes, then add the remainder of the ice cream mix. Set timer to 8 minutes, turn on refrigeration and begin batch. When the batch is complete, add in the Irish whiskey, turn off refrigeration and extrude finished product.

Chocolate-Covered Coffee Bean Ice Cream

Different varieties of coffee beans (vanilla, almond, hazelnut, Irish Cream) will impart a different flavor to this ice cream, so create a flavor for your favorite taste buds.

INGREDIENTS

10-Qt Batch	20-Qt Batch	40-Qt Batch	
2½ oz	5 oz	10 oz	Freeze-dried coffee (B)
1 oz	2 oz	4 oz	Hot water (B)
2 tsp	4 tsp	8 tsp	Cocoa (22–24% fat) (B)
1¼ gal	2½ gal	5 gal	Ice cream mix (B)
2 oz	4 oz	8 oz	Two-fold vanilla extract (B)
1¼ lb	2½ lb	5 lb	Chocolate-covered coffee beans: ⅓ (B), ⅔ (O)
10 oz	20 oz	40 oz	Dark rum (E)
½ oz	1 oz	2 oz	Cinnamon (E)

PREPARATION   Batch time: 8–10 minutes

Mix freeze-dried coffee with as little hot water as possible. Add cocoa and blend until mixture is very smooth with no dry coffee or cocoa visible. Pour coffee mix- ture, ice cream mix, vanilla and ⅓ of the coffee beans into the batch freezer. Turn on dasher, set timer to 8 minutes, turn on refrigeration and begin batch. When batch is almost com- plete, add in rum and cinnamon, turn off refrigeration, add in remaining coffee beans and extrude finished product. Decorate tops of tubs with coffee beans.

Mexican Coffee Ice Cream

It's amazing what a touch of cinnamon can do for a flavor. This flavor delivers a terrific sensual punch for anyone who likes coffee.

INGREDIENTS

10-Qt Batch	20-Qt Batch	40-Qt Batch	
2½ oz	5 oz	10 oz	Freeze-dried coffee (B)
1 oz	2 oz	4 oz	Hot water (B)
2 tsp	4 tsp	6 tsp	Cocoa (22–24% fat) (B)
1¼ gal	2½ gal	5 gal	Ice cream mix (B)
2 oz	4 oz	8 oz	Two-fold vanilla extract (B)
1¼ lb	2½ lb	5 lb	Chocolate-covered coffee beans: ⅓ (B), ⅔ (O)
½ oz	1 oz	2 oz	Cinnamon (E)
6 oz	12 oz	24 oz	Kahlua or Tia Maria (E)

PREPARATION   Batch time: 8–10 minutes

Mix freeze-dried coffee with as little hot water as possible. Add cocoa and blend thoroughly until mixture is very smooth with no dry coffee or cocoa visible. Pour the coffee mixture, ice cream mix, vanilla extract and ⅓ of the coffee beans into the batch freezer. Turn on dasher, set timer to 8 minutes, turn on refrigeration and begin the batch. When the batch is almost complete, add in the cinnamon and Kahlua (or Tia Maria), turn off the refrigeration, add in the remaining chocolate-covered coffee beans and extrude the finished product. Decorate tops of tubs with coffee beans.

 Homemade Version

INGREDIENTS

½ oz	Freeze-dried coffee	16 oz	Heavy cream
½ tsp	Cocoa	1 Tbsp	Vanilla extract
8	Egg yolks	¼ tsp	Cinnamon
8 oz	Sugar	2 oz	Kahlua or Tia Maria
16 oz	Milk	5 oz	Chocolate-covered coffee beans

PREPARATION

Mix freeze-dried coffee with as little hot water as possible. Add cocoa and blend until mixture is very smooth with no dry coffee or cocoa visible. Use a double boiler to create a custard base. Pour egg yolks, sugar and milk into the pot and heat slowly but do *not* bring to a boil. When a film forms over the back of your spoon, remove custard base from heat and place the pot into a larger pot filled with cold water to cool. Add in heavy cream and place in refrigerator until cold (at least 2 hours). Then stir in the coffee mixture, vanilla and cinnamon and transfer to an ice cream maker. Freeze according to manufacturer's instructions. Then add in Kahlua and chocolate-covered coffee beans, turn off refrigeration and extrude the finished product. Yield: 1½ quarts of ice cream

Mocha Fudge Pie Ice Cream

INGREDIENTS

10-Qt Batch	20-Qt Batch	40-Qt Batch	
2 oz	4 oz	8 oz	Freeze-dried coffee (B)
1 oz	2 oz	4 oz	Hot water (B)
1 Tbsp	2 Tbsp	4 Tbsp	Cocoa (22–24% fat) (B)
1¼ gal	2½ gal	5 gal	Ice cream mix (B)
1 oz	2 oz	4 oz	Two-fold vanilla extract (B)
½ lb	1 lb	2 lb	Graham crackers (E)
8 oz	16 oz	32 oz	Chocolate chips (E)
8 oz	16 oz	32 oz	Chocolate chip cookies (E)
1 qt	2 qt	4 qt	Hot fudge (O)

PREPARATION
Batch time: 8–10 minutes

Mix freeze-dried coffee with as little hot water as possible. Add cocoa and blend until mixture is smooth with no dry coffee or cocoa visible. Pour coffee mixture, ice cream mix and vanilla into batch freezer, turn on dasher, set timer to 8 minutes, turn on refrigeration and begin batch. While batch is running, spread inner lining of tubs with fudge. When the batch is complete, add in graham crackers, chocolate chips and cookies, then turn off refrigeration and slowly swirl fudge into tubs as you extrude finished product. Decorate tops of tubs with chocolate chips, cookies and fudge.

Mocha Almond Fudge Ice Cream

INGREDIENTS

10-Qt Batch	20-Qt Batch	40-Qt Batch	
2½ oz	5 oz	10 oz	Freeze-dried coffee (B)
1 oz	2 oz	4 oz	Hot water (B)
3 tsp	1½ Tbsp	3 Tbsp	Cocoa (22–24% fat) (B)
1¼ gal	2½ gal	5 gal	Ice cream mix (B)
2 oz	4 oz	8 oz	Two-fold vanilla extract (B)
4 oz	8 oz	1 lb	Sliced almonds (E)
24 oz	48 oz	3 qt	Hot fudge (O)

PREPARATION
Batch time: 8–10 minutes

Mix freeze-dried coffee with as little hot water as possible. Add cocoa and blend until mixture is smooth with no dry pieces of coffee or cocoa visible. Pour all ingredients except almonds and fudge into batch freezer. Turn on dasher and run for 2 minutes, set timer to 8 minutes, turn on refrigeration and begin the batch. While batch is running, spread inner lining of tubs with fudge. When batch is complete, add in almonds, turn off refrigeration and slowly swirl fudge into the tubs as you extrude the finished product. Decorate tops of tubs with almonds and fudge.

Mocha Chip Ice Cream

INGREDIENTS

10-Qt Batch	20-Qt Batch	40-Qt Batch	
1½ oz	3 oz	6 oz	Freeze-dried coffee (B)
2 Tbsp	4 Tbsp	8 Tbsp	Cocoa (22–24% fat) (B)
1 oz	2 oz	4 oz	Hot water (B)
1¼ gal	2½ gal	5 gal	Ice cream mix (B)
2 oz	4 oz	8 oz	Two-fold vanilla extract (B)
1½ lb	3 lb	6 lb	Dark chocolate chunks (E)

PREPARATION
Batch time: 8–10 minutes

Mix freeze-dried coffee with as little hot water as possible. Add cocoa and blend thoroughly until mixture is very smooth with no dry pieces of coffee or cocoa visible. Pour all ingredients except the dark chocolate chunks into the batch freezer. Turn on dasher and run for 2 minutes, set timer to 8 minutes, turn on refrigeration and begin the batch. When the batch is almost complete, add in the dark chocolate chunks, turn off refrigeration and extrude the finished product.

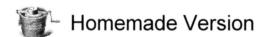 Homemade Version

INGREDIENTS

½ Tbsp	Freeze-dried coffee
½ Tbsp	Cocoa
8	Egg yolks
8 oz	Sugar
16 oz	Milk
16 oz	Heavy cream
1 Tbsp	Vanilla extract
6 oz	Chocolate chips

PREPARATION

Mix freeze-dried coffee with as little hot water as possible. Add cocoa and blend thoroughly until mixture is very smooth with no dry coffee or cocoa visible. Use a double boiler to create a custard base. Pour the egg yolks, sugar and milk into the pot and heat slowly but do *not* bring to a boil. When a film forms over the back of your spoon, remove custard base from heat and place the pot into a larger pot filled with cold water to cool. Add in heavy cream and place in refrigerator until cold (at least 2 hours). Then stir in vanilla extract and coffee mixture and transfer to an ice cream maker. Freeze according to manufacturer's instructions. When the ice cream is almost frozen, add in the chocolate chips, turn off the refrigeration and extrude the finished product. Yield: 1½ quarts of ice cream

Mud Pie Ice Cream

Mud Pie is really a sundae with hot fudge, but I have expanded on that idea here.

INGREDIENTS

10-Qt Batch	20-Qt Batch	40-Qt Batch	
2 oz	4 oz	10 oz	Freeze-dried coffee (B)
3 tsp	2 Tbsp	4 Tbsp	Cocoa (22–24% fat) (B)
1 oz	2 oz	4 oz	Hot water (B)
1¼ gal	2½ gal	5 gal	Ice cream mix (B)
1 oz	2 oz	4 oz	Two-fold vanilla extract (B)
8 oz	1 lb	2 lb	Graham crackers: ½ (B), ½ (E)
1 qt	2 qt	4 qt	Hot fudge (O)

PREPARATION   **Batch time: 8–10 minutes**

Mix freeze-dried coffee with as little hot water as possible. Add cocoa and blend thoroughly until mixture is smooth with no dry pieces of coffee or cocoa visible. Pour coffee mixture, ice cream mix, vanilla extract and ½ of the graham crackers into the batch freezer. Turn on dasher and run for 2 minutes, set timer to 8 minutes, turn on refrigeration and begin the batch. While batch is running, spread inner lining of tubs with fudge. When batch is complete, add in the rest of the graham crackers, turn off the refrigeration and slowly swirl fudge into the tubs as you extrude the finished product. Decorate tops of tubs with graham crackers and fudge.

Mocha Praline Almond Ice Cream

INGREDIENTS

10-Qt Batch	20-Qt Batch	40-Qt Batch	
2 oz	4 oz	8 oz	Freeze-dried coffee (B)
1 oz	2 oz	4 oz	Hot water (B)
2 oz	4 oz	8 oz	Cocoa (22–24% fat) (B)
1¼ gal	2½ gal	5 gal	Ice cream mix (B)
2 oz	4 oz	8 oz	Two-fold vanilla extract (B)
¼ oz	½ oz	1 oz	Ground cinnamon (B)
1¼ lb	2½ lb	5 lb	Praline almonds (O)

PREPARATION   **Batch time: 8–10 minutes**

Mix freeze-dried coffee with as little hot water as possible. Add cocoa and blend until mixture is very smooth with no dry coffee or cocoa visible. Pour all ingredients except praline almonds into the batch freezer. Turn on the dasher, set timer to 8 minutes, turn on refrigeration and begin the batch. When the batch is complete, turn off refrigeration, add praline almonds and extrude the finished product. Decorate tops of tubs with praline almonds.

Kahlua Almond Fudge Ice Cream

INGREDIENTS

10-Qt Batch	20-Qt Batch	40-Qt Batch	
½ oz	1 oz	2 oz	Freeze-dried coffee(B)
1 oz	2 oz	4 oz	Hot water (B)
½ oz	1 oz	2 oz	Cocoa (22–24% fat) (B)
1¼ gal	2½ gal	5 gal	Ice cream mix (B)
2 oz	4 oz	8 oz	Two-fold vanilla extract (B)
13 oz	26 oz	52 oz	Kahlua liqueur* (E)
½ lb	1 lb	2 lb	Diced roasted almonds (E)
24 oz	48 oz	3 qt	Hot fudge (O)

*You can substitute Kahlua extract for the Kahlua liqueur. If you do so, use 2–3 ounces for a 20-quart batch and adjust accordingly for other size batches.

PREPARATION   Batch time: 8–10 minutes

Mix freeze-dried coffee with as little hot water as possible. Add cocoa and blend thoroughly until mixture is very smooth with no dry pieces of coffee or cocoa visible. Pour coffee mixture, ice cream mix and vanilla into batch freezer. Turn on dasher and run for 2 minutes, set timer to 8 minutes, turn on refrigeration and begin batch. While batch is running, spread inner lining of tubs with fudge. When batch is complete, add in Kahlua and almonds, turn off refrigeration and swirl fudge into the tubs as you extrude finished product. Decorate tops of tubs with almonds and fudge.

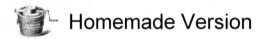 ## Homemade Version

INGREDIENTS

½ oz	Freeze-dried coffee	1 Tbsp	Vanilla extract
½ tsp	Cocoa	¼ tsp	Cinnamon
8	Egg yolks	2 oz	Kahlua or Tia Maria
8 oz	Sugar	5 oz	Almonds
16 oz	Milk	6 oz	Hot fudge
16 oz	Heavy cream		

PREPARATION

Mix freeze-dried coffee with as little hot water as possible. Add cocoa and blend until mixture is very smooth. Use a double boiler to create a custard base. Pour egg yolks, sugar and milk into the pot and heat but do *not* bring to a boil. When a film forms over the back of your spoon, remove base from heat and place pot into a larger pot filled with cold water. Add in heavy cream and place in refrigerator until cold (2 hours). Stir in coffee mixture, vanilla and cinnamon, transfer to an ice cream maker and freeze according to manufacturer's instructions. Add Kahlua and almonds, turn off refrigeration and layer in fudge as you extrude finished product. Yield: 1½ quarts of ice cream

NUT-BASED ICE CREAM FLAVORS

As ice cream producers make more creative use of the many varieties of nuts, these ice cream flavors will become more popular. Until the mid-1980s, butter pecan, maple walnut, burnt almond and pistachio comprised the majority of nut-flavored ice creams produced in the United States, with butter pecan and maple walnut accounting for nearly 70 percent of this market. Recently, the success of such flavors as peanut butter, pecan praline and macadamia nut has spurred the demand for new and exciting ones, resulting in increased sales of nutmeats to the ice cream industry.

We recommend using roasted nuts with no added salt. We prefer no salt for health reasons; we also believe that salt acts as a melting agent during the hardening of the finished product. Be aware that nuts absorb the water in the mix, so it is easy to produce an overprocessed product if your product run goes over the recommended time. To avoid overprocessing when using the batch process, watch closely during the last three minutes of production.

Because the appearance of the product enhances the product itself, always decorate the tops of the packed tubs with some of the nuts of the flavor you are producing.

Absolutely Nuts Ice Cream

This ice cream flavor was one of my all-time favorites when I was at the Ice Cream Extravaganza in New York City during the 1980s. Twenty years later, it still sounds good to me, but add a twist of caramel variegate for a more updated flavor for today's ice cream nut connoisseurs.

INGREDIENTS

10-Qt Batch	20-Qt Batch	40-Qt Batch	
16 oz	32 oz	64 oz	Roasted pecan pieces, praline pecans, cashews, granulated peanuts, walnuts: ½ (B), ½ (E)
1¼ gal	2½ gal	5 gal	Ice cream mix (B)
1 oz	2 oz	4 oz	Two-fold vanilla extract (B)
12 oz	24 oz	48 oz	Butter pecan base (B)

PREPARATION
Batch time: 8–10 minutes

Mix all the nuts together, then pour ½ of them along with the rest of the ingredients into the batch freezer. Turn on the dasher, set the timer to 8 minutes, turn on the refrigeration and begin the batch. When the batch is complete, add in the remaining nuts, turn off the refrigeration and extrude the finished product.

 Homemade Version

The taste is pure, delicious and nutty.

INGREDIENTS

8	Egg yolks	1 Tbsp	Vanilla extract
8 oz	Sugar	1 tsp	Almond extract
16 oz	Milk	8 oz	Assorted nuts (pecan pieces, praline pecans, almonds, cashews, granulated peanuts)
16 oz	Heavy cream		

PREPARATION

Use a double boiler to create a custard base. Pour the egg yolks, sugar and milk into the pot and heat slowly but do *not* bring to a boil. When a film forms over the back of your spoon, remove custard base from heat and place the pot into a larger pot filled with cold water to cool. Add in heavy cream and place in refrigerator until cold (at least 2 hours). Use a blender to blend ½ of the assorted nuts with 8 ounces of custard base, stir in vanilla and almond extracts, add the remaining custard base and transfer to an ice cream maker. Freeze according to manufacturer's instructions. When the ice cream is almost frozen, add in the remaining assorted nuts, turn off refrigeration and extrude the finished product. Yield: 1½ quarts of ice cream

Butter Pecan Ice Cream

This is the most popular of all the nut flavors.

INGREDIENTS

10-Qt Batch	20-Qt Batch	40-Qt Batch	
1¼ gal	2½ gal	5 gal	Ice cream mix (B)
1 oz	2 oz	4 oz	Two-fold vanilla extract (B)
½ qt	1 qt	2 qt	Butter pecan base (B)
1¼ lb	2½ lb	5 lb	Roasted pecan pieces: ⅓ (B), ⅔ (E)

PREPARATION   Batch time: 8–10 minutes

Pour all ingredients except ⅓ of the pecans into the batch freezer. Turn on the dasher, set timer to 8 minutes, turn on refrigeration and begin batch. When the batch is complete, add in the remaining pecans, turn off the refrigeration and extrude the finished product. Decorate tops of tubs with pecan pieces.

 Homemade Version

INGREDIENTS

8 oz	Pecan pieces
2 Tbsp	Sweet butter
8	Egg yolks
8 oz	Sugar
16 oz	Milk
16 oz	Heavy cream
1 Tbsp	Vanilla extract

PREPARATION

Line a baking tray with pecan pieces and sweet butter and heat in oven at 375° F for about 10 minutes. Remove the nuts from the oven and put them in a container. Stir the mixture and place on a paper towel to absorb the remaining butter. Use a double boiler to create a custard base. Pour the egg yolks, sugar and milk into the pot and heat slowly but do *not* bring to a boil. When a film forms over the back of your spoon, remove custard base from heat and place the pot into a larger pot filled with cold water to cool. Add in heavy cream and place in refrigerator until cold (at least 2 hours). Use a blender to blend 4 ounces of the pecan pieces with 8 ounces of the custard base. Then stir in vanilla extract and remainder of the custard base and transfer to an ice cream maker. Freeze according to manufacturer's instructions. When the ice cream is almost frozen, add in the remaining pecan pieces, turn off refrigeration and extrude the finished product. Yield: 1½ quarts of ice cream

Luscious Dolphins Ice Cream

Once you've made this flavor, you'll wonder how you waited so long!

INGREDIENTS

10-Qt Batch	20-Qt Batch	40-Qt Batch	
1¼ gal	2½ gal	5 gal	Ice cream mix (B)
2 oz	4 oz	8 oz	Two-fold vanilla extract (B)
1 lb	2 lb	4 lb	Pignoli nuts: ½ (B), ½ (O)
1¼ qt	2½ qt	5 qt	Caramel or butterscotch variegate (O)

PREPARATION   **Batch time: 8–10 minutes**

Pour ice cream mix, vanilla extract and ½ of the pignoli nuts into the batch freezer. Turn on the dasher, set timer to 8 minutes, turn on refrigeration and begin the batch. While the batch is running, heat the caramel (or butterscotch) variegate in a food warmer or keep at room temperature until creamy. Spread inner lining of tubs with heated variegate. When the batch is complete, turn off refrigeration, add in remain- ing pignoli nuts and slowly swirl caramel variegate into the tubs as you extrude the finished product. Decorate tops of tubs with pignoli nuts and caramel variegate.

Macadamia Nut Ice Cream

This is my favorite nut-flavored ice cream.. It has real gourmet appeal.

INGREDIENTS

10-Qt Batch	20-Qt Batch	40-Qt Batch	
¾ lb	1½ lb	3 lb	Macadamia nut halves: ½ (B), ½ (E)
1¼ gal	2½ gal	5 gal	Ice cream mix (B)
1 oz	2 oz	4 oz	Two-fold vanilla extract (B)
1 oz	2 oz	4 oz	Macadamia extract (B)

PREPARATION   **Batch time: 8–10 minutes**

Using a blender, blend ½ of the macadamia nuts with ¼ of the ice cream mix to granulate the nuts. Chop the other ½ of the nuts into small pieces and set aside for later use. Pour all ingredients except the macadamia-nut pieces into the batch freezer. Turn on the dasher, set timer to 8 minutes, turn on refrigeration and begin the batch. When the batch is complete, add in remaining macadamia nuts, turn off refrigeration and extrude the finished product. Decorate tops of tubs with macadamia-nut pieces.

Maple Walnut Ice Cream

This is a very popular ice cream flavor, especially in the South and New England.

INGREDIENTS

10-Qt Batch	20-Qt Batch	40-Qt Batch	
1½ lb	3 lb	6 lb	Walnuts: ⅓ (B), ⅔ (E)
12 oz	24 oz	48 oz	Pure maple syrup: ⅓ (B), ⅔ (E)
1¼ gal	2½ gal	5 gal	Ice cream mix (B)
1 oz	2 oz	4 oz	Two-fold vanilla extract (B)

PREPARATION   Batch time: 8–10 minutes

Combine the walnuts and maple syrup in a container. Pour all ingredients including ⅓ of the maple syrup/nut mixture into the batch freezer. Turn on dasher, set timer to 8 minutes, turn on refrigeration and begin the batch. When the batch is complete, add in the remaining maple syrup/nut mixture, turn off refrigeration and extrude the finished product. Decorate tops of tubs with walnut pieces.

Moose Tracks Ice Cream

This is a variation of the Moose Tracks ice cream product sold in supermarkets around the country.

INGREDIENTS

10-Qt Batch	20-Qt Batch	40-Qt Batch	
1¼ gal	2½ gal	5 gal	Ice cream mix (B)
2 oz	4 oz	8 oz	Two-fold vanilla extract (B)
¼ lb	½ lb	1 lb	Granulated peanuts (E)
1¾ lb	3½ lb	7 lb	Peanut butter cups (E)
½ qt	1 qt	2 qt	Peanut butter variegate (O)

PREPARATION   Batch time: 8–10 minutes

Pour ice cream mix and vanilla extract into the batch freezer. Turn on the dasher, set the timer to 8 minutes, turn on refrigeration and begin the batch. While the batch is running, spread inner lining of tubs with peanut butter variegate. When the batch is complete, add in granulated peanuts and peanut butter cups. Turn off refrigeration and slowly swirl peanut butter variegate into the tubs as you extrude the finished product. Decorate tops of tubs with peanuts, peanut butter cups and peanut butter variegate.

Nutty Vanilla Chocolate Chunk Ice Cream

INGREDIENTS

10-Qt Batch	20-Qt Batch	40-Qt Batch	
1¼ gal	2½ gal	5 gal	Ice cream mix (B)
2 oz	4 oz	8 oz	Two-fold vanilla extract (B)
1¼ lb	2½ lb	5 lb	Soft chocolate chunks: (E)
½ lb	1 lb	2 lb	Almonds, roasted and diced (E)
8 oz	16 oz	32 oz	Liquid chocolate* (E)

*To make liquid chocolate, melt in a double boiler 5 parts chocolate (any flavor chocolate bar) to 1 part vegetable oil by weight.

PREPARATION   Batch time: 8–10 minutes

Pour ice cream mix and vanilla extract into the batch freezer. Turn on the dasher, set the timer to 8 minutes, turn on refrigeration and begin the batch. When the batch is complete, add in the chocolate chunks and diced almonds, then slowly add in the liquid chocolate. Turn off refrigeration and extrude the finished product. Decorate tops of tubs with chocolate chunks, almonds and liquid chocolate.

Pecan Praline Ice Cream

Over the last five years, Pecan Praline has become increasingly popular. Use large pecan praline pieces; they not only show better, they taste better.

INGREDIENTS

10-Qt Batch	20-Qt Batch	40-Qt Batch	
1¼ gal	2½ gal	5 gal	Ice cream mix (B)
1 oz	2 oz	4 oz	Two-fold vanilla extract (B)
¼ qt	½ qt	1 qt	Butter pecan base (B)
1 oz	2 oz	4 oz	Praline extract (B)
1¼ lb	2½ lb	5 lb	Pecan praline pieces, large: ⅓ (B), ⅔ (E)
1 qt	2 qt	4 qt	Caramel variegate (O)

PREPARATION   Batch time: 8–10 minutes

Pour ice cream mix, vanilla extract, butter pecan base, praline extract and ⅓ of the pecan praline pieces into the batch freezer. Turn on dasher, set timer to 8 minutes, turn on refrigeration and begin the batch. While the batch is running, spread inner lining of tubs with caramel variegate. When the batch is complete, add in the remaining pecan praline pieces, turn off the refrigeration and slowly swirl the caramel variegate into the tubs as you extrude the finished product. Decorate tops of tubs with pecan praline pieces and caramel variegate.

Peanut Butter Cup Ice Cream

INGREDIENTS

10-Qt Batch	20-Qt Batch	40-Qt Batch	
1¼ gal	2½ gal	5 gal	Ice cream mix (B)
1 oz	2 oz	4 oz	Two-fold vanilla extract (B)
1 qt	2 qt	4 qt	Peanut butter variegate: ½ (B), ½ (O)
½ lb	1 lb	2 lb	Granulated peanuts: ¼ (B), ¾ (E)
1¾ lb	3½ lb	7 lb	Peanut butter cups (E)
½ qt	1 qt	2 qt	Hot fudge (O)

PREPARATION   Batch time: 8–10 minutes

Pour the ice cream mix, vanilla extract, ½ of the peanut butter variegate and ¼ of the granulated peanuts into the batch freezer. Turn on dasher, set timer to 8 minutes, turn on refrigeration and begin the batch. While batch is running, spread inner lining of tubs with peanut butter variegate and fudge. When the batch is complete, add in the remaining granulated peanuts and peanut butter cups, turn off refrigeration and slowly swirl peanut butter variegate and fudge into tubs as you extrude the finished product. Decorate tops of tubs with peanuts and peanut butter variegate.

Peanut Brittle Ice Cream

Vanilla-based ice cream with a caramel variegate and peanut brittle candy makes a wonderful winter ice cream flavor.

INGREDIENTS

10-Qt Batch	20-Qt Batch	40-Qt Batch	
1¼ gal	2½ gal	5 gal	Ice cream mix (B)
1 oz	2 oz	4 oz	Two-fold vanilla extract (B)
8 oz	16 oz	32 oz	Kremia caramel fudge (B)
1 lb	2 lb	4 lb	Peanut brittle pieces (E)
¾ qt	1½ qt	3 qt	Caramel variegate (O)

PREPARATION   Batch time: 8–10 minutes

Pour the ice cream mix, vanilla extract and Kremia caramel fudge into batch freezer. Turn on the dasher, set timer to 8 minutes, turn on refrigeration and begin the batch. While batch is running, spread inner lining of tubs with caramel variegate. When the batch is complete, add in the peanut brittle pieces, turn off refrigeration and slowly swirl the caramel variegate into tubs as you extrude the finished product. Decorate tops of tubs with peanut brittle pieces and caramel variegate.

Peanut Butter Ice Cream

The peanut butter craze of the 1980s created a demand for a variety of peanut-butter flavored ice creams and demand is even stronger today. Timing is important in the production process of this flavor to be sure it is not overprocessed.

INGREDIENTS

10-Qt Batch	20-Qt Batch	40-Qt Batch	
1¼ gal	2½ gal	5 gal	Ice cream mix (B)
1 oz	2 oz	4 oz	Two-fold vanilla extract (B)
¾ lb	1½ lb	3 lb	Granulated peanuts: ¼ (B), ¾ (E)
1 qt	2 qt	4 qt	Peanut butter variegate: ½ (B), ½ (O)

PREPARATION   Batch time: 8–10 minutes

Pour the ice cream mix, vanilla extract, ¼ of the granulated peanuts and ½ of the peanut butter variegate into the batch freezer. Turn on the dasher, set the timer to 8 minutes, turn on refrigeration and begin the batch. While batch is running, spread inner lining of tubs with peanut butter variegate. When the batch is complete, add in the remaining granulated peanuts, turn off refrigeration and slowly swirl remaining peanut butter variegate into the tubs as you extrude the finished product. Decorate tops of tubs with peanuts and peanut butter variegate.

FRUIT- AND BERRY-BASED ICE CREAM FLAVORS

From fresh raspberries and strawberries that are rich and intense in flavor to summer-ripened peaches, mangos and pineapple, fruits and berries are an ice cream maker's pot of gold. During the summer, there is such a variety and abundance of fresh fruit that is reasonably priced and readily available, so use the word *fresh* when you market and merchandise these summer flavors.

Ambrosia Ice Cream

This recipe produces a refreshing blend of pineapple ice cream combined with the flavors of orange, coconut and cherries.

INGREDIENTS

10-Qt Batch	20-Qt Batch	40-Qt Batch	
1¼ gal	2½ gal	5 gal	Ice cream mix (B)
1 oz	2 oz	4 oz	Two-fold vanilla extract (B)
16 oz	1 qt	2 qt	Orange-pineapple base (B)
16 oz	1 qt	2 qt	Pineapple base (B)
4 oz	8 oz	16 oz	Shredded coconut (B)
1 pt	2 pt	4 pt	Bordeaux cherry halves (B)

PREPARATION   Batch time: 8–10 minutes

Pour all ingredients into the batch freezer. Turn on dasher, set timer to 8 minutes, turn on refrigeration and begin the batch. When the batch is complete, turn off the refrigeration and extrude the finished product. Decorate tops of tubs with coconut, pineapple base and cherry halves.

Apple Strudel Ice Cream

A wonderful seasonal item to feature in the fall, this ice cream is one of my "set-you-apart-from-the-competition" flavors. It is not easy to prepare, but it is worth the effort.

INGREDIENTS

10-Qt Batch	20-Qt Batch	40-Qt Batch	
1¼ gal	2½ gal	5 gal	Ice cream mix (B)
1 oz	2 oz	4 oz	Two-fold vanilla extract (B)
1½ lb	3 lb	6 lb	Apple pie filling (B)
1 oz	2 oz	4 oz	Cinnamon (B)
8 oz	16 oz	32 oz	Raisins (M)
4 oz	8 oz	16 oz	Graham crackers, broken (M)

PREPARATION   Batch time: 8–10 minutes

Pour all ingredients except raisins and graham crackers into the batch freezer. Turn on dasher, set timer to 8 minutes, turn on refrigeration and begin the batch. Midway through the batch, add the raisins and graham crackers. When the batch is complete, turn off the refrigeration and extrude the finished product. Decorate tops of tubs with some cinnamon, graham cracker pieces and raisins.

MALCOLM SAYS: The apple pie filling and cinnamon are added at the beginning of the batch to create an apple flavor in the mix. The raisins and graham crackers are added while the batch is running to retain larger pieces that will give the finished product more substance.

Pumpkin Ice Cream

A seasonal flavor appropriate from October through December, this ice cream also makes a great dessert for Thanksgiving and Christmas dinners.

INGREDIENTS

10-Qt Batch	20-Qt Batch	40-Qt Batch	
1¼ gal	2½ gal	5 gal	Ice cream mix (B)
1 oz	2 oz	4 oz	Two-fold vanilla extract (B)
1¼ qt	2½ qt	5 qt	Pumpkin puree (B)
1 oz	2 oz	4 oz	Cinnamon (B)

PREPARATION   Batch time: 8–10 minutes

Pour all ingredients into the batch freezer. Turn on dasher, set timer to 8 minutes, turn on refrigeration and begin the batch. When the batch is complete, turn off the refrigeration and extrude the finished product. Decorate tops of tubs with cinnamon.

Cranberry Ice Cream

This is another fall item that has wonderful body and flavor. It makes a suitable finale for Thanksgiving and Christmas dinners.

INGREDIENTS

10-Qt Batch	20-Qt Batch	40-Qt Batch	
5 lb	10 lb	20 lb	Fresh cranberries* (B)
3½ lb	7 lb	14 lb	Sugar (B)
1 qt	2 qt	4 qt	Water (B)
1¼ gal	2½ gal	5 gal	Ice cream mix (B)
1 oz	2 oz	4 oz	Two-fold vanilla extract (B)
3 oz	6 oz	12 oz	Triple Sec liqueur (E)
1 qt	2 qt	4 qt	Whole-berry cranberry sauce (E)

*Frozen cranberries or processed cranberry puree may be substituted for fresh cranberries. If you use frozen cranberries, defrost, combine them with sugar and water, marinate for 6 hours and then puree the mixture.

PREPARATION   Batch time: 8–10 minutes

Combine fresh cranberries, sugar and water, then puree and strain the mixture. This should provide 6 quarts of cranberry puree. Pour all ingredients except the Triple Sec liqueur and whole-berry cranberry sauce into the batch freezer. Turn on dasher, set timer to 8 minutes, turn on the refrigeration and begin the batch. When the batch is complete, add in the Triple Sec liqueur and ½ of the whole-berry cranberry sauce, turn off refrigeration and, as you extrude the finished product, swirl the remaining ½ of the cranberry sauce into the tubs. Decorate tops of tubs with cranberry sauce.

Blueberry Cheesecake Ice Cream

INGREDIENTS

10-Qt Batch	20-Qt Batch	40-Qt Batch	
1¼ gal	2½ gal	5 gal	Ice cream mix (B)
1 oz	2 oz	4 oz	Two-fold vanilla extract (B)
1½ lb	3 lb	6 lb	Cheesecake powder (B)
1 qt	2 qt	4 qt	Processed blueberries (E)
4 oz	8 oz	16 oz	Graham crackers, broken (E)

PREPARATION   **Batch time: 8–10 minutes**

Pour ¼ of the ice cream mix into the batch freezer, then add the vanilla extract and cheesecake powder. Turn on the dasher and let it run for a few minutes. Pour the balance of the ice cream mix into the batch freezer, set timer to 8 minutes, turn on refrigeration and begin the batch. When the batch is complete, add in the processed blueberries and graham crackers, turn off the refrigeration and extrude the finished product. Decorate tops of tubs with blueberries and graham crackers.

Blueberry Honey Graham Ice Cream

This honey-flavored ice cream with a swirl of blueberry sauce and graham crackers is bound to attract attention. Be sure to use a quality honey to flavor the mix.

INGREDIENTS

10-Qt Batch	20-Qt Batch	40-Qt Batch	
1¼ gal	2½ gal	5 gal	Ice cream mix (B)
1 oz	2 oz	4 oz	Two-fold vanilla extract (B)
8 oz	16 oz	32 oz	Honey (B)
8 oz	16 oz	32 oz	Graham crackers (E)
1 qt	2 qt	4 qt	Processed blueberries, sliced (O)

PREPARATION   **Batch time: 8–10 minutes**

Pour ice cream mix, vanilla extract and honey into the batch freezer. Turn on dasher, set timer to 8 minutes, turn on refrigeration and begin the batch. When the batch is complete, add in the graham crackers, turn off the refrigeration and slowly swirl the processed blueberries into the tubs as you extrude the finished product. Decorate tops of tubs with graham crackers and blueberries.

Coconut Ice Cream

This rich flavor rich is a favorite in the South as well as on the West Coast where tropical flavors sell very well. Taste the product for sweetness during production because you don't want the finished product to be too sweet.

INGREDIENTS

10-Qt Batch	20-Qt Batch	40-Qt Batch	
1¼ gal	2½ gal	5 gal	Ice cream mix (B)
1 oz	2 oz	4 oz	Two-fold vanilla extract (B)
1 lb	2 lb	4 lb	Coconut fruit base (B)
7 oz	14 oz	28 oz	Cream of Coconut (B)
8 oz	16 oz	32 oz	Shredded coconut (E)

PREPARATION   **Batch time: 8–10 minutes**

Pour ice cream mix, vanilla extract, coconut fruit base and cream of Coconut into batch freezer. Turn on dasher, set timer to 8 minutes, turn on refrigeration and begin the batch. Midway through the batch, check the mix for sweetness and taste. If needed, add more coconut fruit base. When the batch is complete, add in shredded coconut, turn off the refrigeration and extrude the finished product. Decorate tops of tubs with shredded coconut.

Carole's Apple Pie Ice Cream

Since Carole and Malcolm make apple pie, I created this recipe based on the pie.

INGREDIENTS

10-Qt Batch	20-Qt Batch	40-Qt Batch	
1¼ gal	2½ gal	5 gal	Ice cream mix (B)
1 oz	2 oz	4 oz	Two-fold vanilla extract (B)
¼ oz	½ oz	1 oz	Cinnamon (B)
2	4	8	Apple pies: ½ (B), ½ (E)
6 oz	12 oz	24 oz	Graham crackers, crumbled (E)

PREPARATION   **Batch time: 8–10 minutes**

Pour ice cream mix, vanilla extract, cinnamon and ½ of the apple pies into the batch freezer. Turn on dasher, set timer to 8 minutes, turn on refrigeration and begin the batch. When batch is complete, add in the remaining apple pies and the crumbled graham crackers, turn off refrigeration and extrude the finished product. Decorate tops of tubs with pieces of apple pie and cinnamon.

Cherry Jubilee Ice Cream

INGREDIENTS

10-Qt Batch	20-Qt Batch	40-Qt Batch	
1 qt	2 qt	4 qt	Cherry halves: ⅓ (B), ⅔ (M)
1¼ gal	2½ gal	5 gal	Ice cream mix (B)
1 oz	2 oz	4 oz	Two-fold vanilla extract (B)
½ lb	1 lb	2 lb	Chocolate chunks (M)

PREPARATION   Batch time: 8–10 minutes

Drain and discard ½ of the juice from the cherry halves. Pour ice cream mix, vanilla extract and ⅓ of the cherry halves into the batch freezer. Turn on dasher, set timer to 8 minutes, turn on refrigeration and begin the batch. Midway through the batch, add in the remaining cherry halves and chocolate chunks. When batch is complete, turn off refrigeration and extrude the finished product. Decorate tops of tubs with cherry halves and chocolate chunks.

Papaya Ice Cream

A delightful, exotic summer dessert, this flavor is very good for wholesale use.

INGREDIENTS

10-Qt Batch	20-Qt Batch	40-Qt Batch	
6	12	24	Ripe papayas (B)
1 lb	2 lb	4 lb	Sugar (B)
1 oz	2 oz	4 oz	Lemon juice (B)
1¼ gal	2½ gal	5 gal	Ice cream mix (B)
1 oz	2 oz	4 oz	Two-fold vanilla extract (B)

PREPARATION   Batch time: 8–10 minutes

Peel, seed and cut the ripe papayas into pieces. Cook papaya flesh for 10 minutes to deactivate the enzymes, then puree the cooked papaya to yield 4 quarts. Add sugar and lemon juice and marinate this mixture for 3 hours. Pour all ingredients into the batch freezer. Turn on dasher, set timer to 8 minutes, turn on refrigeration and begin the batch. When the batch is complete, turn off the refrigeration and extrude the finished product. Decorate tops of tubs with papaya pieces.

Marionberry Cobbler Ice Cream

INGREDIENTS

10-Qt Batch	20-Qt Batch	40-Qt Batch	
1¼ gal	2½ gal	5 gal	Ice cream mix (B)
1 oz	2 oz	4 oz	Two-fold vanilla extract (B)
16 oz	1 qt	2 qt	Marionberry base (B)
¼ oz	½ oz	1 oz	Cinnamon (B)
6 oz	12 oz	24 oz	Graham crackers in pieces (E)
24 oz	1½ qt	3 qt	Marionberry variegate (O)

PREPARATION   Batch time: 8–10 minutes

Pour the ice cream mix, vanilla extract, Marionberry base and cinnamon into the batch freezer. Turn on the dasher and run for 1 minute, set timer to 8 minutes, turn on refrigeration and begin the batch. While batch is running, spread inner lining of tubs with marionberry variegate. When the batch is complete, add in graham cracker pieces, turn off refrigeration and slowly swirl Marionberry variegate into the tubs as you extrude the finished product. Decorate tops of tubs with graham cracker pieces and Marionberry variegate.

Peach Cobbler Ice Cream

From the state of Georgia comes a wintertime ice cream that goes perfectly over fresh apple pie.

INGREDIENTS

10-Qt Batch	20-Qt Batch	40-Qt Batch	
1¼ gal	2½ gal	5 gal	Ice cream mix (B)
1 oz	2 oz	4 oz	Two-fold vanilla extract (B)
16 oz	1 qt	2 qt	Peach base (B)
½ oz	1 oz	2 oz	Peach extract (B)
¼ oz	½ oz	1 oz	Cinnamon (B)
6 oz	12 oz	24 oz	Graham crackers in pieces (E)
24 oz	1½ qt	3 qt	Peach variegate (O)

PREPARATION   Batch time: 8–10 minutes

Pour the ice cream mix, vanilla extract, peach base, peach extract and cinnamon into the batch freezer. Turn on dasher, set timer to 8 minutes, turn on refrigeration and begin the batch. While the batch is running, spread inner lining of tubs with peach variegate. When the batch is complete, add in the graham cracker pieces, turn off the refrigeration and swirl the peach variegate into the tubs as you extrude the finished product. Decorate tops of tubs with graham cracker pieces and peach variegate.

Key Lime Ice Cream

If you think key limes make a wonderful pie, just. wait until you try this ice cream!

INGREDIENTS

10-Qt Batch	20-Qt Batch	40-Qt Batch	
1¼ gal	2½ gal	5 gal	Ice cream mix (B)
1 oz	2 oz	4 oz	Two-fold vanilla extract (B)
5 oz	10 oz	20 oz	Key lime juice (from fresh key limes) (B)
8 oz	16 oz	32 oz	Graham crackers, crumbled (O)

PREPARATION   Batch time: 8–10 minutes

Pour ice cream mix, vanilla extract and key lime juice into the batch freezer. Turn on dasher, set timer to 8 minutes, turn on refrigeration and begin the batch. When the batch is almost complete, turn off the refrigeration and add in the crumbled graham crackers as you extrude the finished product. Decorate tops of tubs with graham crackers.

Mango Ice Cream

This is a very refreshing summertime flavor. Since fresh mangoes are called for, plan on a longer preparation time. Frozen mango puree can be used, but the flavor difference is significant.

INGREDIENTS

10-Qt Batch	20-Qt Batch	40-Qt Batch	
2 qt	4 qt	8 qt	Fresh mangoes (B)
16 oz	32 oz	4 lb	Sugar (B)
1¼ gal	2½ gal	5 gal	Ice cream mix (B)
1 oz	2 oz	4 oz	Two-fold vanilla extract (B)
8 oz	16 oz	32 oz	Pineapple juice (B)
4 oz	8 oz	16 oz	Mango paste (B)

PREPARATION   Batch time: 8–10 minutes

Peel, seed and puree the mangoes. Combine sugar with mango puree and marinate for 6 hours at room temperature. (If you use frozen mango puree, do not add sugar.) Pour all ingredients into the batch freezer. Turn on dasher, set timer to 8 minutes, turn on refrigeration and begin the batch. When batch is complete, turn off refrigeration and extrude the finished product. Decorate tops of tubs with fresh mango pieces or mango puree.

Strawberry Ice Cream

There's nothing like the fresh taste of strawberries to make wonderful ice cream!

INGREDIENTS

10-Qt Batch	20-Qt Batch	40-Qt Batch	
5 lb	10 lb	20 lb	Frozen strawberries: ½ (B), ½ (M)
1¼ lb	2½ lb	5 lb	Sugar (B)
1¼ gal	2½ gal	5 gal	Ice cream mix (B)
1 oz	2 oz	4 oz	Two-fold vanilla extract (B)
8 oz	16 oz	1 qt	Processed strawberries (B)
4 oz	8 oz	16 oz	Prepared strawberry puree (B)

PREPARATION   Batch time: 8–10 minutes

Defrost frozen strawberries, add sugar and marinate at least 8 hours or overnight. At the end of the marination period, drain off and discard excess juice and divide the mixture in half. Puree ½ of the mixture and set aside the other ½ for later use. Pour all ingredients except the unpureed strawberries into the batch freezer. Turn on dasher, set timer to 8 minutes, turn on refrigeration and begin the batch. Midway through the batch, add in the unpureed strawberries. When batch is complete, turn off the refrigeration and extrude the finished product. Decorate tops of tubs with marinated strawberry pieces.

MALCOLM SAYS: I use frozen strawberries because they are not as expensive as fresh berries and the end result is almost as good.

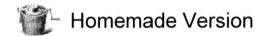 ## Homemade Version

INGREDIENTS

2 lb	Fresh or frozen strawberries	16 oz	Heavy cream
16 oz	Sugar	1 Tbsp	Vanilla extract
8	Egg yolks	6 oz	Strawberry preserves
16 oz	Milk		

PREPARATION

Cut up the strawberries and combine with 8 ounces of sugar. Marinate this mixture for 8 hours, then drain off the excess juice. Use a double boiler to create a custard base. Pour the egg yolks, remainder of sugar and milk into the pot. Heat the mixture slowly but do *not* bring to a boil. When a film forms over the back of your spoon, remove custard base from heat and place the pot into a larger pot filled with cold water to cool. Add in heavy cream and place in refrigerator until cold (at least 2 hours). Stir in the vanilla extract and strawberry preserves, then transfer all to an ice cream maker. Freeze according to manufacturer's instructions. When the ice cream is almost frozen, add in the strawberry mixture, turn off the refrigeration and extrude the finished product. Yield: 2 quarts of ice cream

Banana Ice Cream

Banana is an easy fresh fruit flavor to produce because of the availability of bananas year round.

INGREDIENTS

10-Qt Batch	20-Qt Batch	40-Qt Batch	
1¼ gal	2½ gal	5 gal	Ice cream mix (B)
1 oz	2 oz	4 oz	Two-fold vanilla extract (B)
4 lb	8 lb	16 lb	Fresh ripe bananas, peeled (B)
½ oz	1 oz	2 oz	Lemon juice (B)

PREPARATION   Batch time: 8–10 minutes

Pour all ingredients into the batch freezer. Turn on dasher, set timer to 8 minutes, turn on the refrigeration and begin the batch. When the batch is complete, turn off the refrigeration and extrude the finished product. Decorate tops of tubs with banana pieces.

 Homemade Version

If you like bananas, you'll love making this flavor at home!

INGREDIENTS

2 lb	Fresh ripe bananas, peeled	16 oz	Heavy cream
16 oz	Sugar	1 Tbsp	Vanilla extract
8	Egg yolks	1 Tbsp	Lemon juice
16 oz	Milk		

PREPARATION

Cut up the bananas and combine with 8 ounces of sugar. Marinate this mixture for 8 hours, then drain off the excess juice. Use a double boiler to create a custard base. Pour the egg yolks, remainder of sugar and milk into the pot. Heat the mixture slowly but do *not* bring to a boil. When a film forms over the back of your spoon, remove custard base from heat and place the pot into a larger pot filled with cold water to cool. Add in heavy cream and place in refrigerator until cold (at least 2 hours). Stir in vanilla extract, lemon juice and ½ of the banana mixture and transfer all to an ice cream maker. Freeze according to manufacturer's instructions. When the ice cream is almost frozen, add in remaining banana mixture, turn off refrigeration and extrude the finished product. Yield: 1½ quarts of ice cream

Banana Daiquiri Ice Cream

Adults will love this sophisticated summer flavor that is as tasty and refreshing as the drink.

INGREDIENTS

10-Qt Batch	20-Qt Batch	40-Qt Batch	
5 lb	10 lb	20 lb	Fresh ripe bananas, peeled (B)
1¼ gal	2½ gal	5 gal	Ice cream mix (B)
1 oz	2 oz	4 oz	Two-fold vanilla extract (B)
½ oz	1 oz	2 oz	Lemon juice (B)
8 oz	16 oz	32 oz	Dark rum (E)

PREPARATION   Batch time: 8–10 minutes

Cut the bananas into pieces. Pour all ingredients except rum into the batch freezer. Turn on dasher, set timer to 8 minutes, turn on refrigeration and begin the batch. When the batch is complete, add in the rum, turn off refrigeration and extrude the finished product. Decorate tops of tubs with bananas.

Bananas Foster Ice Cream

New Orleans claims to own this creation, but it really originated in the Caribbean. This is a "knock-your-socks-off" flavor.

INGREDIENTS

10-Qt Batch	20-Qt Batch	40-Qt Batch	
5 lb	10 lb	20 lb	Fresh ripe bananas, peeled (B)
1¼ gal	2½ gal	5 gal	Ice cream mix (B)
1 oz	2 oz	4 oz	Two-fold vanilla extract (B)
½ oz	1 oz	2 oz	Lemon juice (B)
3 oz	6 oz	12 oz	Brown sugar (B)
5 oz	10 oz	20 oz	Dark rum (E)
1 qt	2 qt	4 qt	Caramel cinnamon variegate (O)

PREPARATION   Batch time: 8–10 minutes

Cut the bananas into pieces. Pour all ingredients except rum and caramel cinnamon variegate into the batch freezer. Turn on the dasher, set timer to 8 minutes, turn on refrigeration and begin the batch. When the batch is almost complete, add in the dark rum and continue freezing for 2–3 minutes. Turn off the refrigeration and, as you extrude the finished product, slowly swirl the caramel cinnamon variegate into the tubs. Decorate tops of tubs with banana pieces.

Banana Macadamia Nut Ice Cream

The combination of bananas and macadamia nuts makes a great flavor!

INGREDIENTS

10-Qt Batch	20-Qt Batch	40-Qt Batch	
1¼ gal	2½ gal	5 gal	Ice cream mix (B)
1 oz	2 oz	4 oz	Two-fold vanilla extract (B)
5 lb	10 lb	20 lb	Fresh ripe bananas, peeled (B)
½ lb	1 lb	2 lb	Macadamia nut pieces (M)

PREPARATION   Batch time: 8–10 minutes

Pour all ingredients except the macadamia nuts into the batch freezer. Turn on the dasher, set timer to 8 minutes, turn on refrigeration and begin the batch. Midway through the batch, add in the macadamia nuts. When the batch is complete, turn off refrigeration and extrude the finished product. Decorate tops of tubs with banana and macadamia-nut pieces.

Banana Split Ice Cream

This is just the kind of flavor the whole family loves!

INGREDIENTS

10-Qt Batch	20-Qt Batch	40-Qt Batch	
1¼ gal	2½ gal	5 gal	Ice cream mix (B)
1 oz	2 oz	4 oz	Two-fold vanilla extract (B)
3 lb	6 lb	12 lb	Fresh bananas, peeled (B)
1 lb	2 lb	4 lb	Processed strawberries (E)
½ lb	1 lb	2 lb	Bordeaux cherry halves (E)
4 oz	8 oz	16 oz	Sliced almonds (E)
4 oz	8 oz	16 oz	Shredded coconut (E)

PREPARATION   Batch time: 8–10 minutes

Pour the ice cream mix, vanilla extract and bananas into the batch freezer. Turn on dasher, set timer to 8 minutes, turn on refrigeration and begin the batch. When the batch is complete, add in processed strawberries, Bordeaux cherries, sliced almonds and shredded coconut, then turn off refrigeration and extrude the finished product. Decorate tops of tubs with bananas, strawberries, cherries and shredded coconut.

Jackfruit Cashew Ice Cream

This very popular Vietnamese fruit is a wonderful, distinctive flavor to have after a Vietnamese dinner.

INGREDIENTS

10-Qt Batch	20-Qt Batch	40-Qt Batch	
2 lb	4 lb	8 lb	Frozen jackfruit: ½ (B), ½ (E)
½ lb	1 lb	2 lb	Sugar (B)
1¼ gal	2½ gal	5 gal	Ice cream mix (B)
1 oz	2 oz	4 oz	Two-fold vanilla extract (B)
½ lb	1 lb	2 lb	Cashew pieces (E)

PREPARATION   Batch time: 8–10 minutes

Defrost the jackfruit, combine with sugar and marinate for 8 hours. At the end of the marination process, puree ½ of the jackfruit mixture and cut the balance into small cubes. Pour the pureed jackfruit, ice cream mix and vanilla extract into batch freezer. Turn on dasher, set timer to 8 minutes, turn on refrigeration and begin the batch. When the batch is complete, add in the jackfruit cubes and cashews, turn off the refrigeration and extrude the finished product. Decorate tops of tubs with jackfruit cubes and cashews.

Orange-Pineapple-Macaroon Ice Cream

If you are operating an old-fashioned ice cream parlor, then this ice cream flavor of the 1940–50s will sell very well.

INGREDIENTS

10-Qt Batch	20-Qt Batch	40-Qt Batch	
1¼ gal	2½ gal	5 gal	Ice cream mix (B)
1 oz	2 oz	4 oz	Two-fold vanilla extract (B)
1½ qt	3 qt	6 qt	Orange-pineapple base (B)
12 oz	1½ lb	3 lb	Macaroons (E)
1½ lb	3 lb	6 lb	Pineapple topping (E)

PREPARATION   Batch time: 8–10 minutes

Pour ice cream mix, vanilla extract and orange-pineapple base into the batch freezer. Turn on the dasher, set timer to 8 minutes, turn on refrigeration and begin the batch. When batch is almost complete, add in the macaroons and pineapple topping, turn off the refrigeration and extrude the finished product. Decorate tops of tubs with macaroons and pineapple topping.

Peach Ice Cream

INGREDIENTS

10-Qt Batch	20-Qt Batch	40-Qt Batch	
5 lb	10 lb	20 lb	Frozen peaches: ½ (B), ½ (E)
1 lb	2 lb	4 lb	Sugar (B)
1¼ gal	2½ gal	5 gal	Ice cream mix (B)
1 oz	2 oz	4 oz	Two-fold vanilla extract (B)
6 oz	12 oz	24 oz	Peche (peach) paste (B)
½ oz	1 oz	2 oz	Natural peach extract (B)

PREPARATION   Batch time: 8–10 minutes

Defrost peaches, combine with sugar and marinate for 8 hours. At the end of the marination process, puree ½ of the peach mixture and cut the other ½ into small cubes. Pour all ingredients except the peach cubes into the batch freezer. Turn on dasher, set timer to 8 minutes, turn on refrigeration and begin the batch. When the batch is complete, add in the peach cubes, turn off the refrigeration and extrude the finished product. Decorate tops of tubs with peach cubes.

Pineapple Ice Cream

Becoming increasingly hard to find in a dipping shop, this sweet and tart summer flavor sells well.

INGREDIENTS

10-Qt Batch	20-Qt Batch	40-Qt Batch	
1½	3	6	Pineapples (E)
4 oz	8 oz	16 oz	Sugar (B)
8 oz	16 oz	32 oz	Pineapple juice (B)
1¼ gal	2½ gal	5 gal	Ice cream mix (B)
1 oz	2 oz	4 oz	Two-fold vanilla extract (B)

PREPARATION   Batch time: 8–10 minutes

Core and pare the pineapples, cut them into pieces and cook on medium heat for 30 minutes. Add sugar and pineapple juice, divide the mixture in half, puree ½ and set aside the other ½ for later use. Pour ice cream mix and vanilla extract into the batch freezer. Turn on the dasher, set timer to 8 minutes, turn on refrigeration and begin the batch. When the batch is almost complete, add in the pineapple puree. When the batch is complete, add in the pineapple pieces, turn off refrigeration and extrude the finished product. Decorate tops of tubs with cooked pineapple pieces.

MALCOLM SAYS: The reason to cook the pineapples *first* is to prevent them from curdling.

Red Raspberry Ice Cream

A refreshing, delicious summer ice cream flavor!

INGREDIENTS

10-Qt Batch	20-Qt Batch	40-Qt Batch	
2½ lb	5 lb	10 lb	Frozen raspberries (O)
8 oz	16 oz	32 oz	Sugar (O)
1¼ gal	2½ gal	5 gal	Ice cream mix (B)
1 oz	2 oz	4 oz	Two-fold vanilla extract (B)
2 qt	4 qt	8 qt	Red raspberry base (B)

PREPARATION   Batch time: 8–10 minutes

Defrost raspberries, combine with sugar and marinate for 6–8 hours. Then drain off the juice and discard. Pour all ingredients except the marinated raspberries into the batch freezer. Turn on dasher, set timer to 8 minutes, turn on refrigeration and begin the batch. When batch is complete, turn off the refrigeration, add in the marinated raspberries and extrude the finished product. Decorate tops of tubs with raspberry pieces.

Tropical Paradise Ice Cream

This recipe combines the flavor of pineapple with that of banana and rum.

INGREDIENTS

10-Qt Batch	20-Qt Batch	40-Qt Batch	
2 lb	4 lb	8 lb	Ripe bananas, peeled (B)
1¼ gal	2½ gal	5 gal	Ice cream mix (B)
1 oz	2 oz	4 oz	Two-fold vanilla extract (B)
24 oz	1½ qt	3 qt	Pineapple ice cream base (B)
6 oz	13 oz	26 oz	Dark rum* (M)

*If you use rum extract in place of the rum, use 3 ounces for a 20-quart batch and adjust accordingly for other size batches.

PREPARATION   Batch time: 8–10 minutes

Puree the bananas. Pour all ingredients except the rum into the batch freezer. Turn on dasher, set timer to 8 minutes, turn on refrigeration and begin the batch. Midway through the batch, add in the rum. When the batch is complete, turn off the refrigeration and extrude finished product. Decorate tops of tubs with banana pieces.

Strawberry Cheesecake Ice Cream

Without a doubt, cheesecake is the #1-selling restaurant dessert in the U.S. What better idea than taking this great-tasting dessert and making some variations in the form of ice cream! In 1991 my associate Lisa Tanner and I did just that—we created Raspberry Cheescake Frozen Yogurt Cake and won 1ˢᵗ place for Penguin Frozen Yogurt's best new foodservice dessert of the year.

INGREDIENTS

10-Qt Batch	20-Qt Batch	40-Qt Batch	
1¼ gal	2½ gal	5 gal	Ice cream mix (B)
1½ lb	3 lb	6 lb	Cheesecake powder (B)
1 oz	2 oz	4 oz	Two-fold vanilla extract (B)
1 qt	2 qt	4 qt	Processed strawberries (E)
4 oz	8 oz	16 oz	Graham crackers, broken (E)

PREPARATION   Batch time: 8–10 minutes

Pour ½ of the ice cream mix, dry cheesecake powder and vanilla extract into the batch freezer. Turn on dasher and let it run for a few minutes. Pour the remainder of the ice cream mix into the batch freezer, set timer to 8 minutes, turn on refrigeration and begin batch. When the batch is complete, add in the processed strawberries and graham crackers, turn off refrigeration and extrude the finished product. Decorate tops of tubs with strawberries and graham crackers.

VARIATION

RASPBERRY CHEESECAKE ICE CREAM: For 20-quart batch, substitute 2 quarts of raspberry topping or raspberry variegate for the strawberries. Swirl it into the tubs as you extrude the finished product. Adjust accordingly for other size batches.

Ube Ice Cream

The term Ube refers to the purple yam that is grown in the Philippines. It is similar in size to a sweet potato and has a sweet taste that I am sure you will like.

INGREDIENTS

10-Qt Batch	20-Qt Batch	40-Qt Batch	
1½ lb	3 lb	6 lb	Ube, frozen or canned (B)
6 oz	12 oz	24 oz	Sugar (B)
1¼ gal	2½ gal	5 gal	Ice cream mix (B)
1 oz	2 oz	4 oz	Two-fold vanilla extract (B)

PREPARATION   Batch time: 8–10 minutes

Defrost the ube, add sugar to it and marinate the mixture for 2–3 hours. Pour all ingredients into the batch freezer. Turn on dasher, set timer to 8 minutes, turn on refrigeration and begin the batch. When the batch is complete, turn off refrigeration and extrude the finished product.

CANDY-BASED ICE CREAM FLAVORS

The continued popularity of candy based flavors has enabled batch freezer producers to create a niche producing a superior product because we can control the amount of candy based ingredients that go into a batch.

This category of flavors is relatively new to the ice cream industry, becoming popular at about the same time as the craze for super-premium ice cream began in the early 1980s. These flavors were created to satisfy consumers who enjoyed chilled or frozen candy bars and ultimately craved their favorite candy in a frozen dairy creation.

For the most part, candy manufacturers are now producing for the ice cream industry bulk packaging of small broken pieces of their candies for inclusion into ice cream flavors. If you are using whole candy bars, they should be broken into pieces that can be seen in the finished ice cream, but the pieces should not be larger than ⅜-inch square. Temperature at time of usage should be 40 degrees F. Larger pieces are likely to jam the fruit feeder equipment. In using candies in a batch freezing operation, don't add the candy to the freezer all at once. Add it at frequent intervals during the freezing process to prevent the candy from sticking together and forming clumps.

This category lends itself to experimentation, so don't be afraid to ask yourself "What if?" and then try it and see!

English Toffee Ice Cream

This flavor is very popular in the Midwest, but for some reason it has not caught on in the rest of the country. It tastes very good and it is not difficult to make.

INGREDIENTS

10-Qt Batch	20-Qt Batch	40-Qt Batch	
1¼ gal	2½ gal	5 gal	Ice cream mix (B)
1 oz	2 oz	4 oz	Two-fold vanilla extract (B)
1½ oz	3 oz	6 oz	Rum extract (B)
1¼ lb	2½ lb	5 lb	English Toffee candy: ½ (B), ½ (E)

PREPARATION   Batch time: 8–10 minutes

Pour all ingredients except ½ of the English Toffee candy into the batch freezer. Turn on dasher and run for 5 minutes to blend ingredients, set timer to 8 minutes, turn on refrigeration and begin the batch. When the batch is complete, add in the remaining candy, turn off refrigeration and extrude the finished product. Decorate tops of tubs with pieces of toffee candy.

Butter Brickle Ice Cream

I have always been fond of this flavor and I enjoy tasting it right out of the batch freezer. This flavor has universal appeal whether produced in half-gallon sizes for supermarket shelves or for an ice cream shop in Des Moines, Iowa.

INGREDIENTS

10-Qt Batch	20-Qt Batch	40-Qt Batch	
1¼ gal	2½ gal	5 gal	Ice cream mix (B)
1 oz	2 oz	4 oz	Two-fold vanilla extract (B)
1 oz	2 oz	4 oz	Freeze-dried coffee (B)
1 Tbsp	2 Tbsp	4 Tbsp	Hot water (B)
1½ oz	3 oz	6 oz	Butter flavor (B)
1¼ lb	2½ lb	5 lb	Butter Brickle candy: ½ (B), ½ (E)

PREPARATION   Batch time: 8–10 minutes

Pour all ingredients except ½ of the Butter Brickle candy into the batch freezer. Turn on dasher for 3 minutes to allow candy to blend into the ice cream mix, set timer to 8 minutes, turn on refrigeration and begin the batch. When the batch is complete, add in the remaining Butter Brickle candy, turn off refrigeration and extrude the finished product. Decorate tops of tubs with pieces of Butter Brickle candy.

Heath Bar Ice Cream

Heath Bar is one of the best-selling candy flavors in the ice cream market because of its great taste and ease of production.

INGREDIENTS

10-Qt Batch	20-Qt Batch	40-Qt Batch	
1¼ gal	2½ gal	5 gal	Ice cream mix (B)
1 oz	2 oz	4 oz	Two-fold vanilla extract (B)
1 oz	2 oz	4 oz	Freeze-dried coffee (B)
1 oz	2 oz	4 oz	Hot water (B)
1 lb	2 lb	4 lb	Heath Bar candy pieces: ½ (B), ½ (E)

PREPARATION   Batch time: 8–10 minutes

Pour all ingredients except ½ of the granulated Heath Bar pieces into the batch freezer. Turn on dasher for 3 minutes to allow candy to blend into the mix. Turn on refrigeration, set the timer to 8 minutes and begin the batch. When the batch is complete, add in the remaining candy pieces, turn off refrigeration and extrude the finished product. Decorate tops of tubs with Heath Bar pieces.

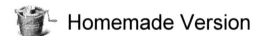 ## Homemade Version

INGREDIENTS

½ Tbsp	Freeze-dried coffee	16 oz	Milk
1 tsp	Hot water	16 oz	Heavy cream
½ Tbsp	Cocoa	1 Tbsp	Vanilla extract
8	Egg yolks	6 oz	Heath Bar candy pieces
8 oz	Sugar	6 oz	Chocolate chips

PREPARATION

Mix freeze-dried coffee with as little hot water as possible. Add cocoa and blend thoroughly until mixture is very smooth with no dry pieces of coffee or cocoa visible. Use a double boiler to create a custard base. Pour the egg yolks, sugar and milk into the pot. Heat the mixture slowly but do *not* bring to a boil. When a film forms over the back of your spoon, remove custard base from heat and place the pot into a larger pot filled with cold water to cool. Add in the heavy cream and place in refrigerator until cold (at least 2 hours). Then stir in the vanilla extract and transfer to an ice cream maker. Freeze according to manufacturer's instructions. When the ice cream is semifrozen, add in the Heath Bar pieces and chocolate chips. When the batch is complete, turn off refrigeration and extrude the finished product. Yield: 2 quarts of ice cream

M&M Ice Cream

Kids love M&M's as either a candy to eat or an ice cream topping, and they especially love them when they are part of an ice cream flavor. If you want to create excitement in your shop, make this flavor. Some of the candy pieces are added at the beginning of the batch to add the candy flavor to the ice cream.

INGREDIENTS

10-Qt Batch	20-Qt Batch	40-Qt Batch	
1¼ gal	2½ gal	5 gal	Ice cream mix (B)
1 oz	2 oz	4 oz	Two-fold vanilla extract (B)
1 lb	2 lb	4 lb	M&M's mini chocolate candies: ½ (B), ½ (E)
4 oz	8 oz	1 lb	Chocolate chips (E)

PREPARATION   Batch time: 8–10 minutes

Pour the ice cream mix, vanilla extract and ½ of the M&M's into the batch freezer. Turn on dasher, set timer to 8 minutes, turn on refrigeration and begin the batch. When the batch is complete, add in the remaining M&M's and chocolate chips, turn off refrigeration, and extrude finished product. Decorate tops of tubs with M&M's.

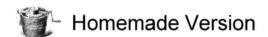 Homemade Version

INGREDIENTS

8	Egg yolks
8 oz	Sugar
16 oz	Milk
16 oz	Heavy cream
1 Tbsp	Vanilla extract
8 oz	M&M's mini chocolate candies
2 oz	Chocolate chips

PREPARATION

Use a double boiler to create a custard base. Pour the egg yolks, sugar and milk into the pot. Heat the mixture slowly but do *not* bring to a boil. When a film forms over the back of your spoon, remove custard base from heat and place the pot into a larger pot filled with cold water to cool. Add in heavy cream and place in refrigerator until cold (at least 2 hours). Then stir in vanilla extract and transfer to an ice cream maker. Freeze according to manufacturer's instructions. When the ice cream is semifrozen, add in the M&M's and chocolate chips. When the batch is complete, turn off the refrigeration and extrude the finished product. Yield: 1½ quarts of ice cream

Extraterrestrial Ice Cream

The movie ET made this flavor very popular with children. Some of the candy pieces are added at the beginning of the batch for extra candy flavor.

INGREDIENTS

10-Qt Batch	20-Qt Batch	40-Qt Batch	
1¼ gal	2½ gal	5 gal	Ice cream mix (B)
1 oz	2 oz	4 oz	Two-fold vanilla extract (B)
1 lb	2 lb	4 lb	Reeses's Pieces candy: ½ (B), ½ (E)

PREPARATION   Batch time: 8–10 minutes

Pour all ingredients except ½ of the Reese's Pieces into the batch freezer. Turn on dasher, set timer to 8 minutes, turn on refrigeration and begin the batch. When the batch is complete, add in the remaining candy, turn off refrigeration and extrude the finished product. Decorate tops of tubs with Reese's Pieces.

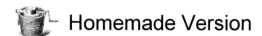 Homemade Version

Kids love this flavor.

INGREDIENTS

8	Egg yolks
8 oz	Sugar
16 oz	Milk
16 oz	Heavy cream
1 Tbsp	Vanilla extract
8 oz	Reese's Pieces candy

PREPARATION

Use a double boiler to create a custard base. Pour the egg yolks, sugar and milk into the pot. Heat the mixture slowly but do *not* bring to a boil. When a film forms over the back of your spoon, remove the custard base from heat and place the pot into a larger pot filled with cold water to cool. Add in heavy cream and place in refrigerator until cold (at least 2 hours). Then stir in the vanilla extract and transfer to an ice cream maker. Freeze according to manufacturer's instructions. When the ice cream is semifrozen, add in the Reese's Pieces. Then turn off the refrigeration and extrude the finished product. Yield: 1½ quarts of ice cream

Milky Way Ice Cream

For years before any ice cream maker ever thought of using the Milky Way candy bar as an ice cream flavor, consumers were freezing and eating them as a frozen dessert. Today it is a very popular ice cream flavor and is one of my "set-me-apart-from-the-competition" flavors.

INGREDIENTS

10-Qt Batch	20-Qt Batch	40-Qt Batch	
12	24	48	Milky Way candy bars (2.15 oz each)**:** ½ (B), ½ (E)
1¼ gal	2½ gal	5 gal	Ice cream mix (B)
1 oz	2 oz	4 oz	Two-fold vanilla extract (B)
4 oz	8 oz	1 lb	Chocolate chips (E)

*Milky Way candy bars can also be purchased in pieces. If you use this product, you'll need 3 pounds for a 20-quart batch. Adjust accordingly for other size batches.

PREPARATION   Batch time: 8–10 minutes

Cut candy bars into small pieces. Pour all ingredients except ½ of the Milky Way pieces into the batch freezer. Turn on dasher for 5 minutes to allow candy pieces to blend into the mix, set timer to 8 minutes, turn on refrigeration and begin the batch. When the batch is complete, add in the remaining candy pieces and chocolate chips, turn off refrigeration and extrude the finished product. Decorate tops of tubs with candy pieces.

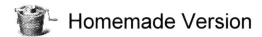 ## Homemade Version

INGREDIENTS

5	Milky Way candy bars (2.15 oz each)	16 oz	Heavy cream
8	Egg yolks	1 Tbsp	Vanilla extract
8 oz	Sugar	1 oz	Malt powder
16 oz	Milk	2 oz	Chocolate chips

PREPARATION

Cut Milky Way candy bars into small pieces. Pour ½ of the pieces and ½ of the milk into a blender and blend thoroughly. Use a double boiler to create a custard base. Pour the egg yolks, sugar and milk into the pot. Heat the mixture slowly but do *not* bring to a boil. When a film forms over the back of your spoon, remove custard base from heat and place the pot into a larger pot filled with cold water to cool. Add in the heavy cream and place in refrigerator until cold (at least 2 hours). Then stir in vanilla extract and malt powder and transfer to an ice cream maker. Freeze according to manufacturer's instructions. When the ice cream is semifrozen, add in remaining candy pieces and chocolate chips, turn off refrigeration and extrude finished product. Yield: 1½ quarts of ice cream

Snickers Ice Cream

This flavor is as popular as Milky Way. It is a must flavor for any gourmet operation. Granulated peanuts and chocolate chips are included for added flavor.

INGREDIENTS

10-Qt Batch	20-Qt Batch	40-Qt Batch	
1¼ lb	2½ lb	5 lb	Ground Snickers bars: ⅓ (B), ⅔ (E)
1¼ gal	2½ gal	5 gal	Ice cream mix (B)
1 oz	2 oz	4 oz	Two-fold vanilla extract (B)
4 oz	½ lb	1 lb	Chocolate chips (B)
4 oz	½ lb	1 lb	Granulated peanuts: ½ (M), ½ (E)

PREPARATION   Batch time: 8–10 minutes

Pour ⅓ of the ground Snickers bars and ¼ of the ice cream mix into the batch freezer. Turn on dasher and blend for 2–3 minutes. Add remainder of the ice cream mix, vanilla extract and chocolate chips into the batch freezer, set timer to 8 minutes, turn on refrigeration and begin the batch. Midway through the batch, add ½ of the granulated peanuts. When the batch is complete, add in remaining ground Snickers bars and the rest of the granulated peanuts, turn off the refrigeration and extrude the finished product. Decorate tops of tubs with ground Snickers bars.

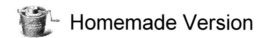 ## Homemade Version

INGREDIENTS

5	Snickers bars	16 oz	Heavy cream
16 oz	Milk	1 Tbsp	Vanilla extract
8	Egg yolks	1 oz	Granulated peanuts
8 oz	Sugar	2 oz	Chocolate chips

PREPARATION

Cut Snickers bars into small pieces. Pour ½ of the pieces into a blender with ½ of the milk and blend thoroughly. Use a double boiler to create a custard base. Pour the egg yolks, sugar and milk into the pot. Heat the mixture slowly but do *not* bring to a boil. When a film forms over the back of your spoon, remove custard base from heat and place the pot into a larger pot filled with cold water to cool. Add in the heavy cream and place in refrigerator until cold (at least 2 hours). Then stir in the vanilla extract and transfer to an ice cream maker. Freeze according to manufacturer's instructions. When the ice cream is semifrozen, add in the remainder of the Snickers bar pieces and chocolate chips, turn off the refrigeration and extrude the finished product. Yield:1½ quarts of ice cream

Gummy Bear Ice Cream

The secret to selling this flavor is the deep blue color of the ice cream.

INGREDIENTS

10-Qt Batch	20-Qt Batch	40-Qt Batch	
1¼ gal	2½ gal	5 gal	Ice cream mix (B)
1 oz	2 oz	4 oz	Two-fold vanilla extract (B)
2½ oz	5 oz	10 oz	Cotton candy flavor (B)
2½ lb	5 lb	10 lb	Gummy bear candy (O)
¾ oz	1½ oz	3 oz	Blue food coloring (B)

PREPARATION   Batch time: 8–10 minutes

Pour all ingredients except the gummy bears into the batch freezer. Turn on dasher, set timer to 8 minutes, turn on refrigeration and begin the batch. When the batch is complete, add in the gummy bears, turn off refrigeration, and extrude the finished product. Decorate tops of tubs with gummy bear pieces.

LIQUOR- & LIQUEUR-BASED ICE CREAM FLAVORS

What succeeds as a beverage often succeeds as an ice cream flavor, and sometimes even better. Ice cream makers have experimented with nearly every liquor and liqueur flavor imaginable, and recipes for the most popular results are presented here.

Care should be taken when using liquors, wines or liqueurs because their alcohol content can inhibit the freezing process. Alcoholic ingredients are usually added to the ice cream in production in the middle or at the end of the freezing stage. The use of alcoholic ingredients in a batch-freezing operation will increase the freezing time by about 2–3 minutes. Natural or artificial liquor or liqueur extracts or flavorings can be added anytime during the freezing process.

Ice cream flavors with liquor should be sold to adults only.

Grand Marnier Ice Cream

In the liqueur category of flavors, Grand Marnier stands out for its sophisticated flavor. It is very popular in restaurants and gourmet ice cream operations.

INGREDIENTS

10-Qt Batch	20-Qt Batch	40-Qt Batch	
1¼ gal	2½ gal	5 gal	Ice cream mix (B)
1 oz	2 oz	4 oz	Two-fold vanilla extract (B)
13 oz	26 oz	52 oz	Grand Marnier liqueur* (M)
2	4	8	Zest from oranges (M)

PREPARATION   Batch time: 9–11 minutes

Pour all ingredients except the Grand Marnier liqueur into the batch freezer. Turn on dasher, set timer to 9 minutes, turn on refrigeration and begin the batch. When the batch is almost complete, add in the Grand Marnier and continue freezing for 2–3 minutes, then turn off the refrigeration and extrude the finished product.

Peach Cognac Ice Cream

I enjoy eating peaches and Peach ice cream during the summer, so this flavor was a natural for me to create.

INGREDIENTS

10-Qt Batch	20-Qt Batch	40-Qt Batch	
1¼ gal	2½ gal	5 gal	Ice cream mix (B)
1 oz	2 oz	4 oz	Two-fold vanilla extract (B)
1 oz	2 oz	4 oz	Peach ice cream flavor (B)
7 oz	14 oz	28 oz	Cognac* (M)
1 lb	2 lb	4 lb	Processed stabilized peaches (M)

PREPARATION   Batch time: 9–11 minutes

Pour all ingredients except the cognac and processed stabilized peaches into the batch freezer. Turn on dasher, set timer to 8 minutes, turn on refrigeration and begin the batch. When the batch is almost complete, add in the processed peaches and Cognac and continue freezing for 2–3 minutes, then turn off the refrigeration and extrude the finished product. Decorate tops of tubs with processed peaches.

*Sometimes liqueur flavors take 2–3 minutes longer to freeze properly because of the alcohol content. Also, liqueur inhibits the freezing process if added early in the process, so it is important to wait to add it.

Cherry Amaretto Ice Cream

This recipe is a variation of Amaretto ice cream. The flavor of cherries marries well with amaretto, and this flavor is a good addition to any seasonal line.

INGREDIENTS

10-Qt Batch	20-Qt Batch	40-Qt Batch	
1¼ gal	2½ gal	5 gal	Ice cream mix (B)
1 oz	2 oz	4 oz	Two-fold vanilla extract (B)
2 oz	4 oz	8 oz	Amaretto extract (B)
16 oz	1 qt	2 qt	Bordeaux cherry halves (M)
4 oz	½ lb	1 lb	Sliced roasted almonds (M)

PREPARATION   Batch time: 9–11 minutes

Pour all ingredients except the cherry halves and sliced almonds into the batch freezer. Turn on dasher, set timer to 9 minutes, turn on refrigeration and begin the batch. Midway through the batch, add in the cherry halves and sliced almonds. When the batch is complete, turn off the refrigeration and extrude the finished product. Decorate tops of tubs with cherry halves and sliced almonds.

Crème de Cacao Ice Cream

INGREDIENTS

10-Qt Batch	20-Qt Batch	40-Qt Batch	
1¼ gal	2½ gal	5 gal	Ice cream mix (B)
1 oz	2 oz	4 oz	Two-fold vanilla extract (B)
12 oz	1½ lb	3 lb	Chocolate chips: ½ (B), ½ (E)
8 oz	16 oz	32 oz	Crème de Cacao (M)

PREPARATION   Batch time: 9–11 minutes

Pour the ice cream mix, vanilla extract and ½ of the chocolate chips into the batch freezer. Turn on dasher, set timer to 9 minutes, turn on refrigeration and begin the batch. Midway through the batch, add in the Crème de Cacao. When batch is complete, add in the remaining chocolate chips, turn off the refrigeration and extrude the finished product. Decorate tops of tubs with chocolate chips.

Crème de Menthe Ice Cream

Geared toward an adult market, this flavor sells very well in gourmet operations and restaurants.

INGREDIENTS

10-Qt Batch	20-Qt Batch	40-Qt Batch	
1¼ gal	2½ gal	5 gal	Ice cream mix (B)
1 oz	2 oz	4 oz	Two-fold vanilla extract (B)
1 lb	2 lb	4 lb	Chocolate chips: ½ (B), ½ (E)
13 oz	26 oz	52 oz	Crème de Menthe liqueur (M)

PREPARATION   Batch time: 9–11 minutes

Pour the ice cream mix, vanilla extract and ½ of the chocolate chips into the batch freezer. Turn on dasher, set timer to 9 minutes, turn on refrigeration and begin the batch. Midway through the batch, add in the Crème de Menthe. When the batch is complete, add in the remaining chocolate chips, turn off refrigeration and extrude the finished product. Decorate tops of tubs with chocolate chips.

8

ITALIAN GELATO RECIPES

The secret to making any great frozen dessert product is the ingredients used and the "effort and care" taken by the person making the product. Italian gelato is the perfect restaurant frozen dairy dessert because of its freshness, flavor and foreign mystique as well as the way in which it is served—soft. When made in Italy, gelato typically contains 5.7% butterfat and is produced at 20–30% overrun. In the United States, consumers prefer a creamier flavor with the gelato having approximate 5–10% butterfat produced at 30–35% overrun.

Preparing a gelato flavor is like venturing into fantasyland. Because gelato is really a European-based product, most of the flavor ingredients that are used in Europe are foreign to us. But that's exactly what *I* like— venturing into the unknown.

To freeze gelato it is imperative that you use a low-speed batch freezer from either an American or Italian batch freezer manufacturer such as Carpigiani, Emery Thompson, Frigomat, Electro-Freeze, Bravo or Technogel.

The basic ingredients of a gelato-mix base are milk, fresh cream, sugar and with or without egg yolks.

There are a number of reputable Italian gelato ingredient manufacturers selling flavor ingredients in the United States, each one selling excellent ingredients. Every manufacturer of gelato ingredients has a number of special pastes that distinguish it from the competition. The only way for you, the producer, to find out what each has that is special is to try their samples. Once you are in business for a number of years, you will discover that you can make great gelato with ingredients from no particular manufacturer. What will cause you to buy from one vs. another is service and reliability of the product being delivered as promised. How you use these gelato ingredients will determine how you can get a leg up on your competition—It's up to you how you eventually produce the flavor, freeze it properly and present it to your customers in the most attractive way possible.

The following recipes are each on their own "outstanding flavors." A general rule of thumb for using flavor ingredients for gelato production is 13 ounces of flavor for each gallon of gelato mix (a 2½-gallon batch needs 32 ounces of flavor). Sometimes you might want to use these gelato flavors to produce an ice cream flavor with either 14% or 16% butterfat. To do so, increase the usage level by 15% (an additional 5 ounces per each 2½-gallon batch, or 37 ounces of flavor used).

We have created a coding system to help you follow, at a glance, the recipes in an exact sequence so you'll know when to put in specific ingredients (beginning, middle, end or out of the batch). Please refer to the Introduction to the Recipes on page 62 for an explanation of the codes.

Vanilla Gelato

A very unique, intense flavor. When comparing Vanilla gelato to Vanilla ice cream, the difference is remarkable. The finished gelato product is smooth, textured and has a show of little black flecks of the vanilla bean.

INGREDIENTS

10-Qt Batch	20-Qt Batch	40-Qt Batch	
1¼ gal	2½ gal	5 gal	5–10% gelato mix (B)
4 oz	8 oz	16 oz	Italian vanilla flavor (B)
1 oz	2 oz	4 oz	Madagascar Bourbon vanilla (B)
1½ tsp	1 Tbsp	2 Tbsp	Vanilla specks (B)

PREPARATION   Batch time: 8–10 minutes

Pour all ingredients into the batch freezer. Turn on dasher, set timer to 8 minutes, turn on refrigeration and begin the batch. When the batch is complete, turn off the refrigeration and extrude the finished product.

MALCOLM SAYS: I use both an Italian vanilla flavor (with a slight caramel note) and pure vanilla extract (Madagascar Bourbon) to create an authentic Italian vanilla gelato similar to what you might taste in Italy with an American slant to it.

 ## Homemade Version

There's nothing better than the taste of a creamy vanilla gelato!

INGREDIENTS

3	Egg yolks
5 oz	Sugar
1 qt	Half-and-half*
1 Tbsp	Vanilla extract

*You can substitute 24 ounces of whole milk and 8 ounces of heavy cream for half-and-half.

PREPARATION

Use a double boiler to create a custard base for the gelato. Pour the egg yolks, sugar and half-and-half into the pot. Heat the mixture slowly but do *not* bring to a boil. When a film forms over the back of your spoon, remove gelato base from the heat and place the pot into a larger pot filled with cold water to cool. When the base is cold, stir in vanilla extract, transfer the whole mixture to an ice cream maker and freeze according to the manufacturer's instructions. Then turn off refrigeration and extrude the finished product. Yield: 1½ quarts of gelato

Real Italian Espresso Gelato

INGREDIENTS

10-Qt Batch	20-Qt Batch	40-Qt Batch	
1¼ gal	2½ gal	5 gal	5–10% gelato mix (B)
1 oz	2 oz	4 oz	Two-fold vanilla extract (B)
16 oz	32 oz	64 oz	Espresso paste flavoring (B)
1½ tsp	1 Tbsp	2 Tbsp	Espresso beans, ground (B)

PREPARATION   Batch time: 8–10 minutes

Pour all ingredients into the batch freezer. Turn on the dasher, set timer to 8 minutes, turn on refrigeration and begin the batch. When batch is complete, turn off refrigeration and extrude the finished product.

MALCOLM SAYS: I suggest using ground espresso beans so that when your customers taste the espresso they get to taste a "bite of espresso." You can grind your own espresso beans instead of buying a prepared espresso at a much lower cost to you.

 ## Homemade Version

This Espresso gelato can be as strong as you want it to be. It's your call!

INGREDIENTS

½ oz	Freeze-dried coffee
½ tsp	Cocoa
3	Egg yolks
5 oz	Sugar
1 qt	Half-and-half*
1 Tbsp	Vanilla extract

*You can substitute 24 ounces of whole milk and 8 ounces of heavy cream for half-and-half.

PREPARATION

Mix freeze-dried coffee with as little hot water as possible. Add cocoa and blend thoroughly until mixture is very smooth with no dry coffee or cocoa visible. Use a double boiler to create a custard base for the gelato. Pour the coffee mixture, egg yolks, sugar and half-and-half into the pot and heat slowly but do *not* bring to a boil. When a film forms over the back of your spoon, remove gelato base from heat and place the pot into a larger pot filled with cold water to cool. When the base is cold, stir in vanilla extract, transfer the whole mixture to an ice cream maker and freeze according to the manufacturer's instructions. Then turn off refrigeration and extrude finished product. Yield: 1½ quarts of gelato

Fragola (Strawberry) Gelato

INGREDIENTS

10-Qt Batch	20-Qt Batch	40-Qt Batch	
1 lb	2 lb	4 lb	Frozen strawberries, defrosted (E)
4 oz	8 oz	16 oz	Sugar (E)
1¼ gal	2½ gal	5 gal	5–10% gelato mix (B)
1 oz	2 oz	4 oz	Two-fold vanilla extract (B)
8 oz	16 oz	32 oz	Fragola paste (B)
8 oz	16 oz	32 oz	Processed strawberries (B)

PREPARATION   Batch time: 8–10 minutes

Combine defrosted strawberries with sugar and marinate for 8 hours. Drain off and discard excess juice. Pour the gelato mix, vanilla extract, fragola paste and processed strawberries into the batch freezer. Turn on the dasher, set timer to 8 minutes, turn on refrigeration and begin the batch. Just before the batch is complete, add in marinated strawberries and continue freezing for 1–2 minutes. Then turn off the refrigeration and extrude finished product. Decorate tops of gelato pans or tubs with strawberry pieces.

MALCOLM SAYS: I use a prepared processed strawberry in the gelato base to give the flavor a zing. The marinated strawberries give this flavor a very fresh-tasting note.

 Homemade Version

INGREDIENTS

2 lb	Fresh or frozen strawberries	1 qt	Half-and-half*
13 oz	Sugar	1 Tbsp	Vanilla extract
3	Egg yolks	6 oz	Strawberry preserves

*You can substitute 24 ounces of whole milk and 8 ounces of heavy cream for half-and-half.

PREPARATION

Cut up strawberries, combine with 8 ounces of sugar and marinate for 8 hours. Drain off and discard excess juice. Use a double boiler to create a custard base for the gelato. Pour the egg yolks, sugar and half-and-half into the pot and heat slowly but do *not* bring to a boil. When a film forms over the back of your spoon, remove gelato base from heat and place the pot into a larger pot filled with cold water to cool. When the base is cold, stir in vanilla extract and strawberry preserves, transfer the whole mixture to an ice cream maker and freeze according to manufacturer's instructions. When the gelato is semifrozen, add in marinated strawberries, turn off refrigeration and extrude finished product. Yield: 1½ quarts of gelato

Strawberry Cheesecake Gelato

INGREDIENTS

10-Qt Batch	20-Qt Batch	40-Qt Batch	
1¼ gal	2½ gal	5 gal	5–10% gelato mix (B)
1 oz	2 oz	4 oz	Two-fold vanilla extract (B)
1½ lb	3 lb	6 lb	Commercial cheesecake powder* (B)
1 qt	2 qt	4 qt	Processed strawberries (E)
¼ lb	½ lb	1 lb	Graham crackers, broken (E)

*You can substitute prepared cheesecakes for the cheesecake powder. If you do so, use 4 cakes for a 20-quart batch and adjust accordingly for other size batches. Break up the cakes and puree them before putting them in the batch freezer.

PREPARATION
Batch time: 8–10 minutes

Pour the gelato mix, vanilla extract and cheesecake powder into the batch freezer. Turn on dasher for 2 minutes to blend ingredients, set timer for 8 minutes, turn on refrigeration and begin the batch. As the mixture firms up and looks wavy, add in processed strawberries and graham crackers, turn off refrigeration and extrude finished product.

MALCOLM SAYS: I have been using a commercial cheesecake powder similar to the one produced by Precision Foods because this powder comes closest in taste to that of a baked cheesecake.

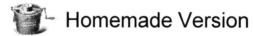 ## Homemade Version

This is as close to eating the real cheesecake in a frozen form as you will ever get!

INGREDIENTS

3	Egg yolks	1	Cheesecake, crumbled
5 oz	Sugar	4 oz	Graham crackers, broken
1 qt	Half-and-half*	6 oz	Strawberry preserves
1 Tbsp	Vanilla extract		

*You can substitute 24 ounces of whole milk and 8 ounces of heavy cream for half-and-half.

PREPARATION

Use a double boiler to create a custard base for the gelato. Pour the egg yolks, sugar and half-and-half into the pot. Heat the mixture slowly but do *not* bring to a boil. When a film forms over the back of your spoon, remove gelato base from heat and place the pot into a larger pot filled with cold water to cool. When the base is cold, stir in vanilla extract, transfer the whole mixture to an ice cream maker and freeze according to the manufacturer's instructions. When the gelato is almost frozen, add in crumbled cheese cake, broken graham crackers and strawberry preserves. Turn off the refrigeration and extrude the finished product. Yield: 1½ quarts of gelato

Creamsicle Gelato

INGREDIENTS

10-Qt Batch	20-Qt Batch	40-Qt Batch	
3 qt	1½ gal	3 gal	Fresh orange juice with pulp (B)
1¼ gal	2½ gal	5 gal	5–10% gelato mix (B)
1 oz	2 oz	4 oz	Two-fold vanilla extract (B)
4	8	16	Zest of oranges (B)

PREPARATION   Batch time: 8–10 minutes

Pour all ingredients into the batch freezer. Turn on the dasher for 2 minutes to blend ingredients, set timer to 8 minutes, turn on the refrigeration and begin the batch. As the mixture firms up and looks wavy, turn off refrigeration and extrude finished product.

MALCOLM SAYS: How do you know when a mixture "looks wavy"? Place a spatula under the extrusion opening of the batch freezer. When the mixture stands up on top of the spatula without sliding off, consider it "wavy."

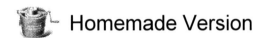 Homemade Version

INGREDIENTS

2	Egg yolks
4 oz	Sugar
26 oz	Half-and-half*
1 Tbsp	Vanilla extract
1 Tbsp	Triple Sec liqueur
12 oz	Orange juice with pulp
3	Zest of oranges

*You can substitute 24 ounces of whole milk and 8 ounces of heavy cream for the half-and-half.

PREPARATION

Use a double boiler to create a custard base for the gelato. Pour the egg yolks, sugar and half-and-half into the pot. Heat the mixture slowly but do *not* bring to a boil. When a film forms over the back of your spoon, remove gelato base from heat and place the pot into a larger pot filled with cold water to cool. When the base is cold, stir in vanilla extract, Triple Sec liqueur, orange juice and orange zest, transfer the whole mixture to an ice cream maker and freeze according to the manufacturer's instructions. Then turn off refrigeration and extrude the finished product. Yield: 1½ quarts of gelato

Gingered Apricot Gelato

The accent of the ginger with the tenderness of the apricots makes for a wonderful sensual eating experience. Simply another way to be creative with ginger.

INGREDIENTS

10-Qt Batch	20-Qt Batch	40-Qt Batch	
1¼ gal	2½ gal	5 gal	5–10% gelato mix (B)
1¼ oz	2½ oz	5 oz	Two-fold vanilla extract (B)
16 oz	32 oz	64 oz	Apricot paste (B)
8 oz	1 lb	2 lb	Candied ginger pieces (E)
			A few dried apricots for decoration

PREPARATION   **Batch time: 8–10 minutes**

Pour ice cream mix, vanilla extract and apricot paste into the batch freezer. Turn on dasher, set timer to 8 minutes, turn on refrigeration and begin the batch. When the batch is complete and looks wavy, pour in candied ginger pieces, turn off refrigeration and extrude the finished product. Decorate tops of gelato pans or tubs with slices of dried apricots and candied ginger pieces.

MALCOLM SAYS: Royal Pacific Foods has terrific dark sweet cuts of ginger, ginger pulp and ginger juice

Apricot White Chocolate Gelato

This is a very unique, subtle apricot flavor with white chocolate chunks dispersed throughout. You will love it!

INGREDIENTS

10-Qt Batch	20-Qt Batch	40-Qt Batch	
1¼ gal	2½ gal	5 gal	5–10% gelato mix (B)
1¼ oz	2½ oz	5 oz	Two-fold pure vanilla extract (B)
16 oz	32 oz	64 oz	Apricot paste (B)
1 lb	2 lb	4 lb	Soft white chocolate chunks (E)
			A few dried apricots for decoration

PREPARATION   **Batch time: 8–10 minutes**

Pour ice cream mix, vanilla extract and apricot paste into the batch freezer. Turn on dasher, set timer to 8 minutes, turn on refrigeration and begin the batch. When batch is complete and looks wavy, add in the white chocolate chunks, turn off the refrigeration and extrude the finished product. Decorate tops of gelato pans or tubs with slices of dried apricots and white chocolate chunks.

Sinful Mint Gelato

INGREDIENTS

10-Qt Batch	20-Qt Batch	40-Qt Batch	
1¼ gal	2½ gal	5 gal	5–10% gelato mix (B)
1 oz	2 oz	4 oz	Two-fold vanilla extract (B)
10 oz	20 oz	40 oz	Menta flavoring (B)
8 oz	16 oz	32 oz	Liquid chocolate* (E)
			A few drops of green food coloring

PREPARATION   Batch time: 8–10 minutes

Pour the gelato mix, vanilla extract and menta flavoring into the batch freezer. Turn on the dasher, set timer to 8 minutes, turn on refrigeration and begin the batch. As the product firms up and gets wavy, slowly pour in liquid chocolate chip*. Then turn off refrigeration and extrude the finished product. Decorate tops of gelato pans or tubs with a little swirl of liquid chocolate.

 Homemade Version

INGREDIENTS

4 oz	Liquid chocolate*	1 Tbsp	Vanilla extract
3	Egg yolks	1 oz	Mint extract
5 oz	Sugar	A few drops	Green food
1 qt	Half-and-half**		coloring

PREPARATION

In a double boiler, heat the semisweet chocolate with vegetable oil to 95° F. Using a spatula, mix thoroughly and then pour the liquid chocolate chip* into a measuring container. Use a double boiler to create a custard base for the gelato. Pour the egg yolks, ¾ sugar and half-and-half into the pot. Heat the mixture slowly but do *not* bring to a boil. When a film forms over the back of your spoon, remove gelato base from heat and place the pot into a larger pot filled with cold water to cool. When the base is cold, stir in the vanilla and mint extracts and green food coloring, transfer the whole mixture to an ice cream maker, and freeze according to the manufacturer's instructions. When the gelato is almost frozen, slowly pour in the liquid chocolate, turn off the refrigeration and extrude the finished product. Yield: 1½ quarts of gelato

*To make liquid chocolate, heat in a double boiler 5 parts chocolate to 1 part vegetable oil by weight up to 95° F. Mix thoroughly with a spatula, then pour the liquid chocolate into a measuring container. It's important to use a double boiler to prevent scorching the chocolate.

**You can substitute 24 ounces of whole milk and 8 ounces of heavy cream for half-and-half.

Kahlua Almond Fudge Gelato

INGREDIENTS

10-Qt Batch	20-Qt Batch	40-Qt Batch	
1 oz	2 oz	4 oz	Freeze-dried coffee (B)
1 oz	2 oz	4 oz	Hot water (B)
1 tsp	2 tsp	4 tsp	Cocoa (B)
1¼ gal	2½ gal	5 gal	5 or 10% gelato mix (B)
1 oz	2 oz	4 oz	Two-fold vanilla extract (B)
9 oz	18 oz	36 oz	Kahlua liqueur (or 2–3 oz Kahlua extract) (E)
8 oz	1 lb	2 lb	Diced roasted almonds (E)
1 qt	2 qt	4 qt	Fudge (O)

PREPARATION   Batch time: 8–10 minutes

Mix freeze-dried coffee with as little hot water as possible. Add cocoa and blend until mixture is smooth with no dry coffee or cocoa visible. Pour all ingredients *except* Kahlua, almonds and fudge into the batch freezer. Turn on the dasher and run for 2 minutes to blend ingredients, set timer to 8 minutes, turn on refrigeration and begin the batch. When the batch is complete and looks wavy, add in the Kahlua and almonds, turn off refrigeration and extrude the finished product as you swirl in the fudge.

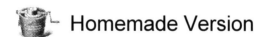 Homemade Version

INGREDIENTS

½ oz	Freeze-dried coffee	1 Tbsp	Vanilla extract
½ tsp	Cocoa	4 oz	Kahlua or Tia Maria
3	Egg yolks		liqueur
5 oz	Sugar	2 oz	Diced roasted almonds
1 qt	Half-and-half *	5 oz	Fudge topping

*You can substitute 24 ounces of whole milk and 8 ounces of heavy cream for half-and-half.

PREPARATION

Mix freeze-dried coffee with as little hot water as possible. Add cocoa and blend thoroughly until mixture is very smooth with no dry coffee or cocoa visible. Use a double boiler to create a custard base for the gelato. Pour the coffee mixture, egg yolks, sugar and half-and-half into the pot and heat slowly but do *not* bring to a boil. When a film forms over the back of your spoon, remove gelato base from the heat and place the pot into a larger pot filled with cold water to cool. When base is cold, stir in vanilla extract, transfer the whole mixture to an ice cream maker and freeze according to manufacturer's instructions. Just before the batch is complete, add in the Kahlua or Tia Maria and diced almonds and continue freezing for 1–2 minutes. Then turn off refrigeration and extrude finished product as you swirl in fudge topping. Yield: 1½ quarts of gelato

Jerry Garcia Gelato

INGREDIENTS

10-Qt Batch	20-Qt Batch	40-Qt Batch	
1¼ gal	2½ gal	5 gal	5–10% gelato mix (B)
1 oz	2 oz	4 oz	Two-fold vanilla extract (B)
1 qt	2 qt	4 qt	Bordeaux cherry halves (B)
½ lb	1 lb	2 lb	Chocolate chips (E)

PREPARATION   Batch time: 8–10 minutes

Pour gelato mix, vanilla extract and Bordeaux cherry halves into the batch freezer. Turn on the dasher for 2 minutes to blend the ingredients, set timer to 8 minutes, turn on refrigeration and begin the batch. As the mixture firms up and looks wavy, add in the chocolate chips, turn off the refrigeration and extrude the finished product.

 Homemade Version

Save money and make your own version of "Jerry Garcia."

INGREDIENTS

3	Egg yolks
5 oz	Sugar
1 qt	Half-and-half*
1 Tbsp	Vanilla extract
6 oz	Sweet dark Bing cherry pieces
4 oz	Chocolate chips

*You can substitute 24 ounces of whole milk and 8 ounces of heavy cream for half-and-half.

PREPARATION

Use a double boiler to create a custard base for the gelato. Pour the egg yolks, sugar and half-and-half into the pot. Heat the mixture slowly but do *not* bring to a boil. When a film forms over the back of your spoon, remove gelato base from heat and place the pot into a larger pot filled with cold water to cool. When the base is cold, stir in vanilla extract, transfer the whole mixture to an ice cream maker and freeze according to the manufacturer's instructions. When the gelato is almost frozen, add in the dark Bing cherry pieces and chocolate chips. Then turn off refrigeration and extrude the finished product. Yield: 1½ quarts of gelato

MALCOLM SAYS: You can use any kind of dark cherry when making this flavor. You'll find these in the canned fruit section of your supermarket.

Amaretto Gelato

INGREDIENTS

10-Qt Batch	20-Qt Batch	40-Qt Batch	
1¼ gal	2½ gal	5 gal	5–10% gelato mix (B)
1 oz	2 oz	4 oz	Two-fold vanilla extract (B)
16 oz	32 oz	64 oz	Amaretto paste (B)
¼ lb	½ lb	1 lb	Almond pieces: ½ (B), ½ (E)
8 oz	16 oz	32 oz	Liquid chocolate* (E)

PREPARATION   Batch time: 8–10 minutes

Pour the gelato mix, vanilla extract, amaretto paste and ½ of the almond pieces into the batch freezer. Turn on the dasher, set the timer to 8 minutes, turn on refrigeration and begin the batch. Just before the batch is complete, pour in the liquid chocolate and remainder of almond pieces and continue freezing for 1–2 minutes. Then turn off the refrigeration and extrude the finished product. Decorate tops of gelato pans with a little swirl of liquid chocolate and almond pieces.

*To make liquid chocolate, heat in a double boiler 5 parts semisweet chocolate to 1 part vegetable oil up to 95° F. Mix thoroughly with a spatula, then pour the liquid chocolate into a measuring container.

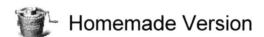 Homemade Version

INGREDIENTS

3	Egg yolks	1 Tbsp	Almond extract
5 oz	Sugar	4 oz	Roasted almond pieces
1 qt	Half-and-half*	4 oz	Almond liqueur
1 Tbsp	Vanilla extract	2 oz	Chocolate chips

*You can substitute 24 ounces of whole milk and 8 ounces of heavy cream for half-and-half.

PREPARATION

Use a double boiler to create a custard base for the gelato. Pour the egg yolks, sugar and half-and-half into the pot. Heat the mixture slowly but do *not* bring to a boil. When a film forms over the back of your spoon, remove gelato base from heat and place the pot into a larger pot filled with cold water to cool. When the base is cold, stir in the vanilla and almond extracts, transfer the whole mixture to an ice cream maker and freeze according to the manufacturer's instructions. When the gelato is almost frozen, add in the roasted almond pieces, almond liqueur and chocolate chips. Then turn off the refrigeration and extrude the finished product. Yield: 1½ quarts of gelato

Gianduja (Chocolate & Hazelnut) Gelato

A perfect match—a chocolate and hazelnut flavor side by side with the crunch of a Biscotti cookie.

INGREDIENTS

10-Qt Batch	20-Qt Batch	40-Qt Batch	
1¼ gal	2½ gal	5 gal	5–10% gelato mix (B)
1 oz	2 oz	4 oz	Two-fold vanilla extract (B)
18 oz	36 oz	72 oz	Gianduja paste (B)
8 oz	16 oz	32 oz	Liquid chocolate* (M)
¼ lb	½ lb	1 lb	Granulated hazelnut pieces (M)

*To make liquid chocolate, heat in a double boiler 5 parts semisweet chocolate to 1 part vegetable oil to 95° F. Mix with a spatula and pour the liquid chocolate into a container.

PREPARATION   Batch time: 8–10 minutes

Pour gelato mix, vanilla extract and gianduja paste into the batch freezer. Turn on dasher, set timer to 8 minutes, turn on the refrigeration and begin the batch. Midway through the batch, add in liquid chocolate and hazelnuts. When the batch is complete, turn off refrigeration and extrude the finished product. Decorate tops of gelato pans or tubs with liquid chocolate and hazelnut pieces.

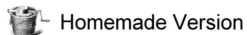 Homemade Version

This is my favorite gelato flavor. I hope it's yours too!

INGREDIENTS

6 oz	Chopped hazelnut pieces, dry roasted, no salt	5 oz	Sugar
		2 oz	Cocoa
1 qt	Half-and-half*	1 Tbsp	Vanilla extract
3	Egg yolks	4 oz	Frangelica liqueur

*You can substitute 24 ounces of whole milk and 8 ounces of heavy cream for half-and-half.

PREPARATION

Using a blender, blend 4 ounces of roasted hazelnuts with 3 ounces of the half-and-half to create a creamy hazelnut paste. Use a double boiler to create a custard base for the gelato. Pour the hazelnut paste, egg yolks, sugar, half-and-half and cocoa into the pot. Heat the mixture slowly but do *not* bring to a boil. When a film forms over the back of your spoon, remove gelato base from heat and place the pot into a larger pot filled with cold water to cool. When the base is cold, stir in the vanilla extract, transfer the whole mixture to an ice cream maker and freeze according to the manufacturer's instructions. When the gelato is almost frozen, add in the remaining hazelnut pieces and Frangelica liqueur. Turn off refrigeration and extrude finished product. Yield: 1½ quarts of gelato

Gianduja Biscotti Gelato
(Chocolate & Hazelnut Cookies)

This is a perfect match: a chocolate and hazelnut flavor side by side with the crunch of a Biscotti cookie.

INGREDIENTS

10-Qt Batch	20-Qt Batch	40-Qt Batch	
1¼ gal	2½ gal	5 gal	5–10% gelato mix (B)
1 oz	2 oz	4 oz	Two-fold vanilla extract (B)
18 oz	36 oz	72 oz	Gianduja paste (B)
8 oz	1 lb	2 lb	Biscotti cookies (M)
4 oz	8 oz	1 lb	Granulated, roasted hazelnut pieces* (M)
6 oz	12 oz	24 oz	Frangelica liqueur (E)
8 oz	16 oz	32 oz	Liquid chocolate** (E)

*Place hazelnut pieces in the oven on a baking tray with a small amount of sweet butter or vegetable oil for 10 minutes at 350° F.

**To make liquid chocolate, heat in a double boiler 5 parts semisweet chocolate to 1 part vegetable oil up to 95° F. Mix with a spatula and pour the liquid chocolate into a container.

PREPARATION   Batch time: 8–10 minutes

Pour gelato mix, vanilla extract and gianduja paste into the batch freezer. Turn on the dasher, set the timer to 8 minutes, turn on refrigeration and begin the batch. Midway through the batch, add in biscotti cookies and roasted hazelnut pieces. When the batch is complete and looks wavy, add in the Frangelica liqueur and liquid chocolate, turn off refrigeration and extrude finished product. Decorate tops of gelato pans or tubs with hazelnut and biscotti pieces.

MALCOLM SAYS: Coat the biscotti in melted chocolate so cookies don't become mealy.

Southern Pecan Pie Gelato

This flavor is so simple to make. All you need is some pecan pies from your local bakery.

INGREDIENTS

10-Qt Batch	20-Qt Batch	40-Qt Batch	
1¼ gal	2½ gal	5 gal	5–10% gelato mix (B)
1 oz	2 oz	4 oz	Two-fold vanilla extract (B)
1½	3	6	Pecan pies in small pieces: ⅓ (B), ⅔ (O)

PREPARATION   Batch time: 8–10 minutes

Pour gelato mix, vanilla, and ⅓ of the pecan pie pieces into batch freezer. Turn on the dasher, set timer to 8 minutes, turn on refrigeration and begin the batch. When the batch is almost complete, add in the remaining pecan pieces, turn off refrigeration and extrude finished product. Decorate tops of gelato pans or tubs with pecan pie pieces.

Chocolate Chip Chip Gelato

My editor, Bev Lozoff, has learned so much about ice cream by editing this book that she deserves a flavor named for her! Since she loves chocolate and chocolate chip cookies so much, this is it!

INGREDIENTS

10-Qt Batch	20-Qt Batch	40-Qt Batch	
¾ lb	1½ lb	3 lb	Semisweet chocolate bar (B)
¾ lb	1½ lb	3 lb	Cocoa (22–24% fat) (B)
1¼ lb	2½ lb	5 lb	Sugar (B)
2 pt	4 pt	8 pt	Hot water (B)
1¼ gal	2½ gal	5 gal	5 or 10% gelato mix (B)
2 oz	4 oz	8 oz	Two-fold vanilla extract (B)
½ oz	1 oz	2 oz	Pure chocolate extract (B)
1 lb	2 lb	4 lb	Liquid chocolate* (E)
1 lb	2 lb	4 lb	Chocolate chip cookies (E)

PREPARATION   Batch time: 8–10 minutes

Cut the chocolate bar into pieces and melt it down. Mix cocoa and sugar with extremely hot water in a double boiler to create a smooth paste, then add in the melted chocolate. Pour all ingredients *except* liquid chocolate and cookies into the batch freezer, turn on dasher and run for 5 minutes to blend ingredients. Set the timer to 8 minutes, turn on refrigeration and begin the batch. When the batch is complete, add in liquid chocolate and chocolate chip cookies, turn off refrigeration and extrude the finished product.

*To make liquid chocolate, heat in a double boiler 5 parts semisweet chocolate to 1 part vegetable oil up to 95° F. Mix with a spatula and pour the liquid chocolate into a container.

Cream-a-Latta Gelato

INGREDIENTS

10-Qt Batch	20-Qt Batch	40-Qt Batch	
1¼ gal	2½ gal	5 gal	5–10% gelato mix (B)
1 oz	2 oz	4 oz	Two-fold vanilla extract (B)
1 oz	2 oz	4 oz	Rum extract (B)
¼ oz	½ oz	1 oz	Cinnamon (B)
½ lb	1 lb	2 lb	Diced almonds (B)

PREPARATION   Batch time: 8–10 minutes

Pour all ingredients into the batch freezer. Turn on the dasher for 2 minutes to blend ingredients, set timer to 8 minutes, turn on refrigeration and begin the batch. As the mixture firms up and looks wavy, turn off the refrigeration and extrude the finished product.

Coconut Gelato

INGREDIENTS

10-Qt Batch	20-Qt Batch	40-Qt Batch	
1¼ gal	2½ gal	5 gal	5–10% gelato mix (B)
1 oz	2 oz	4 oz	Two-fold vanilla extract (B)
18 oz	36 oz	72 oz	Coconut paste (B)
2 oz	4 oz	8 oz	Shredded coconut (B)

PREPARATION   Batch time: 8–10 minutes

Pour all ingredients into the batch freezer. Turn on the dasher, set timer to 8 minutes, turn on refrigeration and begin the batch. When the batch is complete, turn off the refrigeration and extrude the finished product. Decorate tops of tubs or gelato pans with shredded coconut.

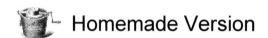 ## Homemade Version

INGREDIENTS

3	Egg yolks
5 oz	Sugar
1 qt	Half-and-half*
1 Tbsp	Vanilla extract
1	Cream of Coconut 15-oz can
2 oz	Shredded coconut

*You can substitute 24 ounces of whole milk and 8 ounces of heavy cream for half-and-half.

PREPARATION

Use a double boiler to create a custard base for the gelato. Pour the egg yolks, sugar and half-and-half into the pot. Heat the mixture slowly but do *not* bring to a boil. When a film forms over the back of your spoon, remove gelato base from heat and place the pot into a larger pot filled with cold water to cool. When the base is cold, stir in the vanilla extract and Cream of Coconut, transfer the whole mixture to an ice cream maker and freeze according to manufacturer's instructions. As the mixture firms up and looks wavy, add in shredded coconut, turn off the refrigeration and extrude the finished product. Yield: 1½ quarts of gelato

160

Piña Colada Gelato

INGREDIENTS

10-Qt Batch	20-Qt Batch	40-Qt Batch	
2 lb	4 lb	8 lb	Pineapple pieces (B)
8 oz	16 oz	32 oz	Sugar (B)
1¼ gal	2½ gal	5 gal	5–10% gelato mix (B)
1 oz	2 oz	4 oz	Two-fold vanilla extract (B)
18 oz	36 oz	72 oz	Coconut paste (B)
2 oz	4 oz	8 oz	Shredded coconut (B)
7½ oz	15 oz	30 oz	Cream of Coconut (B)
16 oz	32 oz	64 oz	Pineapple juice (B)
10 oz	20 oz	40 oz	Rum (E)

PREPARATION   Batch time: 8–10 minutes

Cook pineapple pieces and sugar on medium heat for about 10 minutes. Pour all ingredients *except* the rum into the batch freezer. Turn on dasher, set timer to 8 minutes, turn on the refrigeration and begin the batch. Just before the batch is complete, add in rum and continue freezing for 2 minutes. Then turn off refrigeration and extrude the finished product. Decorate tops of tubs or pans with coconut and pineapple pieces.

MALCOLM SAYS: It's important to cook the pineapple pieces so they don't curdle when mixed with a dairy product.

Tiramisu Gelato

INGREDIENTS

10-Qt Batch	20-Qt Batch	40-Qt Batch	
1¼ gal	2½ gal	5 gal	5–10% gelato mix (B)
1 oz	2 oz	4 oz	Two-fold vanilla extract (B)
16 oz	32 oz	64 oz	Tiramisu gelato flavoring (B)
6 oz	12 oz	24 oz	Marsala wine (E)
8 oz	1 lb	2 lb	Chocolate chunks (E)
½ lb	1 lb	2 lb	Ladyfinger cookies (O)

PREPARATION   Batch time: 8–10 minutes

Pour gelato mix, vanilla extract and tiramisu gelato flavoring into the batch freezer. Turn on the dasher, set timer to 8 minutes, turn on refrigeration and begin the batch. When the batch is almost complete, pour in the marsala and chocolate chunks, then turn off refrigeration and add in the ladyfingers as you extrude the finished prod- uct. Decorate tops of gelato pans or tubs with ladyfinger cookies and chocolate chunks.

MALCOLM SAYS: Marsala gives this flavor an authentic Italian note. Another touch would be adding ground espresso at the rate of ½ ounce per gallon of gelato mix used.

Nocciola (Hazelnut) Gelato

INGREDIENTS

10-Qt Batch	20-Qt Batch	40-Qt Batch	
1¼ gal	2½ gal	5 gal	5–10% gelato mix (B)
1¼ oz	2½ oz	5 oz	Two-fold pure vanilla extract (B)
20 oz	40 oz	80 oz	Nocciola paste (B)
¾ lb	1½ lb	3 lb	Chopped hazelnut pieces, dry roasted, no salt: ½ (B), ½ (E)
8 oz	16 oz	32 oz	Frangelica liqueur (E)

PREPARATION   Batch time: 8–10 minutes

Pour the gelato mix, vanilla extract, nocciola paste and ½ of the chopped hazelnut pieces into the batch freezer. Turn on the dasher, set timer to 8 minutes, turn on the refrigeration and begin the batch. Just before the batch is complete, add in Frangelica liqueur and remaining hazelnut pieces and continue freezing for 1-2 minutes. Then turn off the refrigeration and extrude the finished product. Decorate tops of gelato pans or tubs with hazelnut pieces.

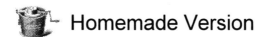 ## Homemade Version

INGREDIENTS

6 oz	Chopped hazelnut pieces, dry roasted, no salt
1 qt	Half-and-half*
3	Egg yolks
5 oz	Sugar
1 Tbsp	Vanilla extract
4 oz	Frangelica liqueur

*You can substitute 24 ounces of whole milk and 8 ounces of heavy cream for the half-and-half.

PREPARATION

Using a blender, blend 4 ounces of roasted hazelnuts with 3 ounces of half-and-half to create a creamy hazelnut paste. Use a double boiler to create a custard base for the gelato. Pour the hazelnut paste, egg yolks, sugar and the rest of the half-and-half into the pot. Heat the mixture slowly but do *not* bring to a boil. When a film forms over the back of your spoon, remove gelato base from heat and place the pot into a larger pot filled with cold water to cool. When the base is cold, stir in vanilla extract, transfer the whole mixture to an ice cream maker and freeze according to manufacturer's instructions. When the gelato is almost frozen, add in the remaining hazelnut pieces and Frangelica liqueur, turn off refrigeration and extrude finished product. Yield: 1½ quarts of gelato

White Chocolate Hazelnut Gelato

INGREDIENTS

10-Qt Batch	20-Qt Batch	40-Qt Batch	
1¼ gal	2½ gal	5 gal	5–10% gelato mix (B)
1¼ oz	2½ oz	5 oz	Two-fold vanilla extract (B)
20 oz	40 oz	80 oz	Nocciola paste (B)
12 oz	1½ lb	3 lb	Chopped hazelnut pieces, dry roasted, no salt: ½ (B), ½ (E)
12 oz	1½ lb	3 lb	White chocolate chunks (E)
8 oz	16 oz	32 oz	Frangelica liqueur (E)

PREPARATION   Batch time: 8–10 minutes

Pour the gelato mix, vanilla extract, nocciola paste and ½ of the chopped hazelnut pieces into the batch freezer. Turn on dasher, set timer to 8 minutes, turn on refrigeration and begin the batch. When the batch is almost complete, add in the remaining hazelnut pieces, white chocolate chunks and Frangelica liqueur. Then turn off refrigeration and extrude finished product. Decorate tops of gelato pans or tubs with hazelnut pieces and white chocolate chunks.

 Homemade Version

INGREDIENTS

6 oz	Chopped hazelnut pieces, dry roasted, no salt
1 qt	Half-and-half*
3	Egg yolks
5 oz	Sugar
1 Tbsp	Vanilla extract
3 oz	White chocolate chips
4 oz	Frangelica liqueur

*You can substitute 24 ounces of whole milk and 8 ounces of heavy cream for half-and-half.

PREPARATION

Using a blender, blend 4 ounces of the chopped hazelnuts with 3 ounces of half-and-half to create a creamy hazelnut paste. Use a double boiler to create a custard base for the gelato. Pour the egg yolks, sugar and half-and-half into the pot. Heat the mixture slowly but do *not* bring to a boil. When a film forms over the back of your spoon, remove gelato base from heat and place the pot into a larger pot filled with cold water to cool. When the base is cold, stir in the vanilla extract, transfer the whole mixture to an ice cream maker and freeze according to manufacturer's instructions. Then add in remaining hazelnut pieces, white chocolate chips and Frangelica liqueur. Turn off the refrigeration and extrude the finished product. Yield: 1½ quarts of gelato

Chocolate Gelato

INGREDIENTS

10-Qt Batch	20-Qt Batch	40-Qt Batch	
½ lb	1 lb	2 lb	Semisweet chocolate bar (B)
¾ lb	1½ lb	3 lb	Cocoa (22–24% fat) (B)
1½ lb	3 lb	6 lb	Hot water (B)
¾ lb	1½ lb	3 lb	Sugar (B)
1¼ lb	2½ gal	5 gal	5–10% gelato mix (B)
1½ oz	3 oz	6 oz	Two-fold vanilla extract (B)
1 Tbsp	1 oz	2 oz	Pure chocolate extract (Star Kay White) (B)

PREPARATION   Batch time: 8–10 minutes

Cut the chocolate bar into small pieces and melt down. Thoroughly mix cocoa and sugar with extremely hot water to create a smooth paste, then add in the melted chocolate. Pour all ingredients into the batch freezer, turn on dasher and let it run for 5 minutes to blend ingredients, set timer to 8 minutes, turn on the refrigeration and begin the batch. When the batch is complete, turn off refrigeration and extrude the finished product.

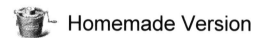 Homemade Version

INGREDIENTS

3	Egg yolks
5 oz	Sugar
1 qt	Half-and-half*
4 oz	Cocoa
4 oz	Semisweet chocolate in small pieces
1 Tbsp	Vanilla extract

*You can substitute 24 ounces of whole milk and 8 ounces of heavy cream for half-and-half.

PREPARATION

Use a double boiler to create a custard base for the gelato. Pour the egg yolks, sugar and half-and-half into the pot. As this mixture is being heated, add in cocoa and chocolate to create a smooth, creamy paste. Heat the mixture slowly but do *not* bring to a boil. When a film forms over the back of your spoon, remove gelato base from the heat and place the pot into a larger pot filled with cold water to cool. When the base is cold, stir in vanilla extract, transfer the whole mixture to an ice cream maker and freeze according to manufacturer's instructions. Then turn off refrigeration and extrude the finished product. Yield: 1½ quarts of gelato

Ricotta Gelato

This flavor, by way of La Sorbetteria in Bologna, Italy, is a must to try. It is rich in cheese flavor and has a wonderful body texture.

INGREDIENTS

10-Qt Batch	20-Qt Batch	40-Qt Batch	
3 lb	6 lb	12 lb	Ricotta cheese (B)
1¼ gal	2½ gal	5 gal	5–10% gelato mix (B)
1¼ oz	2½ oz	5 oz	Two-fold vanilla extract (B)
½ oz	1 oz	2 oz	Cinnamon (B)
½ lb	1 lb	2 lb	Chocolate chunks (B)
½ lb	1 lb	2 lb	Golden raisins (O)
¼ oz	½ oz	1 oz	Lemon zest (O)

PREPARATION   Batch time: 8–10 minutes

In a blender or food processor, process the ricotta cheese until it is smooth. Pour the processed ricotta cheese, gelato mix, vanilla extract, cinnamon and chocolate chunks into the batch freezer. Turn on dasher, set timer to 8 minutes, turn on the refrigeration and begin the batch. When the batch is complete and looks wavy, turn off the refrigeration, add in the golden raisins and lemon zest and extrude the finished product. Decorate tops of tubs or gelato pans with golden raisins and lemon zest.

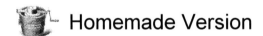 **Homemade Version**

INGREDIENTS

1 lb	Ricotta cheese	¼ oz	Lemon zest
3	Egg yolks	½ tsp	Cinnamon
5 oz	Sugar	4 oz	Golden raisins
1 qt	Half-and-half*	2 oz	Chocolate chips
1 Tbsp	Vanilla extract		

*You can substitute 24 ounces of whole milk and 8 ounces of heavy cream for half-and-half.

PREPARATION

In a blender or food processor, process the Ricotta cheese until smooth. Use a double boiler to create a custard base for the gelato. Pour the egg yolks, sugar and half-and-half into the pot. Heat the mixture slowly but do *not* bring to a boil. When a film forms over the back of your spoon, remove gelato base from heat and place the pot into a larger pot filled with cold water to cool. When the custard base is cold, stir in the processed Ricotta cheese, vanilla extract, lemon zest and cinnamon, then transfer the whole mixture to an ice cream maker and freeze according to the manufacturer's instructions. Add in golden raisins and chocolate chips, turn off the refrigeration and extrude the finished product. Yield: 1½ quarts of gelato

Mint Oreo Gelato

INGREDIENTS

10-Qt Batch	20-Qt Batch	40-Qt Batch	
1¼ gal	2½ gal	5 gal	5–10% gelato mix (B)
1 oz	2 oz	4 oz	Two-fold vanilla extract (B)
10 oz	20 oz	40 oz	Menta flavoring (B)
8 oz	16 oz	32 oz	Liquid chocolate* (E)
1 lb	2 lb	4 lb	Green Mint Oreo cookies (E)

PREPARATION   Batch time: 8–10 minutes

Use a double boiler to heat the chocolate to 95° F. Using a spatula, mix thoroughly and pour out 1¾ quarts of the liquid chocolate chip into a measuring container. Pour the gelato mix, vanilla extract and menta flavoring into the batch freezer. Turn on the dasher, set timer to 8 minutes, turn on refrigeration and begin the batch. As the product firms up and gets wavy, slowly pour in liquid chocolate and Oreo cookies. Turn off refrigeration and extrude finished product. Decorate tops of gelato pans or tubs with a little swirl of liquid chocolate and Oreo cookies.

*To make liquid chocolate, heat in a double boiler 5 parts semisweet chocolate to 1 part vegetable oil up to 95° F. Mix with a spatula and pour the liquid chocolate into a container.

Lauretta (Cherries with Cream) Gelato

INGREDIENTS

10-Qt Batch	20-Qt Batch	40-Qt Batch	
1¼ gal	2½ gal	5 gal	5–10% gelato mix (B)
1¼ oz	2½ oz	5 oz	Two-fold pure vanilla extract (B)
16 oz	32 oz	64 oz	Amarena wild cherries: ⅓ (B), ⅔ (E)

PREPARATION   Batch time: 8–10 minutes

Pour the gelato mix, vanilla extract and ⅓ of the Amarena wild cherries into the batch freezer. Turn on dasher, set timer to 8 minutes, turn on the refrigeration and begin the batch. Just before the batch is complete, pour in the remaining Amarena wild cherries and continue freezing for 1–2 minutes. Then turn off the refrigeration and extrude the finished product. Decorate tops of gelato pans or tubs with Amarena cherries.

MALCOLM SAYS: To highlight the cherries in this recipe, we use only the whole Amarena cherry.

Amarena Wild Cherry Gelato

INGREDIENTS

10-Qt Batch	20-Qt Batch	40-Qt Batch	
1¼ gal	2½ gal	5 gal	5–10% gelato mix (B)
1¼ oz	2½ oz	5 oz	Two-fold vanilla extract (B)
6 oz	12 oz	24 oz	Amarena paste (B)
16 oz	32 oz	64 oz	Amarena wild cherries: ⅓ (B), ⅔ (E)

PREPARATION   Batch time: 8–10 minutes

Pour the gelato mix, vanilla extract, Amarena paste and ⅓ of the wild cherries into the batch freezer. Turn on dasher, set timer to 8 minutes, turn on refrigeration and begin the batch. Just before the batch is complete, pour in the remaining Amarena cherries and continue freezing for 1–2 minutes. Then turn off refrigeration and extrude finished product as you add in the rest of the Amarena cherries. Decorate tops of gelato pans or tubs with Amarena cherries.

 Homemade Version

Crank up your ice cream maker and treat yourself to the best gelato you've ever had!

INGREDIENTS

3	Egg yolks
5 oz	Sugar
1 qt	Half-and-half*
1 Tbsp	Vanilla extract
12 oz	Amarena wild cherries

*You can substitute 24 ounces of whole milk and 8 ounces of heavy cream for half-and-half.

PREPARATION

Use a double boiler to create a custard base for the gelato. Pour the egg yolks, sugar and half-and-half into the pot. Heat the mixture slowly but do *not* bring to a boil. When a film forms over the back of your spoon, remove gelato base from heat and place the pot into a larger pot filled with cold water to cool. When the base is cold, stir in the vanilla extract, transfer the whole mixture to an ice cream maker and freeze according to manufacturer's instructions. Then add in Amarena wild cherries, turn off the refrigeration and extrude the finished product. Yield: 1½ quarts of gelato

MALCOLM SAYS: In my opinion the Amarena cherries from Fabbri are of the highest quality.

Pistachio Gelato (1)

INGREDIENTS

10-Qt Batch	20-Qt Batch	40-Qt Batch	
1 oz	2 oz	4 oz	Confectioners' sugar (B)
¾ lb	1½ lb	3 lb	Chopped pistachio pieces: ⅓ (B), ⅔ (E)
1¼ gal	2½ gal	5 gal	5–10% gelato mix (B)
1¼ oz	2½ oz	5 oz	Two-fold vanilla extract (B)
16 oz	32 oz	64 oz	Pistachio paste (B)

PREPARATION   Batch time: 8–10 minutes

Combine the confectioners' sugar with ⅓ of the chopped pistachio pieces and ¼ of the gelato mix; then blend mixture in a blender. Pour the gelato mix, vanilla extract, pistachio paste and ½ of the pistachio mixture into the batch freezer. Turn on dasher, set timer to 8 minutes, turn on refrigeration and begin the batch. Just before the batch is complete, add in remaining pistachio mixture, turn off the refrigeration and extrude finished product. Decorate tops of gelato pans or tubs with pistachio pieces.

Pistachio Gelato (2)

INGREDIENTS

10-Qt Batch	20-Qt Batch	40-Qt Batch	
3 oz	6 oz	12 oz	Confectioners' sugar, 10X (B)
1½ lb	3 lb	6 lb	Chopped pistachio pieces: ½ (B), ½ (E)
1¼ gal	2½ gal	5 gal	5–10% gelato mix (B)
1¼ oz	2½ oz	5 oz	Two-fold vanilla extract (B)
6 oz	12 oz	24 oz	Pistachio paste (B)
1 oz	2 oz	4 oz	Pistachio extract (B)
4 oz	8 oz	16 oz	Liquid chocolate* (E)

PREPARATION   Batch time: 8–10 minutes

Combine the confectioners' sugar with ⅓ of the pistachio pieces and ¼ of the gelato mix, then blend the mixture in a blender. Pour the gelato mix, vanilla extract, pistachio paste, pistachio extract and ⅓ of the pistachio mixture into the batch freezer. Turn on dasher, set timer to 8 minutes, turn on the refrigeration and begin the batch. Just before the batch is complete, add in the remaining pistachio mixture and liquid chocolate, turn off the refrigeration and extrude the finished product. Decorate tops of gelato pans or tubs with pistachio pieces.

*To make liquid chocolate, heat in a double boiler 5 parts semisweet chocolate to 1 part vegetable oil up to 95° F. Mix with a spatula and pour the liquid chocolate into a container.

Frutta di Bosco (Mixed Berries) Gelato

If you like a fruity gelato flavor, then you can't miss with this one.

INGREDIENTS

10-Qt Batch	20-Qt Batch	40-Qt Batch	
1½ lb	3 lb	6 lb	Mixed fruit (E)
6 oz	12 oz	24 oz	Sugar (E)
1¼ gal	2½ gal	5 gal	5–10% gelato mix (B)
1¼ oz	2½ oz	5 oz	Two-fold vanilla extract (B)
18 oz	36 oz	72 oz	Frutta di Bosco paste (B)

PREPARATION   Batch time: 8–10 minutes

Combine and marinate 3 parts mixed fruit and 1 part sugar for 8 hours. During the marination process blend the mixture so that the sugar is absorbed into the fruit. At the end drain off the remaining liquid and disgard. Pour all ingredients except the fruit mixture into batch freezer. Turn on dasher and let it run for 1 minute to blend ingredients, set timer to 8 minutes, turn on refrigeration and begin the batch. When batch is complete, add in the fruit mixture, turn off refrigeration and extrude the finished product. Decorate tops of gelato pans or tubs with pieces of fruit.

MALCOLM SAYS: When using mixed fruit, combine a variety of berries such as blackberries, strawberries, raspberries and blueberries.

 Homemade Version

INGREDIENTS

12 oz	Mixed fruit (strawberries, blueberries and raspberries)	1 qt	Half-and-half*
		1 Tbsp	Vanilla extract
4 oz	Sugar	6 oz	Mixed berry fruit preserves
3	Egg yolks		
5 oz	Sugar		

*You can substitute 24 ounces of whole milk and 8 ounces of heavy cream for half-and-half.

PREPARATION

Combine and marinate 3 parts mixed fruit and 1 part sugar for 8 hours. During the marination process blend mixture so that sugar is absorbed. At the end drain off liquid and disgard. Pour egg yolks, sugar and half-and-half into a double boiler to create a custard base for the gelato. Heat the mixture slowly but do *not* bring to a boil. When a film forms over the back of your spoon, remove gelato base from heat and place the pot into a larger pot filled with cold water to cool. When base is cold, stir in vanilla extract and preserves. Transfer the whole mixture to an ice cream maker and freeze according to the manufacturer's instructions. Then add in the mixed fruit marinade, turn off refrigeration and extrude the finished product. Yield: 1½ quarts of gelato

Mango Gelato

If you like mangoes, then this gelato is for you!

INGREDIENTS

10-Qt Batch	20-Qt Batch	40-Qt Batch	
1½ lb	3 lb	6 lb	Mangoes (E)
6 oz	12 oz	24 oz	Sugar (E)
1¼ gal	2½ gal	5 gal	5–10% gelato mix (B)
18 oz	36 oz	72 oz	Mango paste (B)
7 oz	14 oz	28 oz	Dark rum (E)

PREPARATION   Batch time: 8–10 minutes

Combine and marinate 3 parts mango pieces and 1 part sugar for 8 hours. During the marination process, blend the mixture so that the sugar is totally absorbed. At the end, drain off and discard the juice. Pour all ingredients except the fruit mixture into batch freezer. Turn on the dasher and let it run for 1 minute to blend ingredients, set timer to 8 minutes, turn on refrigeration and begin the batch. When the batch is complete, add in the fruit mixture and rum, turn off refrigeration and extrude the finished product. Decorate tops of gelato pans or tubs with mango pieces.

 Homemade Version

INGREDIENTS

1½ lb	Mango pieces, frozen
13 oz	Sugar
3	Egg yolks
1 qt	Half-and-half*
1 Tbsp	Vanilla extract
6 oz	Mango fruit preserves

*You can substitute 24 ounces of whole milk and 8 ounces of heavy cream for half-and-half.

PREPARATION

Combine mango pieces with 8 ounces of sugar and marinate for 8 hours. During the marination process, blend the mixture so that the sugar is totally absorbed. At the end, drain off remaining juice and discard. Use a double boiler to create a custard base for the gelato. Pour the egg yolks, remaining sugar and half-and-half into the pot. Heat the mixture slowly but do *not* bring to a boil. When a film forms over the back of your spoon, remove gelato base from heat and place the pot into a larger pot filled with cold water to cool. When the base is cold, stir in the vanilla extract and mango fruit preserves, then transfer the whole mixture to an ice cream maker and freeze according to the manufacturer's instructions. Then add in the mango fruit, turn off refrigeration and extrude the finished product. Yield: 1½ quarts of gelato

Coconut Mango Banana Gelato

By combining mango with banana, you will end up with a very different and fabulous fruit gelato.

INGREDIENTS

10-Qt Batch	20-Qt Batch	40-Qt Batch	
1¼ gal	2½ gal	5 gal	5–10% gelato mix (B)
1¼ oz	2½ oz	5 oz	Two-fold vanilla extract (B)
4 lbs	8 lb	16 lb	Bananas, peeled and cut up (B)
12 oz	24 oz	48 oz	Mango paste (B)
8 oz	1 lb	2 lb	Coconut paste (B)
2 oz	4 oz	8 oz	Shredded coconut (E)

PREPARATION   Batch time: 8–10 minutes

Pour all ingredients except the shredded coconut into the batch freezer. Turn on the dasher, set timer to 8 minutes, turn on refrigeration and begin the batch. When batch is complete and looks wavy, pour in the shredded coconut, turn off the refrigeration and extrude the finished product. Decorate tops of gelato pans or tubs with banana slices and shredded coconut.

 Homemade Version

INGREDIENTS

1 pound	Mango pieces, frozen
10 oz	Sugar
3	Egg yolks
1 qt	Half-and-half*
1 Tbsp	Vanilla extract
3 oz	Mango fruit preserves
8 oz	Bananas, peeled, cut and diced

*You can substitute 24 ounces of whole milk and 8 ounces of heavy cream for half-and-half.

PREPARATION

Defrost the mangoes, combine and marinate mango pieces and ½ of the sugar for 8 hours. During marination process, blend the mixture so that the sugar is totally absorbed. At the end, drain off remaining juice and discard. Use a double boiler to create a custard base for the gelato. Pour the egg yolks, remaining sugar and half-and-half into the pot. Heat the mixture slowly but do *not* bring to a boil. When a film forms over the back of your spoon, remove gelato base from heat and place the pot into a larger pot filled with cold water to cool. When the base is cold, add in vanilla extract and mango fruit preserves, transfer the whole mixture to an ice cream maker and freeze according to manufacturer's instructions. Then add in the marinated mango fruit and bananas, turn off the refrigeration and extrude the finished product. Yield: 1½ quarts of gelato

Stracciatella (Chocolate Chip) Gelato

This is the traditional way of making Italian Vanilla Chocolate Chip gelato—with the use of a liquid chocolate chip called Stracciatella. It has an excellent flavor profile.

INGREDIENTS

10-Qt Batch	20-Qt Batch	40-Qt Batch	
1¼ gal	2½ gal	5 gal	5–10% gelato mix (B)
1¼ oz	2½ oz	5 oz	Two-fold vanilla extract (B)
½ lb	1 lb	2 lb	Chocolate chunks (B)
8 oz	16 oz	32 oz	Liquid chocolate* (E)
			or
12 oz	24 oz	48 oz	Stracciatella liquid chocolate chip* (E)

PREPARATION   Batch time: 8–10 minutes

Pour the gelato mix and vanilla extract into the batch freezer. Turn on the dasher, set the timer to 8 minutes, turn on refrigeration and begin the batch. Just before batch is complete, slowly pour in the liquid chocolate or Stracciatella and continue freezing for for 1–2 minutes. (Liquid chocolate reacts with the semifrozen gelato by solidifying into very thin chocolate flakes.) Then turn off the refrigeration and extrude the finished product. Decorate tops of gelato pans or tubs with little swirls of liquid chocolate or Stracciatella.

 # Homemade Version

INGREDIENTS

3	Egg yolks		1 Tbsp	Vanilla extract
5 oz	Sugar		3 oz	Chocolate chips
1 qt	Half-and-half*		8 oz	Liquid chocolate chip*

PREPARATION

Use a double boiler to create a custard base for the gelato. Pour the egg yolks, sugar and half-and-half into the pot. Heat the mixture slowly but do *not* bring to a boil. When a film forms over the back of your spoon, remove gelato base from heat and place the pot into a larger pot filled with cold water to cool. When the base is cold, stir in the vanilla extract, transfer the whole mixture to an ice cream maker and freeze according to the manufacturer's instructions. Then add in the chocolate chips and slowly pour in the liquid chocolate chip. The turn off refrigeration and extrude the finished product. Yield: 1½ quarts of gelato

*To make your own liquid chocolate, melt in a double boiler 5 parts chocolate to 1 part vegetable oil at 85–90° F. Or you can purchase Stracciatella liquid chocolate chip in a can. If you do so, heat the liquid at 95° F in a double boiler and mix thoroughly before pouring into a measuring container.

Mud Slide Gelato

This is a decadent way to make a coffee-style gelato flavor.

INGREDIENTS

10-Qt Batch	20-Qt Batch	40-Qt Batch	
1½ oz	3 oz	6 oz	Freeze-dried coffee (B)
1 oz	2 oz	4 oz	Hot water (B)
¼ oz	½ oz	1 oz	Cocoa (B)
1¼ gal	2½ gal	5 gal	5–10% gelato mix (B)
1¼ oz	2½ oz	5 oz	Two-fold vanilla extract (B)
1 qt	2 qt	4 qt	Fudge (E)
8 oz	1 lb	2 lb	Graham crackers (E)

PREPARATION   Batch time: 8–10 minutes

Mix freeze-dried coffee with as little hot water as possible. Add cocoa and blend thoroughly until mixture is smooth with no dry coffee or cocoa visible. Pour the coffee mixture, gelato mix and vanilla extract into the batch freezer. Turn on the dasher and let it run for 2 minutes to blend ingredients, set the timer to 8 minutes, turn on the refrigeration and begin the batch. When the batch is complete, add in the fudge and graham crackers, turn off refrigeration and extrude the finished product as you swirl fudge into the pans.

9

SORBET RECIPES

A sorbet is a nondairy product made with fruit and/or chocolate along with sugar, water and a natural stabilizer of guar gum and locust bean gum. Sorbets have reached prime time and are here to stay. Over the last five years, they have become increasingly popular. The most popular flavors are raspberry, lemon, strawberry, chocolate, and mango, followed by passion fruit, banana, strawberry banana, peach, cantaloupe and watermelon.

CHOOSING FRUIT

For overall flavor, frozen fruit is the best to use. Frozen fruit is uniform in flavor, especially if you purchase the fruit from the same manufacturer or distributor. Also, an added feature is that the juice of the fruit, after being defrosted, is free.

The beauty of producing sorbets in the batch freezer is that for many fruits you don't have to puree all the fruit all the time. The batch freezer will do it for you. A good example is strawberry, especially when you use frozen whole strawberries. (*See* recipe for Strawberry Sorbet) Simply pour the defrosted strawberry mixture along with sugar, stabilizer and water into the freezer, turn on the dasher for 1 minute, then the refrigeration and you are off and running. Bar none, this flavor when matched against one produced on a continuous freezer is far superior. The reason is that your sorbet will maintain the fiber texture of the berry while the one produced on the continuous freezer without exception is produced using a puree having no fiber texture at all. Other flavors like banana, pear and pineapple will work just as well.

If you are using fresh fruit, wash the fruit thoroughly with cold water. Next, cut, peel and/or hull the fruit. If you are using frozen fruit, defrost the fruit thoroughly, leaving the juice in the container; do not throw it away. At this point, mix together the dry sugar and stabilizer needed for the recipe. The reason for combining the dry sugar and stabilizer is because otherwise there is a possibility the stabilizer might not immerse itself thoroughly with the fruit. Once they are mixed together, add the mixture to the fruit using a spatula to fully blend everything. The fruit is now ready to begin its marinating process, which will take approximately 8 hours or preferably overnight. When the marinating process is complete, drain off all the juice and set it aside. Take 25% of all the drained fruit and cut it into small pieces. Pour the remaining 75% back into the juice. Puree the juice portion and then pour this mixture into the batch freezer and begin the freezing process.

USING SUGAR AND/OR CORN SYRUP SOLIDS

Corn syrup solids no longer have that taste of grain or corn. Thanks to an incredible improvement in food technology, you can use either 36 DE or 42 DE corn syrup solids. They have a clean sweet flavor that does not obstruct the true taste of fruit used in the production of sorbets, and in some cases actually helps bring out the flavor. DE stands for dextrose equivalent and indicates the percent of sweetness relative to dextrose, so they are about 36% or 42% as sweet as the sugar they replace.

Corn syrup solids are used to make the sorbet smoother and more scoopable. They add body to the product by replacing some of the sugar on a 2 to 1 ratio, thereby increasing the total solids in the finished product.

The big secret to using corn syrup solids is how much to use. Too little is never a problem, but too much can be. We recommend any brand of 36 DE dry corn syrup. Replace 1 part sugar with 2 parts 36 DE to a maximum ratio of no more than 50% sugar to 50% corn syrup; for example, in a recipe that calls for 6 pounds of sugar, replace 2 pounds with 4 pounds of 36 DE. The resulting mixture is now 4 pounds of sugar and 4 pounds of 36 DE, a 50%–50% ratio.

Simply sift the dry corn with the sugar and dissolve in hot water. It's as simple as that. To get the right ratio, start out slow and build up the corn to what you think is a good level. Begin with a ratio of 75% sugar to 25% corn; the reason being that you can always add but you can't subtract once you start a recipe.

USING STABILIZERS

Everyone thinks they know, but very few people actually know how to use one. It's the ingredient that will make your sorbet scoopable. All the recipes in this chapter use the stabilizer CC–917 from Tate & Lyle. Call Tate & Lyle at 631-231-8650 and ask for a sample of CC–917, a cold water stabilizer that is simple to use. It's used at the rate of .75–1.00% by weight.

Stabilizers contain sucrose, guar gum, locust bean gum, citric acid and sodium bicarbonate. Usage level is 3–4 ounces for a 2½-gallon batch and 6–8 ounces for a 5-gallon batch. Simply mix the stabilizer with dry sugar and add to liquid ingredient(s) with good agitation. Allow a few minutes for the stabilizer to hydrate before freezing.

MAKING A TERRIFIC BATCH OF SORBET

The following tricks of the trade will help you prepare a terrific sorbet that in most cases will be far superior to that of your competition.

- The word *gravy* in the Preparation section refers to extruding the finished sorbet product from the batch freezer when it is in a loose "gravy-like" state, not firm and *wavy* as you'd want when making ice cream. Otherwise you run the danger of producing an overprocessed, unscoopable product.

- When mixing stabilizer into the sorbet recipes, ¾ of 1% refers to the total weight of the batch with all ingredients mixed together— it's ¾ of 1% of this amount.

EXAMPLE
INGREDIENTS FOR A 10-QUART BATCH OF CHOCOLATE SORBET:

½ lb   Cocoa (22–24% fat)
2½ lb Sugar
1 gal Water (hot and cold)
1 oz   Vanilla extract
1½ oz Stabilizer (CC–917, ¾ of 1%)
½ lb   Fudge

Total weight of batch: 193 ounces *or* 12.06 pounds
¾ of 1%: 1.45 ounces or 41 grams
(**Note:** Water weighs 8.56 pounds to the gallon
Conversion of ounces to grams: 1 ounce = 28.3 grams)

- When using fresh fruit, in most cases you will have to puree it. Follow this chart for the amount of fruit needed to yield 1 quart of pureed fruit.

FRUIT WEIGHTS

FRUIT	WEIGHT PER FRUIT	AMT PER LB	%LOSS PER LB	AMT PER LB	AMT PER QT
Peach	5 oz	3	12%	3½	7
Banana	5½ oz	3	15%	3½	7
Apple	8 oz	2	10%	2¼	4½
Orange	4 oz	10 juice			14
Grapefruit	2 oz	10 juice			7
Papaya	16 oz	1	15%	1¼	2½
Pineapple	1 oz	3½	20%	4½	1½
Cantaloupe	1 oz	3	20%	3½	1½
Kiwi	4 oz	4	10%	5	10
Tangerine	4 oz	10 juice			14
Lime	5 oz	10 juice			17
Pear	5 oz	3	15%	4	8

Notes About the Table

Weight: Weight in ounces of 1 piece of fruit
Amount Per Pound: Amount of fruit making up 1 pound
Loss: Percent loss of weight after peeling/squeezing fruit
Amount Per Pound: Amount of fruit needed accounting for loss
Yield Per Quart: Amount of fruit making up 1 quart

- When pureeing fruit in the batch freezer, let the dasher run for at least 5 minutes.

- A batch of sorbet mix can be anywhere from 2½ gallons to 3½ gallons of mix per 20-quart batch (or 5 gallons to 7½ gallons for a 40-quart batch), since the overrun of the sorbet product will not exceed 20%.

- Towards the end of the batch, pour the cut-up fruit pieces into the batch freezer and run an additional 1–2 minutes. Turn off refrigeration and extrude the finish-ed product.

- The normal time for producing a batch of sorbet is 11–15 minutes, depending on the amount of sugar used and liquid mix in the barrel. When the recommended batch time is more then 13 minutes, it is usually because more sugar is being used in the recipe. The greater the amount of sugar, the longer the batch time.

- Always use filtered water. Regular tap water has chloride in it which will greatly affect the taste of the sorbet.

We have created a coding system to help you follow the recipes in an exact sequence at a glance so that you know when to put in specific ingredients (beginning, middle, end or out of the batch). Please refer to the Introduction to the Recipes in the Book on page 62 for an explanation of the codes.

Apple Cranberry Sorbet

INGREDIENTS

10-Qt Batch	20-Qt Batch	40-Qt Batch	
2¼ lb	4½ lb	9 lb	Fresh or frozen cranberries (B)
½ qt	1 qt	2 qt	Water (for marinade) (B)
1¾ lb	3½ lb	7 lb	Sugar (for marinade) (B)
5¼ lb	10½ lb	21 lb	Matsu or other eating apples: (B), (E)
1½ oz	3 oz	6 oz	Stabilizer (CC–917, ¾ of 1%) (B)
1 qt	2 qt	4 qt	Unsweetened apple juice (B)
¾ oz	1½ oz	3 oz	Cinnamon (B)
4 lb	8 lb	16 lb	Sugar (B)
1 qt	2 qt	4 qt	Water (hot and cold) (B)
2 Tbsp	4 Tbsp	8 Tbsp	Lemon juice (B)

PREPARATION
Batch time: 13–15 minutes

Combine and marinate cranberries, water and sugar for 3 hours, then puree and strain the cranberry juice and set aside. Peel, core and seed the apples. Under good agitation (using a spatula), slowly sift stabilizer into apples and let it hydrate at least 30 minutes. Puree ¾ of the apples with apple juice, then add cinnamon. Cut the remaining apples into very small pieces and set aside. Thoroughly mix sugar with ½ of the water (hot). Pour the remaining water (cold) and all other ingredients *except* apple pieces into the batch freezer. Turn on dasher, set timer to 13 minutes, turn on the refrigeration and begin the batch. As the mixture firms up, add in the apple pieces, turn off the refrigeration and extrude the finished product. Decorate tops of tubs with cranberries and apple slices (dipped in lemon juice) and cinnamon.

 ## Homemade Version

INGREDIENTS

8 oz	Fresh/frozen cranberries	4 oz	Unsweetened apple juice
4 oz	Water (for marinade)	1 tsp	Cinnamon
8 oz	Sugar (for marinade)	10 oz	Sugar
1½ lb	Matsu or other eating apples	8 oz	Water (hot and cold)

PREPARATION

Marinate cranberries, water and sugar for 3 hours, then puree and strain out the pulp. Peel, core and seed apples. Puree ¾ of the apples with apple juice, then add cinnamon. Cut the remaining apples into very small pieces. Pour all ingredients *except* apple pieces into an ice cream maker and freeze according to manufacturer's instructions. When the batch is almost complete, add in the apple pieces, turn off refrigeration and extrude the finished product. Yield: 2 quarts of sorbet

Apple Brandy Sorbet

INGREDIENTS

10-Qt Batch	20-Qt Batch	40-Qt Batch	
5¼ lb	10½ lb	21 lb	Matsu or other eating apples: (B), (M)
1½ oz	3 oz	6 oz	Stabilizer (CC–917, ¾ of 1%) (B)
2 qt	4 qt	8 qt	Unsweetened apple juice (B)
¾ oz	1½ oz	3 oz	Cinnamon (B)
4 lb	8 lb	16 lb	Sugar (B)
1 qt	2 qt	4 qt	Water (hot and cold) (B)
8 oz	16 oz	32 oz	Apple brandy (M)

PREPARATION
Batch time: 13–15 minutes

Peel, core and seed apples. Under good agitation (using a spatula), slowly sift stabilizer into the apples and let the mixture hydrate. Puree ¾ of the apples with unsweetened apple juice; then add cinnamon. Cut remaining apples into very small pieces. Thoroughly mix sugar with ½ of the water (hot). Pour the remaining water (cold) and all other ingredients *except* apple pieces and brandy into the batch freezer. Turn on the dasher, set timer to 13 minutes, turn on refrigeration and begin the batch. As mixture firms up, add in apple brandy and apple pieces and continue freezing for 2 minutes. Turn off the refrigeration and extrude the finished product. Decorate tops of tubs with apple slices (dipped in lemon juice) and cinnamon.

Apricot Sorbet

This recipe was created by my mentors, Shippen Lebzelter and Guido Magnaguagno, owners of New York Ice. When it comes to creating ices and sorbets, they have more talent than anyone else I know!

INGREDIENTS

10-Qt Batch	20-Qt Batch	40-Qt Batch	
5 lb	10 lb	20 lb	Dried apricots (B)
1 qt	2 qt	4 qt	Water (cold)
2¼ lb	4½ lb	9 lb	Sugar (B)
1½ oz	3 oz	6 oz	Stabilizer (CC–917, ¾ of 1%) (B)
3 qt	6 qt	12 qt	Water (hot and cold) (B)

PREPARATION
Batch time: 13–15 minutes

Pour dried apricots into a pot, cover with cold water, bring to a boil and simmer for ½ hour. Remove apricots from heat, cool and puree. Sift sugar with stabilizer, dissolve in ½ of the water (hot) and let stabilizer hydrate. Pour all ingredients including remaining water (cold) into batch freezer. Turn on the dasher, set timer to 13 minutes, turn on refrigeration and begin batch. As the mixture firms up and looks gravy, turn off refrigeration and extrude the finished product. Decorate tops of tubs with dried apricots.

Apricot Cognac Sorbet

INGREDIENTS

10-Qt Batch	20-Qt Batch	40-Qt Batch	
5 lb	10 lb	20 lb	Dried apricots (B)
1 qt	2 qt	4 qt	Water (cold)
2¼ lb	4½ lb	9 lb	Sugar (B)
1½ oz	3 oz	6 oz	Stabilizer (CC–917, ¾ of 1%) (B)
3 qt	6 qt	12 qt	Water (hot and cold) (B)
6 oz	12 oz	24 oz	Cognac (M)

PREPARATION   Batch time: 13–15 minutes

Pour dried apricots into a pot, cover with cold water, bring to a boil and simmer for ½ hour. Remove from heat, cool and puree apricots. Sift sugar with stabilizer, dissolve in ½ of the water (hot) and let hydrate for ½ hour. Pour remaining water (cold) and all other ingredients *except* cognac into the batch freezer. Turn on dasher, set timer to 13 minutes, turn on refrigeration and begin the batch. As mixture firms up and looks gravy, add in cognac and continue freezing for 2 minutes. Turn off refrigeration and extrude finished product. Decorate tops of tubs with dried apricots.

Apricot Banana Sorbet

INGREDIENTS

10-Qt Batch	20-Qt Batch	40-Qt Batch	
5 lb	10 lb	20 lb	Dried apricots (B)
1 qt	2 qt	4 qt	Water (cold) (B)
2¼ lb	4½ lb	9 lb	Sugar (B)
1½ oz	3 oz	6 oz	Stabilizer (CC–917, ¾ of 1%) (B)
3 qt	6 qt	12 qt	Water (hot and cold) (B)
3 lb	6 lb	12 lb	Bananas, peeled (B)
2 Tbsp	4 Tbsp	8 Tbsp	Lemon juice (B)

PREPARATION   Batch time: 13–15 minutes

Pour dried apricots into a pot, cover with cold water, bring to a boil and simmer for 30 minutes. Remove apricots from heat, cool and puree. Sift sugar with stabilizer, dissolve in ½ of the water (hot) and let stabilizer hydrate for 30 minutes. Pour all ingredients including the remaining water (cold) into the batch freezer. Turn on the dasher, set timer to 13 minutes, turn on refrigeration and begin the batch. As the mixture firms up and looks gravy, turn off refrigeration and extrude the finished product. Decorate tops of tubs with apricot and banana slices.

MALCOLM SAYS: Dried apricots work well in all of these recipes. What's terrific about them is that when they become plump after cooking, they are bursting with flavor.

Apricot Wine Sorbet

The addition of white wine makes this Apricot sorbet the best I've ever made!

INGREDIENTS

10-Qt Batch	20-Qt Batch	40-Qt Batch	
5 lb	10 lb	20 lb	Dried apricots (B)
1 qt	2 qt	4 qt	Water (cold) (B)
2¼ lb	4½ lb	9 lb	Sugar (B)
1½ oz	3 oz	6 oz	Stabilizer (CC–917, ¾ of 1%) (B)
3 qt	6 qt	12 qt	Water (hot and cold) (B)
½ oz	1 oz	2 oz	Vanilla extract (B)
13 oz	26 oz	52 oz	Dry white wine (M)

PREPARATION   Batch time: 13–15 minutes

Pour dried apricots into a pot, cover with cold water, bring to a boil and simmer for 30 minutes. Remove apricots from heat, cool and puree. Sift sugar with stabilizer, dissolve in ½ of the water (hot) and let stabilizer hydrate. Pour remaining water and all other ingredients *except* white wine into the batch freezer. Turn on dasher, set timer to 13 minutes, turn on refrigeration and begin the batch. As the mixture firms up and looks gravy, add in white wine and continue freezing for 2 minutes. Turn off refrigeration and extrude the finished product. Decorate tops of tubs with dried apricots.

Banana Blueberry Sorbet

INGREDIENTS

10-Qt Batch	20-Qt Batch	40-Qt Batch	
2 qt	4 qt	8 qt	Fresh or frozen blueberries (E)
1 lb	2 lb	4 lb	Sugar (for marinade) (E)
9 lb	18 lb	36 lb	Ripe bananas, peeled (B)
1½ lb	3 lb	6 lb	Sugar (B)
1½ oz	3 oz	6 oz	Stabilizer (CC–917, ¾ of 1%) (B)
3 qt	6 qt	12 qt	Water (hot and cold) (B)
2 Tbsp	4 Tbsp	8 Tbsp	Lemon juice (B)

PREPARATION   Batch time: 13–15 minutes

Marinate the blueberries with sugar for 8 hours. Puree the bananas. Sift sugar with stabilizer; then dissolve in ½ of the water (hot). Under good agitation, slowly agitate the mixture for 1 minute and let hydrate for 30 minutes. Pour remaining water (cold) and all other ingredients *except* marinated blueberries into the batch freezer. Turn on the dasher, set the timer to 13 minutes, turn on the refrigeration and begin the batch. As the mixture firms up, add in blueberries, turn off refrigeration and extrude the finished product. Decorate tops of tubs with blueberries and banana slices.

Banana Coconut Fudge Sorbet

Bananas, coconut and fudge—how can you go wrong!

INGREDIENTS

10-Qt Batch	20-Qt Batch	40-Qt Batch	
8¼ lb	16½ lb	33 lb	Ripe bananas, peeled (B)
12 oz	24 oz	48 oz	Coconut fruit base (B)
9½ oz	19 oz	38 oz	Cream of coconut (B)
1½ lb	3 lb	6 lb	Sugar (B)
1 oz	2 oz	4 oz	Stabilizer (CC–917, ¾ of 1%) (B)
3½ qt	7 qt	14 qt	Water (hot and cold) (B)
2 Tbsp	4 Tbsp	8 Tbsp	Lemon juice (B)
1¼ oz	2½ oz	5 oz	Shredded coconut (E)
1 qt	2 qt	4 qt	Fudge variegate (O)

PREPARATION   Batch time: 13–15 minutes

Puree bananas and mix with coconut fruit base and cream of coconut. Sift sugar with stabilizer, dissolve in ½ of the water (hot) and let stabilizer hydrate for 30 minutes. Pour the remaining water (cold) and all other ingredients *except* shredded coconut and fudge variegate into the batch freezer. Turn on dasher, set timer to 13 minutes, turn on refrigeration and begin the batch. As the mixture firms up and looks gravy, add in the shredded coconut and turn off refrigeration. Fill a pastry bag with fudge variegate and squeeze it into semifrozen mixture as you extrude the finished product. Decorate tops of tubs with banana slices, shredded coconut and fudge.

 ## Homemade Version

INGREDIENTS

2 lb	Bananas, peeled
8 oz	Cream of coconut
6 oz	Sugar
22 oz	Water (hot and cold)
½ oz	Shredded coconut
8 oz	Fudge sauce

PREPARATION

Puree the bananas and mix with cream of coconut. Thoroughly mix sugar with ½ of the water (hot). Pour remaining water (cold) and all other ingredients *except* shredded coconut and fudge sauce into an ice cream freezer and freeze according to manufacturer's instructions. When batch is almost complete, add in shredded coconut and turn off refrigeration. Fill a pastry bag with fudge sauce and squeeze it into the semifrozen mixture as you extrude the finished product. Decorate top of container with banana slices, shredded coconut and fudge. Yield: 1½–2 quarts of sorbet

Banana Colada Fudge Sorbet

Take some pineapple, coconut and fudge. What do you get? A Piña Colada Extravaganza!

INGREDIENTS

10-Qt Batch	20-Qt Batch	40-Qt Batch	
8¼ lb	16½ lb	33 lb	Ripe bananas, peeled (B)
1 lb	2 lb	4 lb	Sweet ripe pineapple (B)
12 oz	24 oz	48 oz	Coconut fruit base (B)
9½ oz	19 oz	38 oz	Cream of coconut (B)
1½ lb	3 lb	6 lb	Sugar (B)
1 oz	2 oz	4 oz	Stabilizer (CC-917, ¾ of 1%) (B)
3½ qt	7 qt	14 qt	Water (hot and cold) (B)
1¼ oz	2½ oz	5 oz	Shredded coconut (E)
1 qt	2 qt	4 qt	Fudge variegate (O)

PREPARATION   Batch time: 13–15 minutes

Puree bananas and pineapple. Mix bananas with the coconut fruit base and cream of coconut. Sift sugar with stabilizer, dissolve in ½ of the water (hot) and let stabilizer hydrate for 30 minutes. Pour remaining water (cold) and all other ingredients *except* shredded coconut and fudge variegate into the batch freezer. Turn on dasher, set timer to 13 minutes, turn on refrigeration and begin the batch. As the mixture firms up and looks gravy, add in shredded coconut and turn off refrigeration. Fill a pastry bag with fudge variegate and squeeze it into the semifrozen mixture as you extrude finished product. Decorate tops of tubs with shredded coconut, fudge, pineapple and banana slices.

 Homemade Version

INGREDIENTS

2 lb	Bananas, peeled	8 oz	Pineapple juice
8 oz	Cream of coconut	8 oz	Crushed pineapple pieces
6 oz	Sugar	½ oz	Shredded coconut
22 oz	Water (hot and cold)	8 oz	Fudge sauce

PREPARATION

Puree bananas and combine with cream of coconut. Thoroughly mix sugar with 11 ounces of hot water. Pour the remaining cold water and all other ingredients *except* shredded coconut and fudge sauce into an ice cream freezer and freeze according to manufacturer's instructions. Turn off refrigeration and add in shredded coconut. Fill a pastry bag with fudge sauce and squeeze it into the semifrozen mixture as you extrude the finished product. Decorate top of container with banana slices, shredded coconut, pineapple and fudge. Yield: 1½–2 quarts of sorbet

Cappuccino Sorbet

This sophisticated flavor is served in many Italian-style cafés and restaurants.

INGREDIENTS

10-Qt Batch	20-Qt Batch	40-Qt Batch	
6 oz	12 oz	24 oz	Espresso extract (B)
½ oz	1 oz	2 oz	Cocoa (22–24% fat) (B)
1 oz	2 oz	4 oz	Hot water (B)
2¼ lb	4½ lb	9 lb	Sugar (B)
1½ gal	3 gal	6 gal	Water (hot and cold) (B)
1½ oz	3 oz	6 oz	Stabilizer (CC–917, ¾ of 1%) (B)
24 oz	1½ qt	3 qt	Ice cream mix (B)
6 oz	12 oz	24 oz	Kahlua liqueur (M)

PREPARATION   Batch time: 13–15 minutes

Mix espresso extract and cocoa with extremely hot water to create a paste. Sift together sugar and stabilizer, dissolve in ½ of the water (hot) and then add in remaining water (cold). Under good agitation, slowly sift the stabilizer into the espresso mixture and let it hydrate for 30 minutes. Pour all ingredients *except* the Kahlua into the batch freezer, turn on the dasher, set timer to 13 minutes, turn on the refrigeration and begin the batch. As the mixture firms up, add in the Kahlua and continue freezing for 2 minutes. Turn off refrigeration and extrude the finished product.

 ## Homemade Version

INGREDIENTS

1 oz	Freeze-dried instant espresso
½ tsp	Cocoa
1 tsp	Hot water
10 oz	Sugar
48 oz	Water (hot and cold)
6 oz	Heavy cream
2 oz	Kahlua liqueur

PREPARATION

Mix freeze-dried espresso and cocoa with extremely hot water to create a paste. Thoroughly mix sugar with 24 ounces of hot water, then add in the remaining cold water. Pour all ingredients *except* Kahlua into an ice cream freezer and freeze according to manufacturer's instructions. As mixture firms up and looks gravy, pour in the Kahlua, turn off refrigeration and extrude the finished product. Yield: 1½–2 quarts of sorbet

MALCOLM SAYS: You can use half-and-half in place of the heavy cream.

The Ultimate Chocolate Sorbet

My favorite sorbet, bar none! This one, made with cocoa and fudge, has great body texture.

INGREDIENTS

10-Qt Batch	20-Qt Batch	40-Qt Batch	
½ lb	1 lb	2 lb	Cocoa (22–24% fat) (B)
1 gal	2 gal	4 gal	Water (hot and cold) (B)
2½ lb	5 lb	10 lb	Sugar (B)
1½ oz	3 oz	6 oz	Stabilizer (CC–917, ¾ of 1%) (B)
1 oz	2 oz	4 oz	Vanilla extract (B)
½ lb	1 lb	2 lb	Fudge (B)

PREPARATION   Batch time: 13–15 minutes

Pour cocoa and ¼ of the water (hot) into a double boiler and heat. Sift sugar with stabilizer and dissolve in another ¼ of the water (hot). Add this mixture to the cocoa mixture and create a paste. Pour all ingredients including the remaining water (cold) into the batch freezer. Turn on dasher and run for 2 minutes to blend ingredients, set timer to 13 minutes, turn on refrigeration and begin the batch. As the mixture firms up and looks gravy, turn off refrigeration and extrude the finished product.

MALCOLM SAYS: Make sure there is no dry cocoa powder in the cocoa paste. It will take away from the flavor profile and texture of your finished product.

 # Homemade Version

If you like dark chocolate, than this recipe is a must to try!

INGREDIENTS

4 oz	Cocoa (22–24% fat)
10 oz	Sugar
32 oz	Water (hot and cold)
1 tsp	Vanilla extract
2 oz	Fudge

PREPARATION

Create a paste with cocoa, sugar and 16 ounces of hot water. Pour all ingredients including the remaining cold water into an ice cream maker and freeze according to manufacturer's instructions. As the mixture firms up and looks gravy, turn off the refrigeration and extrude the finished product. Yield: 1½–2 quarts of sorbet

Chocolate Sorbet

INGREDIENTS

10-Qt Batch	20-Qt Batch	40-Qt Batch	
¾ lb	1½ lb	3 lb	Cocoa (22–24% fat) (B)
¾ lb	1½ lb	3 lb	Chocolate (B)
1 gal	2 gal	4 gal	Water (hot and cold) (B)
2¾ lb	5½ lb	11 lb	Sugar (B)
1 lb	2 lb	4 lb	36 DE corn (B)
1 oz	2 oz	4 oz	Stabilizer (CC–917, ¾ of 1%) (B)
1 oz	2 oz	4 oz	Vanilla extract (B)
¾ lb	1½ lb	3 lb	Fudge (B)

PREPARATION   Batch time: 13–15 minutes

Heat cocoa, chocolate and ¼ of the water (hot) in a double boiler. Sift together sugar, 36 DC corn and stabilizer; dissolve in another ¼ of the water (hot). Add this to cocoa mixture and create a paste. Pour all ingredients including cold water into batch freezer. Turn on dasher and run for 2 minutes, set timer to 13 minutes, turn on refrigeration and begin the batch. As the mixture firms up and looks gravy, turn off refrigeration and extrude the finished product.

Chocolate Banana Coconut Sorbet

INGREDIENTS

10-Qt Batch	20-Qt Batch	40-Qt Batch	
¼ lb	½ lb	1 lb	Cocoa (22–24% fat) (B)
1 gal	2 gal	4 gal	Water (hot and cold) (B)
2½ lb	5 lb	10 lb	Sugar (B)
1 lb	2 lb	4 lb	36 DE corn (B)
1½ oz	3 oz	6 oz	Stabilizer (CC–917, ¾ of 1%) (B)
3 lb	6 lb	12 lb	Very ripe bananas (B)
16 oz	2 lb	4 lb	Coconut fruit base (B)
8 oz	1 lb	2 lb	Shredded coconut (M)
½ lb	1 lb	2 lb	Fudge (M)

PREPARATION   Batch time: 13–15 minutes

Heat cocoa and ¼ of the water (hot) in a double boiler. Sift together sugar, 36 DE corn and stabilizer; dissolve in another ¼ of the water (hot). Add to cocoa mixture and create a paste. Puree bananas with just enough water until smooth. Pour remaining water (cold) and all other ingredients *except* coconut and fudge into batch freezer. Turn on dasher and run for 3 minutes, set timer to 13 minutes, turn on refrigeration and begin batch. After 2 minutes, slowly add in fudge and coconut. As mixture looks gravy, turn off refrigeration and extrude finished product.

Chocolate Strawberry Sorbet

INGREDIENTS

10-Qt Batch	20-Qt Batch	40-Qt Batch	
2 lb	4 lb	8 lb	Frozen strawberries, defrosted (O)
8 oz	1 lb	2 lb	Sugar (for marinade) (O)
1½ oz	3 oz	6 oz	Stabilizer (CC–917, ¾ of 1%) (B)
2½ lb	5 lb	10 lb	Sugar (B)
½ lb	1 lb	2 lb	Cocoa (22–24% fat) (B)
1 gal	2 gal	4 gal	Water (hot and cold) (B)
1 oz	2 oz	4 oz	Vanilla extract (B)
½ lb	1 lb	2 lb	Fudge (B)

PREPARATION   Batch time: 13–15 minutes

Combine and marinate strawberries and sugar for 3 hours. Sift sugar, stabilizer and cocoa together, dissolve in ¼ of the water (hot) in a double boiler and heat to create a paste. Pour remaining water (cold) and all other ingredients *except* marinated strawberries into the batch freezer. Turn on dasher and refrigeration, set timer to 13 minutes and begin the batch. As the mixture firms up and looks gravy, turn off refrigeration, add in marinated strawberries and extrude the finished product.

Chocolate Coconut Rum Sorbet

The beauty of coconut and rum is that they work well with all kinds of flavor mixtures all year long.

INGREDIENTS

10-Qt Batch	20-Qt Batch	40-Qt Batch	
2¾ lb	5½ lb	11 lb	Sugar (B)
1½ oz	3 oz	6 oz	Stabilizer (CC–917, ¾ of 1%) (B)
6 oz	12 oz	24 oz	Cocoa (22–24% fat) (B)
3 oz	6 oz	12 oz	Semisweet chocolate (B)
1 gal	2 gal	4 gal	Water (hot and cold) (B)
1 oz	2 oz	4 oz	Vanilla extract (B)
½ lb	1 lb	2 lb	Fudge (B)
1 qt	2 qt	4 qt	Coconut fruit base (B)
6 oz	12 oz	24 oz	Dark rum (E)
4 oz	8 oz	1 lb	Shredded coconut (E)

PREPARATION   Batch time: 13–15 minutes

Mix together sugar and stabilizer; combine with cocoa and chocolate in ¼ of the water (hot) in a double boiler and heat. Pour remaining water (cold) and all ingredients *except* rum and coconut into batch freezer. Turn on dasher and refrigeration, set timer to 13 minutes and begin batch. As mixture firms up and looks gravy, add in rum and coconut, freeze for 2 more minutes, turn off refrigeration and extrude the finished product.

Chocolate Raspberry Sorbet

Try it! You'll be very pleased.

INGREDIENTS

10-Qt Batch	20-Qt Batch	40-Qt Batch	
½ lb	1 lb	2 lb	Cocoa (22–24% fat) (B)
1 gal	2 gal	4 gal	Water (hot and cold) (B)
2 ½ lb	5 lb	10 lb	Sugar (B)
1½ oz	3 oz	6 oz	Stabilizer (CC–917, ¾ of 1%) (B)
1 oz	2 oz	4 oz	Vanilla extract (B)
½ lb	1 lb	2 lb	Fudge (B)
1¾ lb	3½ lb	7 lb	Red raspberry puree (B)

PREPARATION   Batch time: 13–15 minutes

Combine cocoa and ¼ of the water (hot) in a double boiler and heat. Sift together sugar and stabilizer and dissolve in another ¼ of the water (hot). Add this mixture to cocoa mixture and create a paste. Pour all ingredients including the remaining water (cold) into the batch freezer. Turn on dasher and run for 2 minutes to blend ingredients, set timer to 13 minutes, turn on refrigeration and begin the batch. As mixture firms up and looks gravy, turn off the refrigeration and extrude the finished product. Swirl raspberry puree on tops of tubs.

 Homemade Version

The smooth, silky taste of raspberries marries very well with chocolate.

INGREDIENTS

8 oz	Raspberries, fresh or frozen	32 oz	Water (hot and cold)
12 oz	Sugar	1 tsp	Vanilla extract
4 oz	Cocoa (22–24% fat	2 oz	Fudge

PREPARATION

Combine and marinate raspberries and 2 ounces of sugar for 4 hours. Create a paste with cocoa, 10 ounces of sugar and 16 ounces of hot water. Pour all ingredients including the remaining cold water into an ice cream maker and freeze according to manufacturer's instructions. As the mixture firms up and looks gravy, turn off refrigeration and extrude the finished product. Yield: 1½–2 quarts of sorbet

Chocolate Orange Sorbet

INGREDIENTS

10-Qt Batch	20-Qt Batch	40-Qt Batch	
2¾ lb	5½ lb	11 lb	Sugar (B)
1½ oz	3 oz	6 oz	Stabilizer (CC–917, ¾ of 1%) (B)
6 oz	12 oz	24 oz	Cocoa (22–24% fat) (B)
1 gal	2 gals	4 gal	Water (hot and cold) (B)
3 oz	6 oz	12 oz	Semisweet chocolate (B)
1 oz	2 oz	4 oz	Vanilla extract (B)
1 qt	2 qt	1 gal	Fresh orange juice (B)
½ lb	1 lb	2 lb	Fudge (B)
4 oz	8 oz	1 lb	Chocolate chunks (O)

PREPARATION   Batch time: 13–15 minutes

Mix together sugar and stabilizer, combine with cocoa and chocolate, dissolve in ¼ of the water (hot) in a double boiler and heat to create a paste. Pour remaining water (cold) and all other ingredients *except* chocolate chunks into the batch freezer. Turn on dasher for 3 minutes, set timer to 13 minutes, turn on refrigeration and begin the batch. As mixture firms up and looks gravy, turn off refrigeration, add in chocolate chunks and extrude the finished product.

Claret Sorbet

INGREDIENTS

10-Qt Batch	20-Qt Batch	40-Qt Batch	
1½ lb	3 lb	6 lb	Fresh or frozen red raspberries (B)
6 oz	12 oz	24 oz	Sugar (for marinade) (B)
1½ oz	3 oz	6 oz	Stabilizer (CC–917, ¾ of 1%) (B)
2¼ lb	4½ lb	9 lb	Sugar (B)
1½ qt	3 qt	6 qt	Water (hot and cold) (B)
3	6	12	Red Bordeaux wine, 26 oz bottles (M)

PREPARATION   Batch time: 13–15 minutes

Marinate raspberries and sugar for 6 hours; then strain off and discard the juice. Sift together stabilizer and sugar, dissolve in ½ of the water (hot) and hydrate for 30 minutes. Pour remaining water (cold) and all other ingredients *except* the wine into batch freezer. Turn on dasher, set timer to 13 minutes, turn on refrigeration and begin the batch. As mixture firms up, add in wine and continue freezing for 2 minutes. Turn off refrigeration and extrude the finished product. Decorate tops of tubs with raspberries.

MALCOLM SAYS: It is very important to add the red Bordeaux wine into the batch at the end because of the freezing point of the wine.

Cranberry Sorbet

INGREDIENTS

10-Qt Batch	20-Qt Batch	40-Qt Batch	
2 qt	4 qt	8 qt	Water (cold)* (B)
7¼ lb	14½ lb	29 lb	Sugar* (B)
9½ lb	19 lb	38 lb	Fresh or frozen cranberries* (B)
1 oz	2 oz	4 oz	Stabilizer (CC–917, ¾ of 1%) (B)
6 oz	12 oz	24 oz	Triple Sec liqueur (M)

*The ingredients for a 20-quart batch should yield about 11½ quarts of juice. Make appropriate adjustments for other size batches.

PREPARATION   Batch time: 13–15 minutes

Combine water, sugar and cranberries and cook on low heat for 15 minutes. Puree mixture and strain thoroughly to yield as much juice as possible. Under good agitation (using a spatula), slowly sift stabilizer into the juice and let the mixture hydrate. Pour all ingredients *except* Triple Sec into the batch freezer. Turn on dasher, set timer to 13 minutes, turn on refrigeration and begin the batch. As the mixture firms up and looks gravy, add in Triple Sec and continue freezing for 2 minutes. Turn off refrigeration and extrude the finished product.

Fresh Fig Sorbet

This sorbet has a sensual feel to its name and, if promoted correctly, will sell very well.

INGREDIENTS

10-Qt Batch	20-Qt Batch	40-Qt Batch	
4½ lb	9 lb	18 lb	Fresh fig puree* (B)
1 qt	2 qt	4 qt	Water (for puree)
2¼ lb	4½ lb	9 lb	Sugar (B)
1 oz	2 oz	4 oz	Stabilizer (CC–917, ¾ of 1%) (B)
3 qt	6 qt	12 qt	Water (hot and cold) (B)
½ oz	1 oz	2 oz	Vanilla extract (B)
1 oz	2 oz	4 oz	Ground nutmeg (B)
1 oz	2 oz	4 oz	Lemon juice (B)

*For a 20-quart batch, you will need about 10 pounds of figs to make 9 pounds of puree.

PREPARATION   Batch time: 13–15 minutes

Bring fresh figs and water to a slow boil and simmer for 30 minutes. Remove, cool, drain water and puree. Sift together sugar and stabilizer, then dissolve in ½ of the water (hot). Pour all ingredients including remaining water (cold) into batch freezer. Turn on dasher, set timer to 13 minutes, turn on refrigeration and begin the batch. As mixture firms up and looks gravy, turn off refrigeration and extrude finished product.

Grapefruit Sorbet

INGREDIENTS

10-Qt Batch	20-Qt Batch	40-Qt Batch	
24	48	96	Fresh ripe grapefruits* (B)
3¾ lb	7½ lb	15 lb	Sugar (B)
2 oz	4 oz	8 oz	Stabilizer (CC–917, ¾ of 1%) (B)
2 qt	4 qt	8 qt	Water (hot and cold) (B)

PREPARATION   Batch time: 13–15 minutes

Squeeze enough grapefruits to obtain the needed amount of juice*, then strain and remove seeds. Save ½ of the pulp and discard rest. Mix together sugar and stabilizer, then dissolve in ½ of the water (hot). Under good agitation (using a spatula), slowly sift this mixture and let it hydrate. Pour juice, pulp and remaining water (cold) into the the batch freezer. Turn on dasher, set timer to 13 minutes, turn on refrigeration and begin the batch. As the mixture firms up and looks gravy, turn off refrigeration and extrude the finished product. Decorate tops of tubs with fresh grapefruit slices.

Grapefruit Menta Sorbet

Consider developing this delicately flavored dessert for your wholesale restaurant accounts.

INGREDIENTS

10-Qt Batch	20-Qt Batch	40-Qt Batch	
24	48	96	Fresh grapefruits* (B)
3¾ lb	7½ lb	15 lb	Sugar (B)
2 oz	4 oz	8 oz	Stabilizer (CC–917, ¾ of 1%) (B)
2 qt	4 qt	8 qt	Water (hot and cold) (B)
8 oz	16 oz	32 oz	White crème de menthe liqueur (M)

PREPARATION   Batch time: 13–15 minutes

Squeeze enough grapefruits to obtain the needed amount of juice*, then strain and remove seeds. Save ½ of the pulp and discard rest. Sift together sugar and stabilizer; then dissolve in ½ of the water (hot). Under good agitation (using a spatula), slowly sift mixture and let it hydrate. Pour remaining water (cold) and all other ingredients *except* the liqueur into the batch freezer. Turn on dasher, set timer to 13 minutes, turn on refrigeration and begin the batch. As the mixture firms up and looks gravy, add in the liqueur and continue freezing for 2 minutes. Turn off refrigeration and extrude finished product. Decorate tops of tubs with grapefruit slices and green mint leaves.

MALCOLM SAYS: Do not discard the pulp; it adds body and texture to the product.

*You will need about 4 quarts of grapefruit juice for a 10-quart batch, 8 quarts for a 20-quart batch and 16 quarts for a 40-quart batch.

Grapefruit Campari Sorbet

INGREDIENTS

10-Qt Batch	20-Qt Batch	40-Qt Batch	
3 qt	1½ gal	3 gal	Fresh grapefruit juice* (B)
2¾ lb	5½ lb	11 lb	Sugar (B)
1 oz	2 oz	4 oz	Stabilizer (CC–917, ¾ of 1%) (B)
1½ qt	3 qt	6 qt	Water (hot and cold) (B)
13 oz	26 oz	52 oz	Campari wine (E)

*For a 20-quart batch, start with about 36 grapefruits. Adjust accordingly for other size batches.

PREPARATION   Batch time: 13–15 minutes

Squeeze enough grapefruits to obtain the needed amount of juice, then strain and remove seeds. Save ½ of the pulp and discard the rest. Mix together sugar and stabilizer, then dissolve in ½ of the water (hot). Under good agitation (using a spatula), slowly sift this mixture and let it hydrate. Pour the remaining water (cold) and other ingredients *except* the wine into the batch freezer. Turn on the dasher, set timer to 13 minutes, turn on refrigeration and begin the batch. As the mixture firms up and looks gravy, add in wine and continue freezing for 2 minutes. Turn off refrigeration and extrude the finished product. Decorate tops of tubs with grapefruit slices.

 Homemade Version

INGREDIENTS

24 oz	Fresh grapefruit juice
12 oz	Sugar
12 oz	Water (hot and cold)
8 oz	Campari wine

PREPARATION

Squeeze enough grapefruits to obtain the needed amount of juice, then strain and remove seeds. Save ½ of the pulp and discard the rest. Thoroughly mix sugar with 6 ounces of hot water. Pour grapefruit juice, pulp and remaining cold water into an ice cream maker and freeze according to manufacturer's instructions. As mixture firms up and looks gravy, add in wine and continue freezing for 2 minutes. Turn off refrigeration and extrude the finished product. Yield: 1½–2 quarts of sorbet

MALCOLM SAYS: If you want a stronger wine taste, increase the amount of wine to 12 ounces.

Green Apple Candied Ginger Sorbet

Truly refreshing! A touch of ginger provides just the kick to make this a flavor to remember.

INGREDIENTS

10-Qt Batch	20-Qt Batch	40-Qt Batch	
2 qt	4 qt	8 qt	Green apple puree* (B)
2 qt	4 qt	8 qt	Unsweetened apple juice (B)
3¾ lb	7½ lb	15 lb	Sugar (B)
1½ oz	3 oz	6 oz	Stabilizer (CC–917, ¾ of 1%) (B)
1 qt	2 qt	4 qt	Water (hot and cold) (B)
2 oz	4 oz	8 oz	Fresh or frozen lime juice (B)
8 oz	1 lb	2 lb	Candied ginger pieces (B)

*You will need about 5–6 apples for each quart of puree.

PREPARATION   Batch time: 13–15 minutes

Peel, core and seed apples; puree with the apple juice. Sift together sugar and stabilizer, then dissolve in ½ of the water (hot). Under good agitation, slowly agitate mixture for 1 minute and let hydrate for 30 minutes. Pour remaining water and all other ingredients into the batch freezer. Turn on dasher, set timer to 13 minutes, turn on refrigeration and begin batch. As mixture firms up and looks gravy, turn off refrigeration and extrude finished product. Decorate tops of tubs with apple and ginger pieces.

Gianduja (Chocolate & Hazelnut) Sorbet

INGREDIENTS

10-Qt Batch	20-Qt Batch	40-Qt Batch	
½ lb	1 lb	2 lb	Cocoa (22–24% fat) (B)
1 gal	2 gal	4 gal	Water (hot and cold) (B)
2½ lb	5 lb	10 lb	Sugar (B)
1½ oz	3 oz	6 oz	Stabilizer (CC–917, ¾ of 1%) (B)
1 oz	2 oz	4 oz	Vanilla extract (B)
½ lb	1 lb	2 lb	Fudge (B)
10 oz	20 oz	40 oz	Gianduja paste (B)
4 oz	8 oz	1 lb	Roasted granulated hazelnuts (O)

PREPARATION   Batch time: 13–15 minutes

Pour cocoa and ¼ of the water (hot) into a double boiler and heat. Sift together sugar and stabilizer and then dissolve in ¼ of the water (hot). Add this mixture to the cocoa mixture and create a paste. Pour remaining water (cold) and other ingredients *except* hazelnuts into the batch freezer. Turn on dasher and run for 2 minutes, set timer for 13 minutes, turn on refrigeration and begin batch. As the mixture firms up and looks gravy, turn off refrigeration, add in hazelnuts and extrude the finished product.

Kiwi Sorbet

Kiwi is sometimes referred to as "Chinese Gooseberry" because it originated in eastern Asia. On the inside a kiwi is firm and sweet with a slight acidic flavor. It is a very easy fruit to use in sorbet production; simply peel off the skin and puree. To stop discoloration and bring out the best taste, add lemon juice (½ lemon for every 15 kiwis).

INGREDIENTS

10-Qt Batch	20-Qt Batch	40-Qt Batch	
19	38	76	Kiwis* (B)
2½ lb	5 lb	10 lb	Sugar (B)
1¾ oz	3½ oz	7 oz	Stabilizer (CC–917, ¾ of 1%) (B)
1½ qt	3 qt	6 qt	Water (hot and cold) (B)
2½ oz	5 oz	10 oz	Lemon or lime juice (B)

PREPARATION   Batch time: 13–15 minutes

Peel and puree the kiwis. Sift together sugar and stabilizer and then dissolve in ½ of the water (hot). Under good agitation (using a spatula), slowly agitate the mixture for 1 minute and let it hydrate. Pour remaining water (cold) and all other ingredients into the batch freezer. Turn on dasher, set timer to 13 minutes, turn on refrigeration and begin the batch. As the mixture firms up and looks gravy, turn off refrigeration and extrude the finished product. Decorate tops of tubs with kiwi slices.

Kiwi Lemon Sorbet

INGREDIENTS

10-Qt Batch	20-Qt Batch	40-Qt Batch	
19	38	76	Kiwis* (B)
3 lb	6 lb	12 lb	Sugar (B)
1¾ oz	3½ oz	7 oz	Stabilizer (CC–917, ¾ of 1%) (B)
2 qt	4 qt	8 qt	Water (hot and cold) (B)
8 oz	16 oz	32 oz	Fresh lemon juice (B)

PREPARATION   Batch time: 13–15 minutes

Peel and puree the kiwis. Sift together sugar and stabilizer; then dissolve in ½ of the water (hot). Under good agitation (using a spatula) allow the mixture to hydrate. Pour the remaining water (cold) and all other ingredients into the batch freezer. Turn on the dasher, set the timer to 13 minutes, turn on refrigeration and begin the batch. As the mixture firms up and looks gravy, turn off refrigeration and extrude the finished product. Decorate tops of tubs with kiwi and lemon slices.

*You will need about 4½ quarts of juice for a 10-quart batch, 9 quarts for a 20-quart batch and 18 quarts for a 40-quart batch.

Kiwi Strawberry Sorbet

The sweetness of the strawberries is a terrific contrast to the tartness of the kiwis. A winner!

INGREDIENTS

10-Qt Batch	20-Qt Batch	40-Qt Batch	
19	38	76	Kiwis (B)
2½ lb	5 lb	10 lb	Sugar (B)
1¾ oz	3½ oz	7 oz	Stabilizer (CC–917, ¾ of 1%) (B)
1½ qt	3 qt	6 qt	Water (hot and cold) (B)
2½ oz	5 oz	10 oz	Lemon or lime juice (B)
2 qt	4 qt	8 qt	Strawberry puree (B)

PREPARATION   Batch time: 13–15 minutes

Peel and puree the kiwis. Sift together sugar and stabilizer, and then dissolve in ½ of the water (hot) using good agitation (a spatula works well) to allow the mixture to hydrate. Pour all ingredients including the remaining water (cold) into the batch freezer. Turn on the dasher, set timer to 13 minutes, turn on the refrigeration and begin the batch. As the mixture firms up and looks gravy, turn off refrigeration and extrude the finished product. Decorate tops of tubs with kiwi and strawberry slices.

Luscious Summer Delight Sorbet

INGREDIENTS

10-Qt Batch	20-Qt Batch	40-Qt Batch	
2 qt	4 qt	8 qt	Blueberries (fresh or frozen) (E)
1 lb	2 lb	4 lb	Sugar (for marinade) (E)
9 lb	18 lb	36 lb	Banana puree* (B)
1½ lb	3 lb	6 lb	Sugar (B)
1½ oz	3 oz	6 oz	Stabilizer (CC–917, ¾ of 1%) (B)
3½ qt	7 qt	14 qt	Water (hot and cold) (B)
2 Tbsp	4 Tbsp	8 Tbsp	Lemon juice (B)
1 qt	2 qt	4 qt	Raspberry puree (B)

*Peel enough bananas to have about 3 peeled bananas for each pound of puree.

PREPARATION   Batch time: 13–15 minutes

Combine and marinate blueberries and sugar for 8 hours. Using a sieve, drain off liquid sugar mixture and set aside. Puree bananas. Sift together sugar and stabilizer, and then dissolve in ½ of the water (hot). Under good agitation (using a spatula), slowly agitate the mixture for 1 minute and let hydrate for 30 minutes. Pour remaining water (cold) and all ingredients *except* marinated blueberries into batch freezer. Turn on dasher, set timer to 13 minutes, turn on refrigeration and begin the batch. As mixture firms up, add in blueberries, turn off refrigeration and extrude finished product.

Lemon Sorbet

Lemon is the most refreshing sorbet, but also the most difficult to produce. Often the finished product is either too sweet or too tart, depending on the lemons used and time of year.

INGREDIENTS

10-Qt Batch	20-Qt Batch	40-Qt Batch	
4	8	16	Zest of fresh lemons (E)
35	70	140	Lemons* (B)
2 lb	4 lb	8 lb	Sugar (B)
8 oz	1 lb	2 lb	36 DE corn (B)
1½ oz	3 oz	6 oz	Stabilizer (CC–917, ¾ of 1%) (B)
3 qt	6 qt	12 qt	Water (hot and cold) (B)
8 oz	16 oz	1 qt	Fresh orange juice (B)

*The number of lemons you will need depends on their ripeness and sweetness. But, generally, 35 lemons will yield about 1¾ quarts of juice, 70 lemons about 3½ quarts and 140 lemons about 7 quarts.

PREPARATION   Batch time: 13–15 minutes

Zest the lemons and use an electric juicer to juice them. Sift together sugar, 36 DE corn and stabilizer, and then dissolve in ½ of the water (hot) until dry powders are completely dissolved and agitated. Pour remaining water (cold) and all other ingredients *except* lemon zest into the batch freezer. Turn on dasher, set timer to 13 minutes, turn on refrigeration and begin the batch. As the mixture firms up and looks gravy, add in lemon zest, turn off refrigeration and extrude the finished product.

MALCOLM SAYS: Orange juice is used to smooth out the flavor tones that hit your tongue. In simple language, it helps to remove the tartness of the lemons.

 Homemade Version

INGREDIENTS

2	Zest of fresh lemons
9	Lemons (12 ounces of juice)
12 oz	Sugar
20 oz	Water (hot and cold)
2 oz	Fresh orange juice

PREPARATION

Zest the lemons, use an electric juicer to juice them, then set aside the pulp. Mix sugar with 10 ounces of hot water. Pour the remaining cold water and all ingredients *except* lemon zest into an ice cream maker and freeze according to manufacturer's instructions. As the mixture firms up and looks gravy, add in lemon zest, turn off refrigeration and extrude the finished product. Yield: 1½–2 quarts of sorbet

Mango Sorbet

I like Mango sorbet more and more each year. You can't go wrong using either fresh or frozen mangoes. I guarantee it!

INGREDIENTS

10-Qt Batch	20-Qt Batch	40-Qt Batch	
9 lb	18 lb	36 lb	Mango puree* (B)
3 lb	6 lb	12 lb	Sugar (B)
1 oz	2 oz	4 oz	Stabilizer (CC–917, ¾ of 1%) (B)
2½ qt	5 qt	10 qt	Water (hot and cold) (B)
6 oz	12 oz	24 oz	Mango paste (B)
1 Tbsp	1 oz	2 oz	Lemon juice (B)

PREPARATION   Batch time: 13–15 minutes

Peel, seed and puree enough fully ripened mangoes to make the mango puree*. Sift together sugar and stabilizer, then dissolve in ½ of the water (hot) and let stabilizer hydrate for about 30 minutes. Pour all ingredients including remaining water (cold) into the batch freezer. Turn on dasher, set timer to 13 minutes, turn on refrigeration and begin the batch. As the mixture firms up and looks gravy, turn off refrigeration and extrude the finished product. Decorate tops of tubs with fresh mango slices.

MALCOLM SAYS: The mango paste gives this sorbet a "flavor boost." The lemon juice brings out the natural flavor of the mango.

 Homemade Version

INGREDIENTS

2½ lb	Frozen or fresh mango puree*
20 oz	Water (hot and cold)
¾ lb	Sugar
1 Tbsp	Lemon juice

PREPARATION

Peel, seed and puree enough fully ripened mangoes to make the mango puree*. Thoroughly mix sugar with 10 ounces of hot water. Pour all ingredients including the remaining cold water into an ice cream maker and freeze according to manufacturer's instructions. As the mixture firms up and looks gravy, turn off the refrigeration and extrude the finished product. Yield: 1½–2 quarts of sorbet

*You will need 3–4 mangoes for each pound of mango puree.

Mango Coconut Sorbet

INGREDIENTS

10-Qt Batch	20-Qt Batch	40-Qt Batch	
9 lb	18 lb	36 lb	Mango puree* (B)
3 lb	6 lb	12 lb	Sugar (B)
1 oz	2 oz	4 oz	Stabilizer (CC–917, ¾ of 1%) (B)
2½ qt	5 qt	10 qt	Water (hot and cold) (B)
6 oz	12 oz	24 oz	Mango paste (B)
2	4	8	Cream of coconut, 15-oz cans (B)
1 Tbsp	1 oz	2 oz	Lemon juice (B)
4 oz	8 oz	16 oz	Shredded coconut (E)

PREPARATION   **Batch time: 13–15 minutes**

Peel, seed and puree enough fully ripened mangoes to make the mango puree*. Sift together sugar and stabilizer, dissolve in ½ of the water (hot) and let hydrate. Pour remaining water (cold) and other ingredients *except* shredded coconut into the batch freezer. Turn on dasher and refrigeration, set timer to 13 minutes and begin the batch. As mixture firms up and looks gravy, add in coconut, turn off refrigeration and extrude the finished product. Decorate tops of tubs with mango and coconut.

Nieve de Mango Limon Sorbet

INGREDIENTS

10-Qt Batch	20-Qt Batch	40-Qt Batch	
9 lb	18 lb	36 lb	Mango puree* (B)
3 lb	6 lb	12 lb	Sugar (B)
1 oz	2 oz	4 oz	Stabilizer (CC–917, ¾ of 1%) (B)
2½ qt	5 qt	10 qt	Water (hot and cold) (B)
6 oz	12 oz	24 oz	Mango paste (B)
8 oz	16 oz	32 oz	Lime juice, fresh or frozen (B)
1 Tbsp	1 oz	2 oz	Lemon juice (B)

PREPARATION   **Batch time: 13–15 minutes**

Peel, seed and puree enough fully ripened mangoes to make the mango puree*. Sift together sugar and stabilizer, dissolve in ½ of the water (hot) and let hydrate. Pour all ingredients including remaining water (cold) into batch freezer. Turn on dasher, set timer to 13 minutes, turn on refrigeration and begin the batch. As the mixture firms up and looks gravy, turn off refrigeration and extrude the finished product.

MALCOLM SAYS: Given its tartness, lime juice may be difficult to work with. Always start with less, taste and increase as needed before you begin the freezing process.

*You will need 3–4 mangoes for each pound of mango puree.

Mango Berry Sorbet

By now you should have figured out that I love Mango sorbet. Here is my newest version of this fabulous sorbet.

INGREDIENTS

10-Qt Batch	20-Qt Batch	40-Qt Batch	
1½ lb	3 lb	6 lb	Mixed fresh berries (strawberries, blueberries, raspberries) (M)
6 oz	12 oz	24 oz	Sugar (for marinade) (M)
3 lb	6 lb	12 lb	Sugar (B)
1 oz	2 oz	4 oz	Stabilizer (CC–917, ¾ of 1%) (B)
2½ qt	5 qt	10 qt	Water (hot and cold) (B)
9 lb	18 lb	36 lb	Mango puree* (B)
6 oz	12 oz	24 oz	Mango paste (B)
1 Tbsp	1 oz	2 oz	Lemon juice (B)

PREPARATION   Batch time: 13–15 minutes

Combine fresh berries with sugar and marinate for 4 hours. At the end of the marination process, drain off and discard the liquid. Sift together sugar and stabilizer, then dissolve in ½ of the water (hot) and let hydrate. Pour remaining water (cold) and all other ingredients *except* marinated berries into the batch freezer. Turn on dasher, set timer to 13 minutes, turn on refrigeration and begin the batch. As the mixture firms up and looks gravy, add in marinated berries, continue freezing for 2 minutes, turn off refrigeration and extrude the finished product. Decorate tops of tubs with berries.

 Homemade Version

INGREDIENTS

2½ lb	Frozen or fresh mango puree*
¾ lb	Sugar
20 oz	Water (hot and cold)
1 Tbsp	Lemon juice
8 oz	Mixed fresh berries (strawberries, blueberries, raspberries)

PREPARATION

Peel, seed and puree enough fully ripened mangoes to make mango puree*. Sift together sugar and 10 ounces of hot water. Pour the remaining cold water and other ingredients *except* mixed berries into an ice cream maker and freeze according to the manufacturer's instructions. As the mixture firms up and looks gravy, add in mixed berries, turn off refrigeration and extrude the finished product. Yield: 1½–2 quarts of sorbet

*You will need 3–4 mangoes for each pound of puree.

Margarita Sorbet

INGREDIENTS

10-Qt Batch	20-Qt Batch	40-Qt Batch	
16 oz	1 qt	2 qt	Fresh lime juice (B)
3 lb	6 lb	12 lb	Sugar (B)
1 lb	2 lb	4 lb	36 DE corn (B)
1½ oz	3 oz	6 oz	Stabilizer (CC–917, ¾ of 1%) (B)
3 qt	6 qt	12 qt	Water (hot and cold) (B)
16 oz	1 qt	2 qt	Tequila (M)
10 oz	20 oz	40 oz	Triple Sec liqueur (M)

PREPARATION   Batch time: 13–15 minutes

Squeeze enough limes for needed amount of juice, strain juice and retain ½ of the pulp. Sift together sugar, 36 DE corn and stabilizer; dissolve in ½ of the water (hot); add in the remaining water (cold) and let stabilizer hydrate for 30 minutes. Pour all ingredients *except* Tequila and Triple Sec into batch freezer. Turn on dasher, set timer to 13 minutes, turn on refrigeration and begin the batch. As the mixture firms up and looks gravy, add Tequila and Triple Sec and continue freezing for 2 minutes. Turn off refrigeration and extrude the finished product. Decorate tops of tubs with lime slices.

Mango Margarita Sorbet

INGREDIENTS

10-Qt Batch	20-Qt Batch	40-Qt Batch	
1 qt	2 qt	4 qt	Fresh lime juice (B)
2½ lb	5 lb	10 lb	Sugar (B)
1 lb	2 lb	4 lb	36 DE corn (B)
1½ oz	3 oz	6 oz	Stabilizer (CC–917, ¾ of 1%) (B)
3 qt	6 qt	12 qt	Water (hot and cold) (B)
1 qt	2 qt	4 qt	Mango puree* (B)
16 oz	1 qt	2 qt	Tequila (M)
12 oz	24 oz	48 oz	Triple Sec (M)

*You will need 3–4 mangoes for each pound of puree.

PREPARATION   Batch time: 13–15 minutes

Squeeze enough limes for needed amount of juice. Strain and retain ½ of the pulp. Sift together sugar, 36 DE corn and stabilizer, dissolve in ½ of the water (hot), add remaining water (cold) and let stabilizer hydrate. Pour all *except* Tequila and Triple Sec into batch freezer. Turn on dasher, set timer to 13 minutes, turn on refrigeration and begin batch. As mixture firms up and looks gravy, add Tequila and Triple Sec and continue freezing for 2 minutes. Turn off refrigeration and extrude finished product.

Orange Sorbet

INGREDIENTS

10-Qt Batch	20-Qt Batch	40-Qt Batch	
5	10	20	Zest of fresh oranges (B)
5 qt	10 qt	20 qt	Fresh orange juice (B)
3¾ lb	7½ lb	15 lb	Sugar (B)
1 oz	2 oz	4 oz	Stabilizer (CC–917, ¾ of 1%) (B)
1½ qt	3 qt	6 qt	Water (hot and cold) (B)
1 oz	2 oz	4 oz	Triple Sec liqueur (B)

PREPARATION   Batch time: 13–15 minutes

Juice oranges after removing the zest; remove seeds and save the pulp. Sift together sugar and stabilizer, then dissolve in ½ of the water (hot) and let hydrate at least 10 minutes. Pour all ingredients including remaining water (cold) into the batch freezer. Turn on dasher, set timer to 13 minutes, turn on refrigeration and begin the batch. As the mixture firms up and looks gravy, turn off refrigeration and extrude the finished product. Decorate tops of tubs with orange slices.

MALCOLM SAYS: The Triple Sec gives the orange sorbet just the burst of flavor it needs, especially during those times of the year when oranges are less sweet.

 ## Homemade Version

INGREDIENTS

2	Zest of fresh oranges
40 oz	Fresh orange juice
15 oz	Sugar
12 oz	Water (hot and cold)
1 oz	Triple Sec liqueur

PREPARATION

Juice oranges after removing the zest; remove seeds and save the pulp. Thoroughly mix sugar with ½ of the water (hot). Pour the remaining water (cold) and other ingredients *except* Triple Sec into an ice cream maker and freeze according to the manufacturer's instructions. As the mixture firms up and and looks gravy, add in the Triple Sec and continue freezing for 2 more minutes. Turn off refrigeration and extrude the finished product. Yield: 1½–2 quarts of sorbet

MALCOLM SAYS: After you have zested the oranges, cut off the white outer skin, cut the oranges into small pieces, and, using some of the liquid from the batch, puree this mixture and add it back into the batch.

Tequila Sunrise Sorbet

This recipe was created in 1982 by Shipen Lebzelter and Guido Magnaguagno, owners of New York Ice. I mention them often in my books because they were not only very talented but also passionate about what they did. They never bought orange juice but rather squeezed it themselves.

INGREDIENTS

10-Qt Batch	20-Qt Batch	40-Qt Batch	
5	10	20	Zest of fresh oranges (B)
5 qt	10 qt	20 qt	Fresh orange juice (B)
3¾ lb	7½ lb	15 lb	Sugar (B)
1 oz	2 oz	4 oz	Stabilizer (CC–917, ¾ of 1%) (B)
1½ qt	3 qt	6 qt	Water (hot and cold) (B)
1 oz	2 oz	4 oz	Triple Sec liqueur (B)
16 oz	1 qt	2 qt	Tequila (M)

PREPARATION
Batch time: **13–15 minutes**

Juice oranges after removing the zest; remove seeds and save the pulp. Sift together sugar and stabilizer, then dissolve in ½ of the water (hot) and let stabilizer hydrate at least 10 minutes. Pour the remaining water (cold) and other ingredients *except* Tequila into the batch freezer. Turn on dasher, set timer to 13 minutes, turn on refrigeration and begin the batch. As mixture firms up, add in Tequila and continue freezing for 2 more minutes. Turn off refrigeration and extrude the finished product. Decorate tops of tubs with fresh orange slices.

Blood Orange Sorbet

Now that blood oranges are available in the United States, they are plentiful and reasonably priced. You can simply substitute blood oranges for regular oranges in your recipes.

INGREDIENTS

10-Qt Batch	20-Qt Batch	40-Qt Batch	
5	10	20	Zest of fresh oranges (B)
5 qt	10 qt	20 qt	Fresh blood orange juice (B)
3¾ lb	7½ lb	15 lb	Sugar (B)
1 oz	2 oz	4 oz	Stabilizer (CC–917, ¾ of 1%) (B)
1½ qt	3 qt	6 qt	Water (hot and cold) (B)
1 oz	2 oz	4 oz	Triple Sec liqueur (B)

PREPARATION
Batch time: **13–15 minutes**

Juice oranges after removing the zest; remove seeds and save the pulp. Sift together sugar and stabilizer, then dissolve in ½ of the water (hot) and let hydrate. Pour all ingredients including the remaining water (cold) into the batch freezer. Turn on the dasher, set timer to 13 minutes, turn on refrigeration and begin the batch. As mixture firms up, turn off refrigeration and extrude the finished product.

Orange Rosemary Sorbet

INGREDIENTS

10-Qt Batch	20-Qt Batch	40-Qt Batch	
5	10	20	Zest of fresh oranges (B)
5 qt	10 qt	20 qt	Fresh orange juice (B)
1 oz	2 oz	4 oz	Stabilizer (CC–917, ¾ of 1%) (B)
3¾ lb	7½ lb	15 lb	Sugar (B)
1½ qt	3 qt	6 qt	Water (hot and cold) (B)
2	4	8	Large rosemary sprigs (B)
1 oz	2 oz	4 oz	Triple Sec liqueur (M)

PREPARATION   Batch time: 13–15 minutes

Juice oranges after removing zest; remove seeds and save pulp. Sift together stabilizer and ½ of the sugar, dissolve in ¼ of the water (hot) and let hydrate. In a saucepan, dissolve remaining sugar and ¼ of the water (hot) and bring to a boil. Add in rosemary sprigs, remove from heat and let infuse for 30 minutes. Strain syrup, discard sprigs and add syrup to mixture. Pour remaining water and all ingredients *except* Triple Sec into batch freezer. Turn on dasher and refrigeration, set timer to 13 minutes and begin batch. As mixture firms up, add in Triple Sec and continue freezing 2 minutes. Turn off refrigeration and extrude finished product. Decorate tubs with orange slices.

Passion Fruit Sorbet

This is an exotic fruit sorbet that adds excitement to any dinner table, especially in restaurants.

INGREDIENTS

10-Qt Batch	20-Qt Batch	40-Qt Batch	
10 lb	20 lb	40 lb	Passion fruit puree* (B)
1¾ lb	3½ lb	7 lb	Sugar (B)
1 oz	2 oz	4 oz	Stabilizer (CC–917, ¾ of 1%) (B)
3 qt	6 qt	12 qt	Water (hot and cold) (B)
2 oz	4 oz	8 oz	Lemon juice and zest (B)

*For a 20-quart batch, you will need 6¾ quarts of juice/pulp. Adjust for other batch sizes.

PREPARATION   Batch time: 13–15 minutes

Cut passion fruit in half and scoop the pulp into a strainer over a bowl. Press pulp through strainer to extract juice. Discard seeds and retain some pulp. Sift together sugar and stabilizer, dissolve in ½ of the water (hot), add in remaining water (cold) and lemon juice and let stabilizer hydrate. Pour all ingredients into batch freezer. Turn on dasher, set timer to 13 minutes, turn on refrigeration and begin batch. As the mixture firms up and looks gravy, turn off refrigeration and extrude the finished product.

Passion Mango Sorbet

It's all about passion and your willingness to be creative!

INGREDIENTS

10-Qt Batch	20-Qt Batch	40-Qt Batch	
7 lb	14 lb	28 lb	Passion fruit puree* (B)
1¾ lb	3½ lb	7 lb	Sugar (B)
1 oz	2 oz	4 oz	Stabilizer (CC–917, ¾ of 1%) (B)
3 qt	6 qt	12 qt	Water (hot and cold) (B)
2 oz	4 oz	8 oz	Lemon juice and zest (B)
3 qt	6 qt	12 qt	Mango puree** (B)

*For a 20-quart batch, you will need about 4½ quarts of juice and pulp.

**You will need 3–4 mangoes for each pound of puree.

PREPARATION   Batch time: 13–15 minutes

Cut passion fruit in half and scoop pulp into strainer over a bowl. Press pulp through strainer to extract juice. Discard seeds and retain some pulp for body and texture. Sift together sugar and stabilizer, dissolve in ½ of the water (hot), add in remaining water (cold) and lemon juice and let stabilizer hydrate for 30 minutes. Pour all ingredients into batch freezer. Turn on dasher, set timer to 13 minutes, turn on refrigeration and begin batch. As mixture firms up and looks gravy, turn off refrigeration and extrude the finished product. Decorate tops of tubs with passion fruit pulp and mango slices.

Pear Sorbet

INGREDIENTS

10-Qt Batch	20-Qt Batch	40-Qt Batch	
1½	3	6	#10 Cans–Pears in heavy syrup* (B)
1 qt	2 qt	4 qt	Water (hot and cold) (B)
1¾ lb	3½ lb	7 lb	Sugar (B)
1 oz	2 oz	4 oz	Stabilizer (CC–917, ¾ of 1%) (B)
½ qt	1 qt	2 qt	Pear nectar (B)
2 oz	4 oz	8 oz	Lemon juice and zest (B)

*For a 20-quart batch, 3 cans of pears will yield 18 pounds of pears. Adjust accordingly.

PREPARATION   Batch time: 13–15 minutes

Drain pears, puree and retain syrup. Sift together sugar and stabilizer, then dissolve in ½ of the water (hot) and let it hydrate. Pour all ingredients including remaining water into the batch freezer. Turn on dasher, set timer to 13 minutes, turn on refrigeration and begin the batch. When the mixture firms up and looks gravy, turn off refrigeration and extrude the finished product. Decorate tops of tubs with pear slices.

Prickly Pear Sorbet

The prickly pear is native to the drier regions of Central America and the great deserts of the U.S. Their fleshy, spiked leaves take the form of flattish discs or pads stacked one on another. Eaten fresh, they are pleasantly sweet. Lime or lemon juice helps bring out the flavor of the fruit.

INGREDIENTS

10-Qt Batch	20-Qt Batch	40-Qt Batch	
3½ lb	7 lb	14 lb	Sugar (B)
1½ oz	3 oz	6 oz	Stabilizer (CC–917, ¾ of 1%) (B)
1 gal	2 gal	4 gal	Water (hot and cold) (B)
½ oz	1 oz	2 oz	Pineapple extract (B)
½ oz	1 oz	2 oz	Strawberry extract (B)
1 oz	2 oz	4 oz	Lemon juice (B)
1 qt	2 qt	4 qt	Prickly pear puree (B)

PREPARATION
Batch time: 13–15 minutes

Sift together sugar and stabilizer, then dissolve in ½ of the water (hot) and let stand for 30 minutes. Pour all ingredients including remaining water (cold) into the batch freezer. Turn on dasher, set timer to 13 minutes, turn on refrigeration and begin the batch. When the mixture firms up and looks gravy, turn off refrigeration and extrude the finished product.

Strawberry Sorbet

Extremely refreshing, popular and easy to prepare.

INGREDIENTS

10-Qt Batch	20-Qt Batch	40-Qt Batch	
10 lb	20 lb	40 lb	Frozen strawberries, thawed (B)
2½ lb	5 lb	10 lb	Sugar (B)
1 oz	2 oz	4 oz	Stabilizer (CC–917, ¾ of 1%) (B)
2 qt	4 qt	7 qt	Water (hot and cold) (B)
4 oz	8 oz	16 oz	Fragola paste (B)

PREPARATION
Batch time: 13–15 minutes

Puree thawed strawberries. Sift together sugar and stabilizer, then dissolve in ½ of the water (hot) and let it hydrate for 30 minutes. Pour all ingredients including remaining water (cold) into the batch freezer. Turn on dasher, set timer to 13 minutes, turn on refrigeration and begin the batch. As the mixture firms up and looks gravy, turn off the refrigeration and extrude the finished product. Decorate tops of tubs with fresh strawberries.

Strawberry Champagne Sorbet

Offer this festive winter sorbet to your restaurant clients. It's a perfect sorbet to feature around the holidays.

INGREDIENTS

10-Qt Batch	20-Qt Batch	40-Qt Batch	
1¼ lb	2½ lb	5 lb	Sugar (B)
1 oz	2 oz	4 oz	Stabilizer (CC–917, ¾ of 1%) (B)
1¾ qt	3½ qt	7 qt	Water (hot and cold) (B)
10 lb	20 lb	40 lb	Frozen strawberries, thawed (B)
2 oz	4 oz	8 oz	Lemon juice and zest (B)
4 oz	8 oz	16 oz	Fragola paste (B)
20 oz	1¼ qt	2½ qt	Champagne (M)

PREPARATION   Batch time: 13–15 minutes

Sift together sugar and stabilizer, then dissolve in ½ of the water (hot). Puree ⅔ of the defrosted strawberries and retain all the juice. Pour the remaining water (cold) and all other ingredients *except* champagne into the batch freezer. Turn on the dasher for 2 minutes to blend ingredients, set timer to 13 minutes, turn on refrigeration and begin the batch. As the mixture firms up and looks gravy, add in champagne and continue freezing for 2 more minutes. Turn off refrigeration and extrude the finished product.

 Homemade Version

INGREDIENTS

6 oz	Sugar
12 oz	Water (hot and cold)
2½ lb	Frozen strawberries, thawed
10 oz	Champagne
½ oz	Lemon juice and zest

PREPARATION

Mix sugar with 6 ounces of hot water. Puree ⅔ of the strawberries and retain all the juice. Pour the remaining cold water and other ingredients *except* champagne into an ice cream maker and freeze according to manufacturer's instructions. As the mixture firms up and looks gravy, add in champagne and continue freezing for 2 more minutes. Turn off refrigeration and extrude the finished product. Yield: 1½–2 quarts of sorbet

Strawberry Banana Sorbet

The addition of bananas is a can't-miss winner!

INGREDIENTS

10-Qt Batch	20-Qt Batch	40-Qt Batch	
10 lb	20 lb	40 lb	Frozen strawberries, thawed (B)
2 lb	4 lb	8 lb	Very ripe bananas, peeled (B)
1¼ lb	2½ lb	5 lb	Sugar (B)
1 oz	2 oz	4 oz	Stabilizer (CC–917, ¾ of 1%) (B)
1¾ qt	3½ qt	7 qt	Water (hot and cold) (B)
4 oz	8 oz	16 oz	Fragola paste (B)
1 oz	2 oz	4 oz	Lemon juice (B)

PREPARATION   Batch time: 13–15 minutes

Defrost and puree the strawberries. Puree the bananas. Sift together sugar and stabilizer, then dissolve in ½ of the water (hot) and let stabilizer hydrate for ½ hour. Pour all ingredients including remaining water (cold) into the batch freezer. Turn on dasher, set timer to 13 minutes, turn on refrigeration and begin the batch. As the mixture firms up and looks gravy, turn off refrigeration and extrude the finished product. Decorate tops of tubs with strawberry and banana slices.

Wine Peach Sorbet

Simply a great-tasting dessert! Red-fleshed peaches are sometimes called "blood" peaches. If you have trouble finding them, just purchase peaches with the reddest-looking skin you can find.

INGREDIENTS

10-Qt Batch	20-Qt Batch	40-Qt Batch	
8 lb	16 lb	32 lb	Red-fleshed peaches or frozen peach slices (B)
3 lb	6 lb	12 lb	Sugar (B)
2 oz	4 oz	8 oz	Stabilizer (CC–917, ¾ of 1%) (B)
1¼ qt	2½ qt	5 qt	Water (hot and cold) (B)
4 oz	8 oz	16 oz	Lemon juice and zest (B)
8 oz	16 oz	2 lb	Honey (B)
4 oz	8 oz	16 oz	Peche paste (B)
1¼ qt	2½ qt	5 qt	Dry red wine (B)

PREPARATION   Batch time: 13–15 minutes

Wash peaches, cut in half, remove stones and puree. Sift together sugar and stabilizer, then dissolve in ½ of the water (hot) and let hydrate. Pour remaining water (cold) and all ingredients *except* red wine into the batch freezer. Turn on dasher, set timer to 13 minutes, turn on refrigeration and begin the batch. As the mixture firms up and looks gravy, add in the wine and continue freezing for 2 more minutes. Turn off refrigeration and extrude the finished product. Decorate tops of tubs with peach slices.

Piña Colada Sorbet

INGREDIENTS

10-Qt Batch	20-Qt Batch	40-Qt Batch	
2 lb	4 lb	8 lb	Sugar (B)
1½ oz	3 oz	6 oz	Stabilizer (CC–917, ¾ of 1%) (B)
1 gal	2 gal	4 gal	Water (hot and cold) (B)
1 qt	2 qt	4 qt	Pineapple juice (B)
40 oz	80 oz	10 lb	Coconut fruit base (B)
40 oz	80 oz	10 lb	Pineapple pieces (B)
4 oz	8 oz	16 oz	Shredded coconut (B)

PREPARATION   Batch time: 13–15 minutes

Sift together sugar and stabilizer, and then dissolve in ½ of the water (hot). Pour all ingredients including remaining water (cold) into the batch freezer. Turn on dasher for 2 minutes to blend ingredients, set timer to 15 minutes, turn on refrigeration and begin the batch. As the mixture firms up and looks gravy, turn off refrigeration and extrude finished product.

Tomato Basil Sorbet

The perfect appetizer or dessert for a sunny June day.

INGREDIENTS

10-Qt Batch	20-Qt Batch	40-Qt Batch	
12	24	48	Tomatoes* (B)
½ tsp	1 tsp	2 tsp	Basil leaves (B)
½ tsp	1 tsp	2 tsp	Chives (B)
2 oz	4 oz	8 oz	Lemon juice (B)
2 lb	4 lb	8 lb	Sugar (B)
1 oz	2 oz	4 oz	Stabilizer (CC–917, ¾ of 1%) (B)
1 qt	2 qt	4 qt	Water (hot and cold) (B)
½ oz	1 oz	2 oz	Tabasco sauce (B)

*For a 20-quart batch, 24 tomatoes should yield about 4 quarts of tomato juice.

PREPARATION   Batch time: 13–15 minutes

Puree tomatoes with basil leaves, chives and lemon juice. Add some salt and pepper for taste. Sift together sugar and stabilizer, then dissolve in ½ of the water (hot). Under good agitation, slowly agitate the mixture for 1 minute and let stand for 30 minutes. Pour all ingredients including remaining water (cold) into the batch freezer. Turn on dasher, set timer to 13 minutes, turn on refrigeration and begin the batch. When the mixture firm ups, turn off refrigeration and extrude the finished product. Decorate tops of tubs with tomato slices.

Jalapeño Lime Sorbet

A flavor that's both tart and sweet.

INGREDIENTS

10-Qt Batch	20-Qt Batch	40-Qt Batch	
1½ qt	3 qt	6 qt	Fresh squeezed lime juice* (B)
2 oz	4 oz	8 oz	Lime zest (B)
1¼ lb	2½ lb	5 lb	Sugar (B)
1 oz	2 oz	4 oz	Stabilizer (CC–917, ¾ of 1%) (B)
2½ qt	5 qt	10 qt	Water (hot and cold) (B)
2	4	8	Jalapeños (B)

*For a 20-quart batch, you'll need about 1 case of limes (if they are juicy) to yield 3 quarts of juice. Adjust accordingly for other size batches.

PREPARATION   Batch time: 13–15 minutes

Juice and zest the limes (preferably the same day you are making the sorbet, but never longer than 24 hours in advance). Allow to dry a bit and chop the zest; then place zest into a strainer and pour boiling water over it. (This removes the bitter taste and leaves a smooth lime taste.) Sift together sugar and stabilizer, then dissolve in ½ of the water (hot). Meanwhile, seed and chop jalapeños into tiny pieces. Combine them with the lime juice mixture and lime zest. (Do not let this sit too long; the heat of the jalapeños intensifies as it sits.) Pour all ingredients including the remaining water (cold) into the batch freezer. Turn on dasher, set timer to 13 minutes, turn on the refrigeration and begin the batch. When mixture firms up and looks gravy, turn off refrigeration and extrude the finished product. Decorate tops of tubs with lime slices and jalapeños.

MALCOLM SAYS: When working with jalapeños, keep these tips in mind: Wear gloves; do not use the batch freezer for any other flavors after you make this one; be sure to clean the batch freezer thoroughly.

10

WATER ICE AND CREAM ICE RECIPES

WATER ICES

There is nothing more refreshing than digging into a cup of Italian water ice on a hot summer day. What New York and Philadelphia Italian ice manufacturers have known for many years is now sweeping the country:

Producing Italian water ice is not difficult. The real key is not merely making a typical Italian water ice with flavor syrup, sugar and water—anybody can do that. The differences between the success stories in the ice cream business and the entrepreneurs who get into the business simply for the money are high-quality flavor ingredients and customer satisfaction.

While flavoring is important in creating a wonderful-tasting water ice, equally important is the use of filtered water. Contact Grainger or even go the nearest Home Depot and purchase a charcoal filtering system. You will be amazed at the difference filtered water makes to your finished water ice product.

If you follow any of the Italian water ice recipes on the following pages, you will, without a doubt, be on the road to success. When I use the words *trust me* in the description of a particular flavor, it means you can take it to the bank!

Ices require the use of stabilizers. In determining the amount of stabilizer to use per batch, weigh all dry and wet ingredients, convert pounds to ounces, then calculate .50–.75% of that total depending on the type of fruit you are using. For citrus flavors, use approximately .75%; fibrous flavors (strawberries, mangoes) will require closer to .50%.

Basic Water Ice Recipe

This recipe is balanced for sugar, water and stabilizer so that you can add any kind of puree or flavor extract that fits your desired flavor profile.

INGREDIENTS

10-Qt Batch	20-Qt Batch	40-Qt Batch	
3 lb	6 lb	12 lb	Sugar (B)
1½ lb	3 lb	6 lb	36 DE corn (B)
1½ oz	3 oz	6 oz	Stabilizer CC–917 (.50%–.75% by weight) (B)
1¾ gal	3½ gal	7 gal	Water (B)
2 oz	4 oz	8 oz	Fruit extract* (B)

*The amount used depends on the manufacturer's recommended usage level.

PREPARATION   **Batch time: 15–18 minutes**

Combine and mix thoroughly sugar, 36 DE corn and stabilizer. Add in ½ of the water (hot) and blend well. Pour this mixture along with remaining water (cold) and fruit extract into the batch freezer. Turn on the dasher and run for 2 minutes to blend ingredients, set timer to 15 minutes, turn on refrigeration and begin the batch. As the mixture firms up and looks gravy, turn off refrigeration and extrude finished product.

MALCOLM SAYS: Always use hot water for mixing dry ingredients; use cold water for everything else.

We have created a coding system to help you follow the recipes in an exact sequence at a glance so that you know when to put in specific ingredients (beginning, middle, end or out of the batch). Please refer to the Introduction to the Recipes on page 62 for an explanation of the codes.

Amarena Cherry Water Ice

Sometimes not having the right ingredients turns a mistake into gold. This is what happened when I created Amarena Cherry water ice. I didn't have tart cherries so I used Amarena cherries instead— and discovered a fabulous flavor.

INGREDIENTS

10-Qt Batch	20-Qt Batch	40-Qt Batch	
3 lb	6 lb	12 lb	Sugar (B)
1½ lb	3 lb	6 lb	36 DE corn (B)
1½ oz	3 oz	6 oz	Stabilizer CC–917 (B)
1¾ gal	3½ gal	7 gal	Water (B)
1 oz	2 oz	4 oz	Lemon juice (B)
1½ lb	3 lb	6 lb	Amarena cherries, drained and chopped (B)
18 oz	36 oz	72 oz	Amarena cherry paste (B)

PREPARATION
Batch time: 15–18 minutes

Mix together thoroughly the sugar, 36 DE corn and stabilizer. Add in ½ of the water (extremely hot). Under good agitation (using a spatula), slowly agitate the mixture for 1 minute, then allow it to stand for 30 minutes. Pour all ingredients including remaining water into the batch freezer. Turn on dasher, set timer to 15 minutes, turn on refrigeration and begin batch. As the mixture firms up and looks gravy, turn off the refrigeration and extrude the finished product. Decorate tops of tubs with cherry pieces.

MALCOLM SAYS: How do you know when a mixture "looks gravy"? Place a spatula under the extrusion opening of the batch freezer. When the mixture stands up on top of the spatula looking firm but wet and starts to slide off, consider it "gravy."

 ## Homemade Version

INGREDIENTS

10 oz	Amarena cherry pieces
8 oz	Sugar
32 oz	Water (hot and cold)

PREPARATION

Puree ½ of the Amarena cherry pieces. Mix together sugar and 16 ounces of water (hot). Pour pureed cherries, sugar-water mixture and remaining 16 ounces of water (cold) into an ice cream maker and freeze according to the manufacturer's instructions. When the batch is complete, add in the rest of the cherry pieces, turn off refrigeration and extrude finished product. Decorate top of container with sliced Amarena cherry pieces. Yield: 1½–2 quarts of water ice

MALCOLM SAYS: You will find Amarena cherries at most specialty food shops.

Banana Water Ice

Not only will you taste the bananas, but you will also smell them in this very fresh water ice flavor.

INGREDIENTS

10-Qt Batch	20-Qt Batch	40-Qt Batch	
3 lb	6 lb	12 lb	Ripe bananas, peeled (B)
1¼ lb	2½ lb	5 lb	Sugar (B)
½ lb	1 lb	2 lb	36 DE corn (B)
1 oz	2 oz	4 oz	Stabilizer CC–917 (B)
1½ gal	3 gal	6 gal	Water (B)
¾ oz	1½ oz	3 oz	Lemon juice (B)

PREPARATION   Batch time: 15–18 minutes

Puree the bananas. Mix together thoroughly the sugar, 36 DE corn and stabilizer. Add in ½ of the water (hot) and blend until the dry powders are completely dissolved and agitated. Pour the pureed bananas, liquefied sugar solution, remaining water (cold) and lemon juice into the batch freezer. Turn on the dasher, set timer to 15 minutes, turn on the refrigeration and begin the batch. As the mixture firms up and looks gravy, turn off refrigeration and extrude the finished product.

 # Homemade Version

INGREDIENTS

1 lb	Ripe bananas, peeled
8 oz	Sugar
32 oz	Water (hot and cold)
1 Tbsp	Lemon juice

PREPARATION

Puree the bananas. Combine sugar with 16 ounces of water (hot) and mix thoroughly. Add in the pureed bananas, remaining water (cold) and lemon juice. Pour all ingredients into an ice cream maker and freeze according to the manufacturer's instructions. When the batch is complete, turn off refrigeration and extrude the finished product. Decorate top of container with banana slices. Yield: 1½–2 quarts of water ice

Cantaloupe Water Ice

INGREDIENTS

10-Qt Batch	20-Qt Batch	40-Qt Batch	
3 lb	6 lb	12 lb	Cantaloupe pieces (E)
12 oz	1½ lb	3 lb	Sugar (E)
3 lb	6 lb	12 lb	36 DE corn (B)
6 lb	12 lb	24 lb	Sugar (B)
1 oz	2 oz	4 oz	Stabilizer CC–917 (B)
4½ qt	2¼ gal	4½ gal	Water (B)
8¾ lb	17½ lb	35 lb	Cantaloupe puree* (B)
1 oz	2 oz	4 oz	Lemon juice (B)
3 oz	6 oz	12 oz	Melon paste (B)

*For a 20-quart batch, use 2 cases (12 per case) of cantaloupes for the puree. Adjust accordingly for other size batches.

PREPARATION
Batch time: 15–18 minutes

Chop cantaloupe into very small pieces and set aside. Combine and marinate cantaloupe pieces and sugar for 8 hours. Mix together thoroughly sugar, 36 DE corn and stabilizer. Add in ½ of the water (hot) and blend until the dry powders are completely dissolved and agitated. Pour liquefied sugar solution, remaining water (cold), cantaloupe puree, lemon juice and melon paste into the batch freezer. Turn on the dasher and run for a few minutes to blend ingredients, set timer to 15 minutes, turn on refrigeration and begin the batch. As mixture firms up and looks gravy, add in cantaloupe pieces, turn off refrigeration and extrude the finished product.

MALCOLM SAYS: When making this flavor, be sure that the cantaloupe puree and pieces are very ripe to ensure the best flavor result.

 # Homemade Version

INGREDIENTS

1 lb	Cantaloupe pieces
8 oz	Sugar
32 oz	Water (hot and cold)

PREPARATION

Puree the cantaloupe pieces. Combine sugar with 16 ounces of water (hot) and mix thoroughly. Add in pureed cantaloupe and remaining water (cold). Pour the mixture into an ice cream maker and freeze according to the manufacturer's instructions. When the batch is complete, turn off the refrigeration and extrude the finished product. Yield: 1½–2 quarts of water ice

Cherry Water Ice

Cherry water ice has always been a popular flavor, as illustrated by this recipe.

INGREDIENTS

10-Qt Batch	20-Qt Batch	40-Qt Batch	
1½ lb	3 lb	6 lb	IQF* Tart cherry pieces (B)
4½ lb	9 lb	18 lb	Sugar (B)
2 lb	4 lb	8 lb	36 DE corn (B)
1 oz	2 oz	4 oz	Stabilizer CC–917 (B)
1¾ gal	3½ gal	7 gal	Water (B)
2 oz	4 oz	8 oz	DS Cherry flavor (B)
1 oz	2 oz	4 oz	Lemon juice (B)

*IQF stands for "individually quick frozen."

PREPARATION   Batch time: 15–18 minutes

Defrost cherries, chop them up into very small pieces and set aside. Combine and mix thoroughly the sugar, 36 DE corn and stabilizer. Add in ½ of the water (hot) and blend well. Pour the cherry pieces, liquefied sugar solution, remaining water (cold), DS cherry flavor and lemon juice into the batch freezer. Turn on dasher and run for 2 minutes to blend ingredients, set timer for 18 minutes, turn on refrigeration and begin the batch. As the mixture firms up and looks gravy, turn off refrigeration and extrude the finished product.

MALCOLM SAYS: I like to use tart cherries because they provide a distinctive cherry taste.

 Homemade Version

INGREDIENTS

8 oz	Sugar
32 oz	Water (hot and cold)
1 lb	Cherry pie filling

PREPARATION

Combine sugar with 16 ounces of water (hot). Add in remaining water (cold) and cherry pie filling. Pour the mixture into an an ice cream maker and freeze according to the manufacturer's instructions. When the batch is complete, turn off refrigeration and extrude the finished product. Yield: 1½–2 quarts of water ice

Chocolate Banana Coconut Water Ice

INGREDIENTS

10-Qt Batch	20-Qt Batch	40-Qt Batch	
2 oz	4 oz	8 oz	Cocoa (22-24% fat) (B)
2½ lb	5 lb	10 lb	Sugar (B)
1 oz	2 oz	4 oz	Stabilizer CC–917 (B)
1 gal	2 gal	4 gal	Water (hot and cold) (B)
3 lb	6 lb	12 lb	Very ripe bananas (B)
11 oz	22 oz	44 oz	Coconut fruit base (B)
1 oz	2 oz	4 oz	Two-fold vanilla extract (B)
½ lb	1 lb	2 lb	Fudge; Shredded coconut (M)

PREPARATION   **Batch time: 15–18 minutes**

Combine cocoa, sugar and stabilizer with ½ of the water (hot). Using a spatula or mixer, mix until dry cocoa is completely dissolved. Next, use a blender to blend bananas with just enough water so that no pieces remain. Pour cocoa mixture, remaining water (cold), blended bananas, coconut fruit base and vanilla extract into the batch freezer. Turn on dasher and run for 3 minutes to blend ingredients, set timer to 15 minutes, turn on refrigeration and begin batch. After 2 minutes, slowly add in fudge and shredded coconut. As mixture firms up and looks gravy, turn off refrigeration and extrude the finished product. Decorate tops of tubs with bananas and shredded coconut.

MALCOLM SAYS: Before freezing this flavor, taste the batch to make sure the coconut flavor is apparent. Sometimes the cocoa overpowers the profile of the flavor.

Papaya Water Ice

INGREDIENTS

10-Qt Batch	20-Qt Batch	40-Qt Batch	
4¼ lb	8½ lb	17 lb	Sugar (B)
1 gal	2 gal	4 gal	Water (B)
1¼ oz	2½ oz	5 oz	Stabilizer CC–917 (B)
3 qt	1½ gal	3 gal	Papaya puree (B)
½ oz	1 oz	2 oz	Lemon juice (B)

PREPARATION   **Batch time: 15–18 minutes**

Mix thoroughly the sugar with ½ of the water (hot), then add in remaining water (cold). Under good agitation (using a spatula), slowly sift stabilizer into the papaya puree. Allow stabilizer to hydrate for at least 30 minutes. Pour sugar-water mixture, papaya puree and lemon juice into the batch freezer. Turn on dasher, set timer to 15 minutes, turn on refrigeration and begin the batch. As the mixture firms up and looks gravy, turn off refrigeration and extrude the finished product.

Coconut Water Ice

INGREDIENTS

10-Qt Batch	20-Qt Batch	40-Qt Batch	
22 oz	2¾ lb	5½ lb	Sugar (B)
1 Tbsp	2 Tbsp	4 Tbsp	Stabilizer CC–917 (B)
1¼ gal	2½ gal	5 gal	Water (B)
4 lb	8 lb	16 lb	Cream of coconut (B)
4 oz	8 oz	16 oz	Shredded coconut (B)

PREPARATION   Batch time: 15–18 minutes

Combine and mix thoroughly the sugar and stabilizer. Add in ½ of the water (hot) and blend well. Pour this mixture, the remaining water (cold), cream of coconut and shredded coconut into the batch freezer. Turn on the dasher and run for 2 minutes to blend ingredients, set timer to 15 minutes, turn on refrigeration and begin the batch. As the mixture firms up and looks gravy, turn off the refrigeration and extrude the finished product.

 Homemade Version

INGREDIENTS

6 oz	Sugar
32 oz	Water (hot and cold)
15 oz	Cream of coconut
1 tbsp	Shredded coconut

PREPARATION

Combine and thoroughly mix sugar and 16 ounces of water (hot). Add in the remaining water, cream of coconut and shredded coconut.. Pour entire mixture into an ice cream maker and freeze according to manufacturer's instructions. When the batch is complete, turn off the refrigeration, and extrude the finished product. Yield: 1½–2 quarts of water ice

Coconut Almond Joy Water Ice

INGREDIENTS

10-Qt Batch	20-Qt Batch	40-Qt Batch	
3 lb	6 lb	12 lb	Sugar (B)
1½ lb	3 lb	6 lb	36 DE corn (B)
2 oz	4 oz	8 oz	Stabilizer CC–917 (B)
1½ gal	3 gal	6 gal	Water (B)
¾ lb	1½ lb	3 lb	Cocoa powder (22–24%) (B)
1 oz	2 oz	4 oz	Two-fold vanilla extract (B)
¾ qt	1½ qt	3 qt	Coconut fruit base (B)
8 oz	1 lb	2 lb	Shredded coconut (B)
¾ lb	1½ lb	3 lb	Diced almonds (B)
¾ lb	1½ lb	3 lb	Hot fudge (O)

PREPARATION   Batch time: 15–18 minutes

Mix together thoroughly the sugar, 36 DE corn and stabilizer. Add in ½ of the water (hot) and blend well. Pour the remaining water (cold) and other ingredients except the fudge into the batch freezer. Turn on the dasher, set timer to 15 minutes, turn on the refrigeration and begin the batch. As the mixture firms up and looks gravy, turn off the refrigeration and swirl the fudge into the tubs as you extrude the finished product. Decorate tops of tubs with fudge, shredded coconut and diced almonds.

Dulce de Leche Water Ice

INGREDIENTS

10-Qt Batch	20-Qt Batch	40-Qt Batch	
2¾ lb	5½ lb	11 lb	Sugar (B)
1½ lb	3 lb	6 lb	36 DE corn (B)
1½ oz	3 oz	6 oz	Stabilizer CC–917 (B)
1½ gal	3 gal	6 gal	Water (B)
10 oz	20 oz	40 oz	Caramel base 8951 SKW (B)
8 oz	16 oz	1 qt	Caramel variegate (O)

PREPARATION   Batch time: 15–18 minutes

Mix together sugar, 36 DE corn, stabilizer and ½ of the water (hot). Pour remaining water (cold) and other ingredients except caramel variegate into batch freezer. Turn on the dasher and run for 2 minutes to blend ingredients, set timer to 15 minutes, turn on refrigeration and begin the batch. As the mixture firms up and looks gravy, turn off the refrigeration and swirl caramel variegate into the tubs as you extrude finished product.

MALCOLM SAYS: I prefer to use the caramel base 8951 and variegate from Star Kay White because they have the best caramel available for a Dulce de Leche-type product.

Granny Apple Water Ice

INGREDIENTS

10-Qt Batch	20-Qt Batch	40-Qt Batch	
½ lb	1 lb	2 lb	Granny Smith apples, peeled and in pieces* (E)
1 oz	2 oz	4 oz	Sugar (E)
¾ lb	1½ lb	3 lb	36 DE corn (B)
1½ lb	3 lb	6 lb	Sugar (B)
¾ oz	1½ oz	3 oz	Stabilizer CC–917 (B)
3½ qt	1¾ gal	3½ gal	Water (B)
1 oz	2 oz	4 oz	Granny Smith apple extract (B)
½ oz	1 oz	2 oz	Lemon juice (B)

*For a 20-quart batch, use 10 apples. Adjust accordingly for other size batches.

PREPARATION   Batch time: 15–18 minutes

Combine and marinate Granny Smith apples with sugar for 8 hours. Mix together thoroughly sugar, 36 DE corn and stabilizer. Add in ½ of the water (hot) and blend until dry powders are completely dissolved and agitated. Pour liquefied sugar solution, remaining water (cold), Granny Smith apple extract and lemon juice into the batch freezer. Turn on dasher and run a few minutes to blend ingredients, set timer to 15 minutes, turn on refrigeration and begin the batch. As the mixture firms up and looks gravy, add in marinated apple pieces, turn off refrigeration and extrude the finished product.

MALCOLM SAYS: **I like to use Granny Smith apples because they are crisp and tart tasting, but, best of all, they are not mealy as other apples tend to be.**

 Homemade Version

INGREDIENTS

1 lb	Granny Smith apple pieces
8 oz	Sugar
32 oz	Water (hot and cold)
1 Tbsp	Lemon juice

PREPARATION

Puree the Granny Smith apple pieces. Thoroughly mix sugar with 16 ounces of water (hot). Pour all ingredients including the remaining water (cold) into an ice cream maker and freeze according to manufacturer's instructions. When the batch is complete, turn off the refrigeration and extrude the finished product. Decorate top of container with apple slices. Yield: 1½–2 quarts of water ice

Grape Water Ice

INGREDIENTS

10-Qt Batch	20-Qt Batch	40-Qt Batch	
3 lb	6 lb	12 lb	Sugar (B)
1½ lb	3 lb	6 lb	36 DE corn (B)
1 oz	2 oz	4 oz	Stabilizer CC–917 (B)
1¾ gal	3½ gal	7 gal	Water (B)
1½ oz	3 oz	6 oz	Grape flavoring (B)
¾ oz	1½ oz	3 oz	Lemon juice (B)
½ qt	1 qt	2 qt	Grape juice (B)
½ lb	1 lb	2 lb	Grape jelly (E)

PREPARATION   Batch time: 15–18 minutes

Mix together thoroughly sugar, 36 DE corn and stabilizer. Add in ½ of the water (hot) and blend until the dry powders are completely dissolved and agitated. Pour liquefied sugar solution, remaining water (cold) and all other ingredients *except* the grape jelly into the batch freezer. Turn on dasher and run for 2 minutes to blend ingredients, set timer to 15 minutes, turn on the refrigeration and begin the batch. As the mixture firms up and looks gravy, add in the grape jelly, turn off refrigeration and extrude the finished product.

Italian Cannoli Water Ice

INGREDIENTS

10-Qt Batch	20-Qt Batch	40-Qt Batch	
2 lb	4 lb	8 lb	Sugar (B)
1 oz	2 oz	4 oz	Stabilizer CC–917 (B)
3 qt	1½ gal	3 gal	Water (B)
1 oz	2 oz	4 oz	Vanilla extract (B)
1½ lb	3 lb	6 lb	Cannoli crème (B)
½ lb	1 lb	2 lb	Cannoli shells (broken) (E)
8 oz	16 oz	2 lb	Pistachio pieces, roasted (E)
4 oz	8 oz	1 lb	Chocolate chips (E)

PREPARATION   Batch time: 15–18 minutes

Mix together thoroughly sugar and stabilizer. Add in ½ of the water (hot) and blend well. Pour the liquified sugar solution, remaining water (cold), vanilla extract and cannoli crème into the batch freezer. Turn on dasher and run for 2 minutes to blend ingredients, set timer to 15 minutes, turn on refrigeration and begin the batch. As the mixture firms up and looks gravy, add in Cannoli shells, pistachio pieces and chocolate chips, turn off refrigeration and extrude the finished product.

Lemon Water Ice

INGREDIENTS

10-Qt Batch	20-Qt Batch	40-Qt Batch	
3¼ lb	6½ lb	13 lb	Sugar (B)
¾ lb	1½ lb	3 lb	36 DE corn (B)
1½ oz	3 oz	6 oz	Stabilizer CC–917 (B)
1½ gal	3 gal	6 gal	Water (B)
24 oz	1½ qt	3 qt	Lemon juice with pulp, freshly squeezed (B)
8 oz	16 oz	32 oz	Fresh orange juice with pulp (B)
5	10	20	Zest of lemons (B)

PREPARATION   Batch time: 15–18 minutes

Mix together thoroughly sugar, 36 DE corn and stabilizer. Add in ½ of the water (hot) and blend until the dry powders are completely dissolved and agitated. Pour the liquefied sugar solution, remaining water (cold), lemon juice, orange juice and lemon zest into the batch freezer. Turn on dasher for a few minutes to blend ingredients, set timer to 15 minutes, turn on refrigeration and begin the batch. As the mixture firms up and looks gravy, turn off the refrigeration and extrude the finished product.

MALCOLM SAYS: I use fresh orange juice with pulp for two reasons: to cut down on the acid taste of the lemons and to create a smoother finished product. The lemon zest gives the product a more distinguishable lemon taste and shows well in the container.

 ## Homemade Version

INGREDIENTS

10 oz	Sugar
32 oz	Water (hot and cold)
2 oz	Lemon juice
1 Tbsp	Orange juice
1	Zest of lemon

PREPARATION

Combine and thoroughly mix sugar with 16 ounces of water (hot). Pour the sugar-water mixture, remaining water (cold), lemon juice, orange juice and lemon zest into an ice cream maker and freeze according to manufacturer's instructions. When the batch is complete, turn off the refrigeration and extrude the finished product. Decorate top of container with lemon slices. Yield: 1½–2 quarts of water ice

Licorice Water Ice

INGREDIENTS

10-Qt Batch	20-Qt Batch	40-Qt Batch	
15 oz	30 oz	60 oz	Black or red licorice strips (B)
3 lb	6 lb	12 lb	Sugar (B)
1½ lb	3 lb	6 lb	36 DE corn (B)
½ oz	1 oz	2 oz	Stabilizer CC–917 (B)
1¾ gal	3½ gal	7 gal	Water (B)
1½ oz	3 oz	6 oz	Licorice extract (B)

PREPARATION   Batch time: 15–18 minutes

Freeze licorice until it is very hard. Place frozen licorice in the blender and blend with some of the water to be used in the batch. Mix together thoroughly sugar, 36 DE corn and stabilizer. Add in ½ of the water (hot) and blend until dry powders are completely dissolved and agitated. Pour licorice pieces, liquefied sugar solution, remaining water (cold) and licorice extract into batch freezer. Turn on dasher for 2 minutes to blend ingredients, set timer to 15 minutes, turn on refrigeration and begin batch. As the mixture firms up and looks gravy, turn off refrigeration and extrude the finished product.

Lime Water Ice

INGREDIENTS

10-Qt Batch	20-Qt Batch	40-Qt Batch	
3¾ lb	7½ lb	15 lb	Sugar (B)
¾ lb	1½ lb	3 lb	36 DE corn(B)
1¼ oz	2½ oz	5 oz	Stabilizer CC–917 (B)
1½ gal	3 gal	6 gal	Water (B)
32 oz	4 lb	8 lb	Lime juice with pulp, freshly squeezed (B)
4 oz	8 oz	16 oz	Orange juice (B)
2	4	8	Zest of limes (B)
¼ tsp	½ tsp	1 tsp	Green food coloring (B)

PREPARATION   Batch time: 15–18 minutes

Mix together thoroughly sugar, 36 DE corn and stabilizer. Add in ½ of the water (hot) and blend until dry powders are completely dissolved and agitated. Pour the liquefied sugar solution, remaining water (cold), lime juice, orange juice, lime zest and green food coloring into the batch freezer. Turn on the dasher and run for a few minutes to blend ingredients, set timer to 15 minutes, turn on refrigeration and begin the batch. As the mixture firms up and looks gravy, turn off refrigeration and extrude finished product.

Mango Water Ice

INGREDIENTS

10-Qt Batch	20-Qt Batch	40-Qt Batch	
1¼ lb	2½ lb	5 lb	Mango pieces, chopped (B)
3 oz	6 oz	12 oz	Sugar (B)
3 qt	1½ gal	3 gal	Water (B)
2¾ lb	5½ lb	11 lb	Sugar (B)
1 oz	2 oz	4 oz	Stabilizer CC–917 (B)
7 lb	14 lb	28 lb	Mango puree (B)
1 oz	2 oz	4 oz	Lemon juice (B)

PREPARATION   Batch time: 15–18 minutes

Chop defrosted mangoes into very small pieces. Combine and marinate mango pieces and sugar for 3 hours. Mix together thoroughly ½ of the water (hot) and sugar, then add in remaining water (cold). Under good agitation (using a spatula), slowly sift stabilizer into the pureed mango and allow stabilizer to hydrate for at least 30 minutes. Pour all ingredients into the batch freezer, turn on the dasher, set timer to 15 minutes, turn on the refrigeration and begin the batch. As the mixture firms up and looks gravy, turn off the refrigeration and extrude the finished product. Decorate tops of tubs with fresh mango slices.

MALCOLM SAYS: Wherever I go, I hear the same thing: Our mangoes are the best. That means the Philippines, Thailand, India or Mexico. Let me set the record straight. Each of these countries produces a terrific, tasty mango. The secret is the sweetness and ripeness of the mango you use. Nothing more, nothing less!

 Homemade Version

INGREDIENTS

1 lb	Mango pieces
8 oz	Sugar
32 oz	Water (hot and cold)
1 Tbsp	Lemon juice

PREPARATION

Puree the mango pieces. Thoroughly mix sugar with 16 ounces of water (hot). Add in the pureed mango, remaining water (cold) and lemon juice. Pour all ingredients into an ice cream maker and freeze according to the manufacturer's instructions. When the batch is complete, turn off the refrigeration and extrude the finished product. Yield: 1½–2 quarts of water ice

Orange Water Ice

INGREDIENTS

10-Qt Batch	20-Qt Batch	40-Qt Batch	
2	4	8	Oranges (B)
3¼ lb	6½ lb	13 lb	Sugar (B)
1 lb	2 lb	4 lb	36 DE sugar (B)
2 qt	1 gal	2 gal	Water (B)
1¼ oz	2½ oz	5 oz	Stabilizer CC–917 (B)
1¼ gal	2½ gal	5 gal	Orange juice with pulp (store bought or fresh) (B)
4 oz	8 oz	16 oz	Triple Sec (B)

PREPARATION   Batch time: 15–18 minutes

Zest and puree the oranges and set aside. Mix together thoroughly the sugar, 36 DE sugar and ½ of the water (hot), then add in the remaining water (cold). Under good agitation (using a spatula), slowly sift stabilizer into the sugar-water mixture and allow stabilizer to hydrate for at least 30 minutes. Pour all ingredients including the orange zest into the batch freezer. Turn on the dasher, set timer to 15 minutes, turn on refrigeration and begin the batch. As the mixture firms up and looks gravy, turn off refrigeration and extrude the finished product. Decorate tops of tubs with orange slices.

MALCOLM SAYS: Whichever kind of orange juice you use (store bought or fresh), make sure you have a lot of pulp in the batch. The pulp will give your finished product more texture and will help in scooping.

 # Homemade Version

INGREDIENTS

10 oz	Sugar
24 oz	Water (hot and cold)
12 oz	Orange juice
1	Zest of orange

PREPARATION

Thoroughly mix the sugar with 12 ounces of water (hot). Add in orange juice, orange zest and remaining water (cold). Pour all ingredients into an ice cream maker and freeze according to the manufacturer's instructions. When the batch is complete, turn off the refrigeration and extrude the finished product. Decorate top of container with orange slices. Yield: 1½–2 quarts of water ice

Guava Water Ice

INGREDIENTS

10-Qt Batch	20-Qt Batch	40-Qt Batch	
4¼ lb	8½ lb	17 lb	Sugar (B)
1¼ oz	2½ oz	5 oz	Stabilizer CC–917 (B)
1 gal	2 gal	4 gal	Water (B)
3 qt	1½ gal	3 gal	Guava puree (B)
½ oz	1 oz	2 oz	Lemon juice (B)

PREPARATION   **Batch time: 15–18 minutes**

Mix together thoroughly sugar and stabilizer. Add in ½ of the water (hot) and blend until dry powders are completely dissolved and agitated. Pour liquefied sugar solution, remaining water (cold), guava puree and lemon juice into the batch freezer. Turn on the dasher and run for a few minutes to blend ingredients, set timer to 15 minutes, turn on refrigeration and begin the batch. As the mixture firms up and looks gravy, turn off the refrigeration and extrude the finished product.

Black Raspberry Water Ice

INGREDIENTS

10-Qt Batch	20-Qt Batch	40-Qt Batch	
3 lb	6 lb	12 lb	Sugar (B)
2 lb	4 lb	8 lb	36 DE corn (B)
1½ oz	3 oz	6 oz	Stabilizer CC–917 (B)
1¾ gal	3½ gal	7 gal	Water (B)
18 oz	36 oz	72 oz	Black raspberry base (B)
1 oz	2 oz	44 oz	Lemon juice (B)
1 lb	2 lb	4 lb	Black raspberry topping (E)

PREPARATION   **Batch time: 15–18 minutes**

Mix together thoroughly sugar, 36 DE corn and stabilizer. Add in ½ of the water (hot) and blend until the dry powders are completely dissolved and agitated. Pour liquefied sugar solution, remaining water (cold), black raspberry base and lemon juice into the batch freezer. Turn on dasher and run for a few minutes to blend ingredients, set timer to 15 minutes, turn on refrigeration and begin the batch. As the mixture firms up and looks gravy, add in the black raspberry topping, turn off the refrigeration and extrude the finished product.

MALCOLM SAYS: For an added twist, you can insert fresh or frozen blackberries into this flavor. If you do so, delete the black raspberry topping.

Pear Water Ice

INGREDIENTS

10-Qt Batch	20-Qt Batch	40-Qt Batch	
3 lb	6 lb	12 lb	Sugar (B)
1½ lb	3 lb	6 lb	36 DE corn (B)
¾ oz	1½ oz	3 oz	Stabilizer CC–917 (B)
1¾ gal	3½ gal	7 gal	Water (B)
2½ oz	5 oz	10 oz	Pear flavoring (B)
2¼ lb	4½ lb	9 lb	Pears, drained (B)
9 oz	18 oz	36 oz	Sugar (B)
¼ tsp	½ tsp	1 tsp	Caramel food coloring (B)

PREPARATION   Batch time: 15–18 minutes

Mix together thoroughly sugar, 36 DE corn and stabilizer. Add in ½ of the water (hot) and blend until the dry powders are completely dissolved and agitated. Pour all ingredients including the remaining water into the batch freezer. Turn on the dasher and run for 2 minutes to blend ingredients, set the timer to 15 minutes, turn on the refrigeration and begin the batch. As the mixture firms up and looks gravy, turn off the refrigeration and extrude the finished product.

Passion Fruit Water Ice

INGREDIENTS

10-Qt Batch	20-Qt Batch	40-Qt Batch	
1 lb	2 lb	4 lb	Passion fruit pieces, seeded (B)
4 oz	8 oz	16 oz	Sugar (B)
1¾ gal	3½ gal	7 gal	Water (B)
1½ lb	3 lb	6 lb	Sugar (B)
¾ lb	1½ lb	3 lb	36 DE corn (B)
1 oz	2 oz	4 oz	Stabilizer CC–917 (B)
½ gal	1 gal	2 gal	Passion fruit base (B)

PREPARATION   Batch time: 15–18 minutes

Combine and marinate the passion fruit pieces and sugar for 8 hours. Mix together thoroughly ½ of the water (hot), sugar and 36 DE corn, then add in remaining water (cold). Under good agitation (using a spatula), slowly sift stabilizer into the passion fruit pieces and allow stabilizer to hydrate for at least 30 minutes. Pour all ingredients into the batch freezer, set timer to 15 minutes, turn on refrigeration and begin the batch. As the mixture firms up and looks gravy, turn off refrigeration and extrude the finished product.

Peach Water Ice

INGREDIENTS

10-Qt Batch	20-Qt Batch	40-Qt Batch	
1 lb	2 lb	4 lb	Peaches, sliced and diced (E)
4 oz	8 oz	1 lb	Sugar (E)
½ lb	1 lb	2 lb	36 DE corn (B)
1¼ lb	2½ lb	5 lb	Sugar (B)
1 oz	2 oz	4 oz	Stabilizer CC–917 (B)
1½ gal	3 gal	6 gal	Water (B)
½ gal	1 gal	2 gal	Peach base (B)
¾ oz	1½ oz	3 oz	Lemon juice (B)

PREPARATION   **Batch time: 15–18 minutes**

Combine and marinate peaches and sugar for 6 hours, then strain off and discard juice. Mix together sugar, 36 DE corn and stabilizer. Add in ½ of the water (hot) and blend until dry powders are completely dissolved and agitated. Pour remaining water (cold) and all other ingredients *except* marinated peaches into the batch freezer. Turn on the dasher, set timer to 15 minutes, turn on refrigeration and begin the batch. As the mixture firms up and looks gravy, add in the marinated peaches, turn off the refrigeration and extrude the finished product.

Strawberry Kiwi Water Ice

INGREDIENTS

10-Qt Batch	20-Qt Batch	40-Qt Batch	
2 lb	4 lb	8 lb	IQF strawberries, sliced (B)
4 oz	8 oz	1 lb	Kiwis, peeled and sliced (B)
1 oz	2 oz	4 oz	Sugar (B)
½ lb	1 lb	2 lb	36 DE corn (B)
1¼ lb	2½ lb	5 lb	Sugar (B)
1 oz	2 oz	4 oz	Stabilizer CC–917 (B)
1½ gal	3 gal	6 gal	Water (B)
½ gal	1 gal	2 gal	Strawberry kiwi base (B)
¾ oz	1½ oz	3 oz	Lemon juice (B)

PREPARATION   **Batch time: 15–18 minutes**

Combine and marinate strawberries, kiwis and sugar for 8 hours. Mix together thoroughly sugar, 36 DE corn and stabilizer. Add in ½ of the water (hot) and blend until powders are dissolved and agitated. Pour remaining water (cold) and all other ingredients into the batch freezer. Turn on dasher, set timer to 15 minutes, turn on refrigeration and begin batch. As mixture firms up and looks gravy, turn off refrigeration and extrude the finished product.

Strawberry Water Ice

INGREDIENTS

10-Qt Batch	20-Qt Batch	40-Qt Batch	
7½ lb	15 lb	30 lb	Frozen strawberries (B)
¾ gal	1½ gal	3 gal	Water (B)
1¾ lb	3½ lb	7 lb	Sugar (B)
¾ oz	1½ oz	3 oz	Stabilizer CC–917 (B)
¾ oz	1½ oz	3 oz	Lemon juice (B)
3 oz	6 oz	12 oz	Fragola paste (B)

PREPARATION   Batch time: 15–18 minutes

Defrost and puree ½ of the strawberries, then combine them with the other ½ that has been thawed. Mix together sugar and ½ of the water (hot), then add in the remaining water (cold). Under good agitation (using a spatula), slowly sift the stabilizer into the strawberry puree, and allow stabilizer to hydrate for at least 30 minutes. Pour all ingredients into the batch freezer, turn on dasher, set timer to 15 minutes, turn on refrigeration and begin the batch. As mixture firms up and looks gravy, turn off refrigeration and extrude finished product. Decorate tops of tubs with fresh strawberries.

 Homemade Version

INGREDIENTS

1 lb	Ripe strawberry pieces (fresh or frozen)
8 oz	Sugar
32 oz	Water (hot and cold)
1 Tbsp	Lemon juice

PREPARATION

Puree the strawberry pieces. Thoroughly mix sugar with ½ of the water (hot). Pour all ingredients including the remaining water (cold) into an ice cream maker and freeze according to the manufacturer's instructions. When the batch is complete, turn off the refrigeration and extrude the finished product. Yield: 1½–2 quarts of water ice

Pineapple Water Ice

INGREDIENTS

10-Qt Batch	20-Qt Batch	40-Qt Batch	
1¾ lb	3½ lb	7 lb	Pineapple pieces (fresh or frozen) (E)
7 oz	14 oz	28 oz	Sugar (E)
1¾ gal	3½ gal	7 gal	Water (B)
1 lb	2 lb	4 lb	Sugar (B)
1 oz	2 oz	4 oz	Stabilizer CC–917 (B)
½ gal	1 gal	2 gal	Pineapple base (B)
1 qt	2 qt	1 gal	Pineapple juice (B)

PREPARATION   Batch time: 15–18 minutes

Chop pineapples into very small pieces. Combine and marinate pineapple pieces and sugar for 8 hours. Mix together thoroughly sugar and stabilizer. Add in ½ of the water (hot) and blend until the dry powders are dissolved and agitated. Pour the liquefied sugar solution, pineapple base, pineapple juice and remaining water (cold) into the batch freezer. Turn on the dasher and run for a few minutes to blend the ingredients, set timer to 15 minutes, turn on the refrigeration and begin the batch. As the mixture firms up and looks gravy, add in marinated pineapple pieces, turn off the refrigeration and extrude the finished product.

MALCOLM SAYS: **Pineapple juice gives this flavor a more natural and refreshing taste.**

 # Homemade Version

INGREDIENTS

1 lb	Pineapple pieces
8 oz	Sugar
24 oz	Water (hot and cold)
12 oz	Pineapple juice

PREPARATION

Puree the pineapple pieces. Thoroughly mix the sugar with 12 ounces of water (hot). Add in the pureed pineapple, remaining water (cold) and pineapple juice. Pour all ingredients into an ice cream maker and freeze according to manufacturer's instructions. When the batch is complete, turn off the refrigeration and extrude the finished product. Yield: 1½–2 quarts of water ice

Pink Lemonade Water Ice

INGREDIENTS

10-Qt Batch	20-Qt Batch	40-Qt Batch	
1¼ lb	2½ lb	5 lb	Sugar (B)
4 oz	8 oz	1 lb	36 DE corn (B)
1 oz	2 oz	4 oz	Stabilizer (CC–917) (B)
½ gal	1 gal	2 gal	Water (B)
1 gal	2 gal	4 gal	Pink lemonade (B)
6 oz	12 oz	24 oz	Fresh lemon juice with pulp (B)
½ tsp	1 tsp	2 tsp	Lemon emulsion (B)
3 oz	6 oz	12 oz	Orange juice (B)
4	8	16	Zest of lemons
1 tsp	2 tsp	4 tsp	Red food coloring (B)
8 oz	16 oz	32 oz	Cranberry juice (B)

PREPARATION Batch time: 15–18 minutes

Mix together thoroughly sugar, 36 DE corn and stabilizer. Add in ½ of the water (hot) and blend until dry powders are dissolved and agitated. Pour all ingredients including the remaining water (cold) into the batch freezer. Turn on the dasher and run for a few minutes to blend ingredients, set timer to 15 minutes, turn on refrigeration and begin the batch. As the mixture firms up and looks gravy, turn off refrigeration and extrude the finished product.

Root Beer Water Ice

INGREDIENTS

10-Qt Batch	20-Qt Batch	40-Qt Batch	
3 lb	6 lb	12 lb	Sugar (B)
1½ lb	3 lb	6 lb	36 DE corn (B)
1 oz	2 oz	4 oz	Stabilizer CC–917 (.5% by weight) (B)
1¾ gal	3½ gal	7 gal	Water (B)
1¾ oz	3½ oz	7 oz	Root beer flavoring (B)
½ tsp	1 tsp	2 tsp	Caramel coloring (B)
¾ oz	1½ oz	3 oz	Vanilla extract (B)

PREPARATION Batch time: 15–18 minutes

Mix together thoroughly sugar, 36 DE corn and stabilizer. Add in ½ of the water (hot) and blend until dry powders are dissolved and agitated. Pour all ingredients including the remaining water (cold) into the batch freezer. Turn on dasher and run a few minutes to blend ingredients, set timer to 15 minutes, turn on refrigeration and begin batch. As the mixture firms up and looks gravy, turn off refrigeration and extrude the finished product.

Vanilla Water Ice

INGREDIENTS

10-Qt Batch	20-Qt Batch	40-Qt Batch	
1½ lb	3 lb	6 lb	Sugar (B)
¾ lb	1½ lb	3 lb	36 DE corn (B)
¾ oz	1½ oz	3 oz	Stabilizer CC–917 (B)
3½ qt	1¾ gal	3½ gal	Water (B)
1½ oz	3 oz	6 oz	Pure vanilla extract (B)
½ tsp	1 tsp	2 tsp	Vanilla specks (B)

PREPARATION   Batch time: 15–18 minutes

Mix together thoroughly sugar, 36 DE corn and stabilizer. Add in ½ of the water (hot) and blend until dry powders are dissolved and agitated. Pour all ingredients including the remaining water into the batch freezer. Turn on dasher and run for a few minutes to blend ingredients, set timer to 15 minutes, turn on refrigeration and begin the batch. As the mixture firms up and looks gravy, turn off refrigeration and extrude the finished product.

Vanilla Chip Water Ice

INGREDIENTS

10-Qt Batch	20-Qt Batch	40-Qt Batch	
1½ lb	3 lb	6 lb	Sugar (B)
¾ lb	1½ lb	3 lb	36 DE corn (B)
¾ oz	1½ oz	3 oz	Stabilizer CC–917 (B)
3½ qt	1¾ gal	3½ gal	Water (B)
2 oz	4 oz	8 oz	Pure vanilla extract (B)
8 oz	16 oz	32 oz	Soft chocolate chunks (O)
4 oz	8 oz	16 oz	Liquid chocolate* (O)

*To make the liquid chocolate, melt in a double boiler 5 parts chocolate (any flavor chocolate bar) to 1 part vegetable oil by weight. Mix thoroughly with a spatula, then pour into a measuring container.

PREPARATION   Batch time: 15–18 minutes

Mix together thoroughly sugar, 36 DE corn and stabilizer. Add in ½ of the water (hot) and blend until dry powders are dissolved and agitated. Pour the liquefied sugar solution, remaining water (cold) and vanilla extract into the batch freezer. Turn on dasher and run for a few minutes to blend ingredients, set timer to 15 minutes, turn on refrigeration and begin the batch. As the mixture firms up and looks gravy, turn off refrigeration, pour in the soft chocolate chunks and liquid chocolate and extrude the finished product.

Watermelon Water Ice

INGREDIENTS

10-Qt Batch	20-Qt Batch	40-Qt Batch	
3 lb	6 lb	12 lb	Sugar (B)
2 lb	4 lb	8 lb	36 DE corn (B)
1½ oz	3 oz	6 oz	Stabilizer CC–917 (B)
½ gal	1 gal	2 gal	Water (B)
¼ oz	½ oz	1 oz	Watermelon extract (B)
8 qt	16 qt	32 qt	Watermelon, seedless (B)
½ oz	1 oz	2 oz	Lemon juice (B)

PREPARATION
Batch time: 15–18 minutes

Mix together thoroughly sugar, 36 DE corn and stabilizer. Add in ½ of the water (hot) and blend until dry powders are dissolved and agitated. Pour all ingredients including remaining water (cold) into the batch freezer. Turn on dasher and run a few minutes to blend ingredients, set timer to 15 minutes, turn on refrigeration and begin the batch. As the mixture firms up and looks gravy, turn off the refrigeration and extrude the finished product.

 **Homemade Version**

INGREDIENTS

1 lb	Watermelon pieces
8 oz	Sugar
32 oz	Water (hot and cold)

PREPARATION

Puree the watermelon pieces. Thoroughly mix the sugar with 16 ounces of water (hot). Add in pureed watermelon and remaining water (cold) Pour the mixture into an ice cream maker and freeze according to manufacturer's instructions. When the batch is complete, turn off refrigeration and extrude the finished product. Yield: 1½–2 quarts of water ice

CREAM ICES (SHERBET)

What started out as a fad a few years ago has become the rage of the water ice business. So what is a cream ice? It is a water ice product with approximately 2% butterfat as part of the basic formula. For the most part, many water ice manufacturers use 10% ice cream mix to create the cream ice flavor. Because of the butterfat content in the cream ice mix, the overrun of the finished product is higher (30%) than the overrun of the same flavor (15–20%) without the addition of butterfat. Also, because butterfat is such an integral part of the cream ice formula, less stabilizer is needed in any of the recipes.

Basic Cream Ice Recipe

This cream ice basic recipe is balanced for sugar, water and stabilizer, meaning that you can add any kind of puree or flavor extract that fits your desired flavor profile.

INGREDIENTS

10-Qt Batch	20-Qt Batch	40-Qt Batch	
26 oz	3¼ lb	6½ lb	Sugar (B)
¾ lb	1½ lb	3 lb	36 DE corn (B)
½ oz	1 oz	2 oz	Stabilizer CC–917 (B)
3 qt	1½ gal	3 gal	Water (B)
24 oz	1½ qt	3 qt	Ice cream mix* (B)
1–2 oz	2–3 oz	3–6 oz	Flavoring (B)

*If you want a richer cream flavor, use 1 quart/10-quart batch, 2 quarts/20-quart batch and 4 quart/40-quart batch.

PREPARATION   Batch time: 15–18 minutes

Thoroughly mix together the dry sweetener ingredients—sugar, 36 DE corn, stabilizer. Add in ½ of the water (hot) and blend well. Pour all ingredients including remaining water (cold) into the batch freezer. Turn on the dasher and run for 2 minutes to blend ingredients, set timer to 15 minutes, turn on refrigeration and begin the batch. As the mixture firms up and looks gravy, turn off refrigeration and extrude finished product.

MALCOLM SAYS: In some parts of the U.S. this frozen dessert is called a sherbet. Any percentage of ice cream mix will work with this recipe, but remember: the lower the fat content of the mix, the lower total fat in the finished product.

Apple Pie Cream Ice

INGREDIENTS

10-Qt Batch	20-Qt Batch	40-Qt Batch	
26 oz	3¼ lb	6½ lb	Sugar (B)
¾ lb	1½ lb	3 lb	36 DE corn (B)
1 oz	2 oz	4 oz	Stabilizer CC–917 (B)
3 qt	1½ gal	3 gal	Water (B)
24 oz	1½ qt	3 qt	Ice cream mix (B)
1 oz	2 oz	4 oz	Vanilla extract (B)
1½ qt	3 qt	6 qt	Apple pie filling (B)
½ lb	1 lb	2 lb	Graham crackers, broken (B)
½ oz	1 oz	2 oz	Cinnamon (B)
1 drop	2 drops	4 drops	Caramel coloring (B)
½ oz	1 oz	2 oz	Lemon juice (B)

PREPARATION   Batch time: 15–18 minutes

Mix together sugar, 36 DE corn and stabilizer. Add in ½ of the water (hot) and blend. Pour all ingredients including remaining water (cold) into batch freezer. Turn on dasher and run 2 minutes, set timer to 15 minutes, turn on refrigeration and begin batch. As mixture firms up and looks gravy, turn off refrigeration and extrude finished product.

MALCOLM SAYS: Use chunky apple sauce for the pie filling for a less sweet product.

Cotton Candy Cream Ice

INGREDIENTS

10-Qt Batch	20-Qt Batch	40-Qt Batch	
26 oz	3¼ lb	6½ lb	Sugar (B)
¾ lb	1½ lb	3 lb	36 DE corn (B)
1 oz	2 oz	4 oz	Stabilizer CC–917 (B)
3 qt	1½ gal	3 gal	Water (B)
24 oz	1½ qt	3 qt	Ice cream mix (B)
1 oz	2 oz	4 oz	Vanilla extract (B)
1¼ oz	2½ oz	5 oz	Cotton candy extract (B)
¼ tsp	½ tsp	1 tsp	Red food coloring (B)
½ lb	1 lb	2 lb	Gummy worm pieces (O)

PREPARATION   Batch time: 15–18 minutes

Mix together sugar, 36 DE corn and stabilizer, blend in ½ of the water (hot). Pour rest of water (cold) and all ingredients *except* gummy worms into batch freezer. Turn on dasher, run 2 minutes, set timer to 15 minutes, turn on refrigeration and begin batch. As mixture firms up, turn off refrigeration, add candy and extrude finished product.

Banana Cream Ice

Tastes just like eating a frozen banana!

INGREDIENTS

10-Qt Batch	20-Qt Batch	40-Qt Batch	
7 lb	14 lb	28 lb	Bananas, very ripe, peeled (B)
26 oz	3¼ lb	6½ lb	Sugar (B)
¾ lb	1½ lb	3 lb	36 DE corn (B)
1 oz	2 oz	4 oz	Stabilizer CC–917 (B)
3 qt	1½ gal	3 gal	Water (B)
24 oz	1½ qt	3 qt	Ice cream mix (B)
1 oz	2 oz	4 oz	Vanilla extract (B)
½ oz	1 oz	2 oz	Lemon juice (B)

PREPARATION   Batch time: 15–18 minutes

Puree the bananas. Mix together thoroughly sugar, 36 DE corn and stabilizer. Add in ½ of the water (hot) and blend well. Pour all ingredients including the remaining water (cold) into the batch freezer. Turn on dasher and run for 2 minutes to blend ingredients, set timer to 15 minutes, turn on the refrigeration and begin the batch. As mixture firms up and looks gravy, turn off refrigeration and extrude the finished product.

 # Homemade Version

INGREDIENTS

1 lb	Bananas, peeled
8 oz	Sugar
32 oz	Water (hot and cold)
8 oz	Heavy cream
1 Tbsp	Lemon juice

PREPARATION

Puree the bananas. Thoroughly mix the sugar with 16 ounces of water (hot). Pour all ingredients including the remaining water (cold) into an ice cream maker and freeze according to manufacturer's instructions. When the batch is complete, turn off refrigeration and extrude the finished product. Decorate top of container with banana slices. Yield: 1½–2 quarts of cream ice

Cappuccino Chunk Cream Ice

INGREDIENTS

10-Qt Batch	20-Qt Batch	40-Qt Batch	
3 oz	6 oz	12 oz	Freeze-dried coffee (B)
½ oz	1 oz	2 oz	Cocoa (B)
48 oz	3 qt	1½ gal	Ice cream mix (B)
3¼ lb	6½ lb	13 lb	Sugar (B)
1 oz	2 oz	4 oz	Stabilizer CC–917 (B)
4½ qt	2¼ gal	4½ gal	Water (B)
1 oz	2 oz	4 oz	Vanilla extract (B)
½ lb	1 lb	2 lb	Chocolate chunks (B)
½ tsp	1 tsp	2 tsp	Italian espresso beans, fine grind (B)

PREPARATION

Batch time: 15–18 minutes

Mix freeze-dried coffee with as little hot water as possible. Add cocoa and blend to create a smooth paste. Combine coffee mixture with ice cream mix. Next, mix together thoroughly sugar and stabilizer. Add in ½ of the water (hot) and blend well. Pour all ingredients including remaining water (cold) into batch freezer. Turn on dasher and run for 2 minutes, set timer to 15 minutes, turn on refrigeration and begin batch. As the mixture firms up and looks gravy, turn off refrigeration and extrude finished product.

Cream-a-Latta Cream Ice

INGREDIENTS

10-Qt Batch	20-Qt Batch	40-Qt Batch	
2¾ lb	5½ lb	11 lb	Sugar (B)
½ oz	1 oz	2 oz	Stabilizer CC–917 (B)
4½ qt	2¼ gal	4½ gal	Water (B)
1½ qt	3 qt	3 lb	Ice cream mix (B)
1 oz	2 oz	4 oz	Vanilla extract (B)
1 oz	2 oz	4 oz	Rum extract* (B)
½ tsp	1 tsp	2 tsp	Cinnamon (B)
1 oz	2 oz	4 oz	Almond extract (B)
8 oz	1 lb	2 lb	Diced almonds (B)

*If you choose to replace the rum extract with dark rum, use 4 ounces for a 10-quart batch, 8 ounces for a 20-quart batch and 16 ounces for a 40-quart batch.

PREPARATION

Batch time: 15–18 minutes

Mix together thoroughly sugar and stabilizer. Add in ½ of the water (hot) and blend well. Pour all ingredients including remaining water (cold) into batch freezer. Turn on dasher for 2 minutes, set timer to 15 minutes, turn on refrigeration and begin batch. As mixture firms up and looks gravy, turn off refrigeration and extrude finished product.

Dulce de Leche Chip Cream Ice

INGREDIENTS

10-Qt Batch	20-Qt Batch	40-Qt Batch	
26 oz	3¼ lb	6½ lb	Sugar (B)
¾ lb	1½ lb	3 lb	36 DE corn (B)
1 oz	2 oz	4 oz	Stabilizer CC–917 (B)
3 qt	1½ gal	3 gal	Water (B)
24 oz	1½ qt	3 qt	Ice cream mix (B)
1 oz	2 oz	4 oz	Vanilla extract (B)
¾ lb	1½ lb	3 lb	Caramel base 8951–Star Kay White (B)
4 oz	½ lb	1 lb	Chocolate chunks (E)
4 oz	½ lb	1 lb	Pecan pralines (E)
1½ lb	3 lb	6 lb	Caramel kremia variegate #1PE–SKW (O)

PREPARATION Batch time: 15–18 minutes

Mix together sugar, 36 DE corn and stabilizer. Add in ½ of the water (hot) and blend well. Pour the liquefied sugar solution, remaining water (cold), ice cream mix, vanilla extract and caramel base into the batch freezer. Turn on dasher and run for 2 minutes, set timer to 15 minutes, turn on refrigeration and begin batch. As the mixture firms up and looks gravy, pour in chocolate chunks and pecan pralines. Turn off refrigeration and swirl the variegate into the tubs as you extrude the finished product.

Peanut Butter Cream Ice

INGREDIENTS

10-Qt Batch	20-Qt Batch	40-Qt Batch	
1 qt	2 qt	4 qt	Peanut butter topping (B)
26 oz	3¼ lb	6½ lb	Sugar (B)
¾ lb	1½ lb	3 lb	36 DE corn (B)
1 oz	2 oz	4 oz	Stabilizer CC–917 (B)
3 qt	6 qt	12 qt	Water (B)
24 oz	1½ qt	3 qt	Ice cream mix (B)
1 oz	2 oz	4 oz	Vanilla extract (B)
½ lb	1 lb	2 lb	Granulated peanuts (B)

PREPARATION Batch time: 15–18 minutes

Mix peanut butter so oil is evenly disbursed. Mix together sugar, 36 DE corn and stabilizer. Add in ½ of the water (hot) and blend well. Pour all ingredients including the remaining water (cold) into batch freezer. Turn on dasher and run for 2 minutes, set timer to 15 minutes, turn on refrigeration and begin batch. As mixture firms up and looks gravy, turn off refrigeration and extrude finished product.

Chocolate Chocolate Chip Cream Ice

INGREDIENTS

10-Qt Batch	20-Qt Batch	40-Qt Batch	
2½ lb	5 lb	10 lb	Sugar (B)
1 oz	2 oz	4 oz	Stabilizer CC–917 (B)
4½ qt	2¼ gal	4½ gal	Water (B)
1½ qt	3 qt	1½ gal	Ice cream mix (B)
1 oz	2 oz	4 oz	Vanilla extract (B)
½ lb	1 lb	2 lb	Cocoa (B)
½ lb	1 lb	2 lb	Brownies, crumbled (B)
8 oz	1 lb	2 lb	Chocolate chunks (M)
4 oz	8 oz	1 lb	Liquid chocolate* (O)

*To make the liquid chocolate, melt in a double boiler 5 parts chocolate (any flavor chocolate bar) to 1 part vegetable oil by weight. Mix thoroughly with a spatula, then pour into a measuring container.

PREPARATION
Batch time: 15–18 minutes

Mix together thoroughly the sugar and stabilizer. Add in ½ of the water (hot) and blend well. Pour water-sugar mixture, ice cream mix, remaining water (cold), vanilla extract, cocoa and brownies into the batch freezer. Turn on the dasher and run for 2 minutes to blend ingredients, set timer to 15 minutes, turn on refrigeration and begin the batch. As the mixture firms up and looks gravy, turn off refrigeration, add in chocolate chunks and liquid chocolate and extrude the finished product.

 # Homemade Version

INGREDIENTS

4 oz	Cocoa
32 oz	Water (hot and cold)
8 oz	Sugar
8 oz	Heavy cream
4 oz	Brownie pieces

PREPARATION

Using a double boiler, heat the cocoa with 4 ounces of water until all the cocoa has dissolved. Combine sugar with 14 ounces of water (hot) and blend well. Pour cocoa mixture, sugar-water solution, remaining water (cold), heavy cream and remaining water (cold) into an ice cream maker and freeze according to the manufacturer's instructions. When the batch is complete, add in the brownie pieces, turn off the refrigeration and extrude the finished product. Yield: 1½–2 quarts of cream ice

Chocolate Cream Ice

INGREDIENTS

10-Qt Batch	20-Qt Batch	40-Qt Batch	
¾ lb	1½ lb	3 lb	Cocoa (B)
¾ lb	1½ lb	3 lb	Chocolate (B)
1 lb	2 lb	4 lb	36 DE sugar (B)
1 oz	2 oz	4 oz	Stabilizer CC–917 (B)
2¾ lb	5½ lb	11 lb	Sugar (B)
1 gal	2 gal	4 gal	Water (B)
24 oz	1½ qt	3 qt	Ice cream mix (B)
1 oz	2 oz	4 oz	Vanilla extract (B)
¾ lb	1½ lb	3 lb	Hot fudge (B)
½ lb	1 lb	2 lb	Chocolate chunks (O)

PREPARATION
Batch time: 15–18 minutes

Combine cocoa, chocolate, 36 DE sugar and stabilizer with ½ of the water (extremely hot). Pour the cocoa-chocolate mixture, remaining water (cold), ice cream mix, vanilla extract and fudge into the batch freezer. Turn on the dasher and run for 3 minutes to stir the mixtures together, set timer to 15 minutes, turn on refrigeration and begin the batch. After 2 minutes, slowly add in the fudge. As the mixture firms up and looks gravy, turn off refrigeration, add in the chocolate chunks and extrude finished product.

 ## Homemade Version

INGREDIENTS

4 oz	Cocoa
32 oz	Water (hot and cold)
8 oz	Sugar
8 oz	Heavy cream
4 oz	Chocolate chips

PREPARATION

Using a double boiler, heat the cocoa with 4 ounces of water until all the cocoa has dissolved into the mixture. Thoroughly mix the sugar with ½ of the water (hot). Add cocoa mixture, heavy cream and remaining water (cold) into an ice cream maker and freeze according to the manufacturer's instructions. When the batch is complete, add in the chocolate chips, turn off the refrigeration and extrude the finished product. Yield: 1½–2 quarts of cream ice

Chocolate Fudge Brownie Cream Ice

INGREDIENTS

10-Qt Batch	20-Qt Batch	40-Qt Batch	
½ lb	1 lb	2 lb	Cocoa (B)
2½ lb	5 lb	10 lb	Sugar (B)
1 oz	2 oz	4 oz	Stabilizer CC–917 (B)
4½ qt	2¼ gal	4½ gal	Water (B)
48 oz	3 qt	1½ gal	Ice cream mix (B)
1 oz	2 oz	4 oz	Vanilla extract (B)
½ lb	1 lb	2 lb	Brownies, crumbled (E)
4 oz	8 oz	1 lb	Chocolate chunks (E)
16 oz	1 qt	2 qt	Hot fudge (O)

PREPARATION   Batch time: 15–18 minutes

Create a paste with cocoa and a small amount of hot water. Mix together sugar and stabilizer. Add in ½ of the water (hot) and blend well. Pour the cocoa paste, liquefied sugar solution, remaining water (cold), ice cream mix and vanilla extract into the batch freezer. Turn on the dasher and run for 2 minutes, set timer to 15 minutes, turn on the refrigeration and begin batch. As mixture firms up, add brownies and chocolate chunks, turn off refrigeration and swirl fudge into the tubs as you extrude the finished product.

Chocolate Mousse Cream Ice

INGREDIENTS

10-Qt Batch	20-Qt Batch	40-Qt Batch	
2¾ lb	5½ lb	11 lb	Sugar (B)
1½ qt	3 qt	1½ gal	Ice cream mix (B)
1 oz	2 oz	4 oz	Stabilizer CC–917 (B)
4½ qts	2¼ gal	4½ gal	Water (B)
1 oz	2 oz	4 oz	Vanilla extract (B)
8 oz	1 lb	2 lb	Cocoa powder 22–24% (B)
7½ oz	15 oz	30 oz	Egg base* (B)
8 oz	1 lb	2 lb	Hot fudge (B)

*You can replace egg base with pasteurized egg yolks: 4 ounces for a 10-quart batch, 8 ounces for a 20-quart batch, and 1 pound for a 40-quart batch.

PREPARATION   Batch time: 15–18 minutes

Mix together sugar and stabilizer. Add in ½ of the water (hot) and blend well. Pour all ingredients including the remaining water (cold) into the batch freezer. Turn on dasher and run for 2 minutes, set timer to 15 minutes, turn on the refrigeration and begin the batch. As the mixture firms up and looks gravy, turn off refrigeration and extrude the finished product.

Coconut Cream Ice

INGREDIENTS

10-Qt Batch	20-Qt Batch	40-Qt Batch	
22 oz	2¾ lb	5½ lb	Sugar (B)
¾ lb	1½ lb	3 lb	36 DE corn (B)
1 oz	2 oz	4 oz	Stabilizer CC–917 (B)
1¼ gal	2½ gal	5 gal	Water (B)
24 oz	1½ qt	3 qt	Ice cream mix (B)
1 oz	2 oz	4 oz	Vanilla extract (B)
4 lb	8 lb	16 lb	Cream of coconut (B)
4 oz	8 oz	1 lb	Shredded coconut (B)

PREPARATION   Batch time: 15–18 minutes

Mix together thoroughly sugar and stabilizer. Add in ½ of the water (hot) and blend well. Pour all ingredients including remaining water (cold) into the batch freezer. Turn on dasher for 2 minutes to blend ingredients, set timer to 15 minutes, turn on refrigeration and begin the batch. As the mixture firms up and looks gravy, turn off refrigeration and extrude the finished product.

 # Homemade Version

INGREDIENTS

6 oz	Sugar
32 oz	Water (hot and cold)
15 oz	Cream of coconut
8 oz	Heavy cream
1 Tbsp	Shredded coconut

PREPARATION

Thoroughly mix the sugar with ½ of the water (hot). Pour all ingredients including the remaining water (cold) into an ice cream maker and freeze according to manufacturer's instructions. When the batch is complete, turn off refrigeration and extrude the finished product. Yield: 1½–2 quarts of cream ice

Coconut Almond Joy Cream Ice

INGREDIENTS

10-Qt Batch	20-Qt Batch	40-Qt Batch	
¾ lb	1½ lb	3 lb	Cocoa (B)
6 oz	12 oz	1½ lb	Sugar (B)
1 oz	2 oz	4 oz	Stabilizer CC–917 (B)
3 qt	1½ gal	3 gal	Water (B)
1 qt	2 qt	1 gal	Ice cream mix (B)
1 oz	2 oz	4 oz	Vanilla extract (B)
¾ lb	1½ lb	3 lb	Diced almonds (B)
1½ qt	3 qt	6 qt	Coconut fruit base (B)
2¼ lb	4½ lb	9 lb	Fudge (O)

PREPARATION   Batch time: 15–18 minutes

Mix together thoroughly cocoa, sugar and stabilizer. Add in ½ of the water (hot) and blend well. Pour the remaining water (cold) and other ingredients *except* the fudge into the batch freezer. Turn on dasher and run for 2 minutes to blend ingredients, set timer to 15 minutes, turn on refrigeration and begin the batch. As the mixture firms up and looks gravy, turn off refrigeration and slowly swirl fudge into the tubs as you extrude the finished product.

Banana Coconut Almond Joy Cream Ice

INGREDIENTS

10-Qt Batch	20-Qt Batch	40-Qt Batch	
¾ lb	1½ lb	3 lb	Cocoa (B)
1½ lb	3 lb	6 lb	Sugar (B)
1 oz	2 oz	4 oz	Stabilizer CC–917 (B)
3 qt	1½ gal	3 gal	Water (B)
1 qt	2 qt	1 gal	Ice cream mix (B)
1 oz	2 oz	4 oz	Vanilla extract (B)
¾ lb	1½ lb	3 lb	Diced almonds (B)
1½ qt	3 qt	6 qt	Coconut fruit base (B)
3 lb	6 lb	12 lb	Peeled bananas (B)
2¼ lb	4½ lb	9 lb	Hot fudge (O)

PREPARATION   Batch time: 15–18 minutes

Mix together thoroughly cocoa, sugar, 36 DE corn and stabilizer. Blend in ½ of the water (hot). Pour remaining water (cold) and other ingredients *except* the fudge into the batch freezer. Turn on dasher and run for 2 minutes, set timer to 15 minutes, turn on refrigeration and begin the batch. As the mixture firms up and looks gravy, turn off the refrigeration and swirl fudge into tubs as you extrude finished product.

Cookies & Crème Cream Ice

Twenty years ago when Cookies & Crème ice cream was first introduced, it became the #3 bestselling ice cream flavor. Today, the same is true with Cookies & Crème Ice.

INGREDIENTS

10-Qt Batch	20-Qt Batch	40-Qt Batch	
26 oz	3¼ lb	6½ lb	Sugar (B)
¾ lb	1½ lb	3 lb	36 DE corn (B)
1 oz	2 oz	4 oz	Stabilizer CC–917 (B)
3 qt	1¼ gal	3 gal	Water (B)
24 oz	1½ qt	3 qt	Ice cream mix (B)
1 oz	2 oz	4 oz	Vanilla extract (B)
1 lb	2 lb	4 lb	Oreo cookies: ½ crushed (B), ½ broken (E)

PREPARATION   Batch time: 15–18 minutes

Mix together thoroughly sugar, 36 DE corn and stabilizer. Add in ½ of the water (hot) and blend well. Pour the liquefied sugar solution, remaining water (cold), ice cream mix, vanilla extract and ½ of the crushed Oreos into the batch freezer. Turn on dasher and run for 2 minutes to blend ingredients, set timer to 15 minutes, turn on refrigeration and begin the batch. As the mixture firms up and looks gravy, add in broken Oreo cookies, turn off refrigeration and extrude the finished product.

 Homemade Version

INGREDIENTS

6 oz	Sugar
32 oz	Water (hot and cold)
1 lb	Oreo cookies, broken
8 oz	Heavy cream

PREPARATION

Thoroughly mix the sugar with ½ of the water (hot). Add Oreo cookies, heavy cream and remaining water (cold). Pour all ingredients into an ice cream maker and freeze according to manufacturer's instructions. When the batch is complete, turn off refrigeration and extrude the finished product. Yield: 1½–2 quarts of cream ice

Cranberry Cream Ice

INGREDIENTS

10-Qt Batch	20-Qt Batch	40-Qt Batch	
5¾ lb	11½ lb	23 lb	Sugar (B)
3 lb	6 lb	12 lb	36 DE corn (B)
1½ oz	3 oz	6 oz	Stabilizer CC–917 (B)
¾ gal	1½ gal	3 gal	Water (B)
8 lb	16 lb	32 lb	Fresh or frozen cranberries* (B)
½ gal	1 gal	2 gal	Ice cream mix (B)
1 oz	2 oz	4 oz	Vanilla extract (B)

PREPARATION   Batch time: 15–18 minutes

Mix together thoroughly sugar, 36 DE corn and stabilizer. Add in ½ of the water (hot) and blend well. Combine cranberries with remaining water (cold) and puree, then strain thoroughly to yield the required amount of cranberry juice,* discard the pulp. Pour all ingredients into batch freezer. Turn on dasher for 2 minutes, set timer to 15 minutes, turn on refrigeration and begin the batch. As the mixture firms up and looks gravy, turn off the refrigeration and extrude the finished product.

*For a 10-quart batch you will need 4 quarts of cranberry juice; for a 20-quart batch, 8 quarts; and for a 40-quart batch, 16 quarts.

Bubble Gum Cream Ice

INGREDIENTS

10-Qt Batch	20-Qt Batch	40-Qt Batch	
26 oz	3¼ lb	6½ lb	Sugar (B)
¾ lb	1½ lb	3 lb	36 DE corn (B)
1 oz	2 oz	4 oz	Stabilizer CC–917 (B)
3 qt	1½ gal	3 gal	Water (B)
24 oz	1½ qt	3 qt	Ice cream mix (B)
1 oz	2 oz	4 oz	Vanilla extract (B)
1 oz	2 oz	4 oz	Bubble gum extract (B)
¼ tsp	½ tsp	1 tsp	Red food coloring (B)
½ lb	1 lb	2 lb	Bubble gum pieces (O)

PREPARATION   Batch time: 15–18 minutes

Mix together sugar, 36 DE corn and stabilizer. Add in ½ of the water (hot) and blend well. Pour remaining water and other ingredients *except* bubble gum pieces into the batch freezer. Turn on dasher and run for 2 minutes, set timer to 15 minutes, turn on refrigeration and begin the batch. As the mixture firms up and looks gravy, turn off refrigeration, add in the bubble gum pieces and extrude the finished product.

Creamsicle Cream Ice

This is just like biting into a Creamsicle bar.

INGREDIENTS

10-Qt Batch	20-Qt Batch	40-Qt Batch	
1½ lb	3 lb	6 lb	Sugar (B)
¾ lb	1½ lb	3 lb	36 DE corn (B)
½ oz	1 oz	2 oz	Stabilizer CC–917 (B)
½ gal	1 gal	2 gal	Water (B)
1¾ qt	3½ qt	1¾ gal	Fresh orange juice with pulp (B)
¾ qt	1½ qt	3 qt	Ice cream mix (B)
1 oz	2 oz	4 oz	Vanilla extract (B)
1 oz	2 oz	4 oz	Orange flavoring (B)

PREPARATION   Batch time: 15–18 minutes

Mix together thoroughly sugar, 36 DE corn and stabilizer. Add in ½ of the water (hot) and blend well. Pour all ingredients including the remaining water (cold) into the batch freezer. Turn on the dasher and run for 2 minutes to blend ingredients, set the timer to 15 minutes, turn on refrigeration and begin the batch. As mixture firms up and looks gravy, turn off refrigeration and extrude the finished product.

 # Homemade Version

INGREDIENTS

10 oz	Sugar
24 oz	Water (hot and cold)
12 oz	Orange juice
8 oz	Heavy cream
1	Zest of orange

PREPARATION

Thoroughly mix the sugar with 12 ounces of water (hot). Add in orange juice, heavy cream, orange zest and remaining water (cold) into an ice cream maker and freeze according to the manufacturer's instructions. When the batch is complete, turn off the refrigeration and extrude the finished product. Yield: 1½–2 quarts of cream ice

Italian Cannoli Cream Ice

INGREDIENTS

10-Qt Batch	20-Qt Batch	40-Qt Batch	
26 oz	3¼ lb	6½ lb	Sugar (B)
12 oz	1½ lb	3 lb	36 DE corn (B)
1 oz	2 oz	4 oz	Stabilizer CC–917 (B)
3 qt	1½ gal	3 gal	Water (B)
24 oz	1½ qt	3 qt	Ice cream mix (B)
1 oz	2 oz	4 oz	Vanilla extract (B)
1½ lb	3 lb	6 lb	Cannoli crème (B)
½ oz	1 oz	2 oz	Cinnamon (B)
½ lb	1 lb	2 lb	Cannoli shells, broken (E)
4 oz	8 oz	1 lb	Liquid chocolate* (E)

*To make the liquid chocolate, melt in a double boiler 5 parts chocolate (any flavor chocolate bar) to 1 part vegetable oil by weight. Mix thoroughly with a spatula, then pour into a measuring container.

PREPARATION   Batch time: 15–18 minutes

Mix together thoroughly sugar, 36 DE corn and stabilizer. Add in ½ of the water (hot) and blend well. Pour remaining water (cold) and all ingredients *except* cannoli shells and liquid chocolate into the batch freezer. Turn on dasher and run for 2 minutes to blend ingredients, set timer to 15 minutes, turn on refrigeration and begin the batch. As the mixture firms up and looks gravy, add in cannoli shells and liquid chocolate, turn off refrigeration and extrude the finished product.

 Homemade Version

INGREDIENTS

16 oz	Sugar
24 oz	Water (hot and cold)
16 oz	Ricotta cheese
8 oz	Heavy cream
1 Tbsp	Cinnamon
1 oz	Chocolate chips
1	Zest of orange

PREPARATION

Thoroughly mix the sugar with ½ of the water (hot). Pour all ingredients including the remaining water (cold) into an ice cream maker and freeze according to manufacturer's instructions. When batch is complete, turn off the refrigeration and extrude the finished product. Decorate top of container with orange slices. Yield: 1½–2 quarts of cream ice

Jerry Garcia Cream Ice

INGREDIENTS

10-Qt Batch	20-Qt Batch	40-Qt Batch	
26 oz	3¼ lb	6½ lb	Sugar (B)
¾ lb	1½ lb	3 lb	36 DE corn (B)
1 oz	2 oz	4 oz	Stabilizer CC–917 (B)
3 qt	1½ gal	3 gal	Water (B)
24 oz	1½ qt	3 lb	Ice cream mix (B)
1 oz	2 oz	4 oz	Vanilla extract (B)
1 lb	2 lb	4 lb	Chocolate chips (E)
2 qt	4 qt	8 qt	Bordeaux cherry halves (E)

PREPARATION   Batch time: 15–18 minutes

Mix together sugar, 36 DE corn, stabilizer. Add in ½ of the water (hot) and blend well. Pour remaining water (cold) and other ingredients *except* chocolate chips and cherry halves into the batch freezer. Turn on dasher and run for 2 minutes, set timer to 15 minutes, turn on refrigeration and begin the batch. When the batch is complete, add in chocolate chips and cherry halves, turn off refrigeration and extrude finished product.

Mint Vanilla Chip Cream Ice

INGREDIENTS

10-Qt Batch	20-Qt Batch	40-Qt Batch	
32 oz	4 lb	8 lb	Sugar (B)
1 oz	2 oz	4 oz	Stabilizer CC–917 (B)
3 qt	1½ gal	3 gal	Water (B)
24 oz	1½ qt	3 qt	Ice cream mix (B)
1 oz	2 oz	4 oz	Vanilla extract (B)
4 oz	8 oz	16 oz	Menta paste (B)
¼ tsp	½ tsp	1 tsp	Green food coloring (B)
1 oz	2 oz	4 oz	Liquid chocolate* (E)
12 oz	1½ oz	3 lb	Chocolate chips (E)

*To prepare liquid chocolate, heat in a double boiler 5 parts chocolate to 1 part vegetable oil by weight.

PREPARATION   Batch time: 15–18 minutes

Mix together sugar and stabilizer. Add in ½ of the water (hot) and blend well. Pour remaining water (cold) and other ingredients *except* liquid chocolate and chocolate chips into the batch freezer. Turn on dasher and run for 2 minutes, set timer to 15 minutes, turn on refrigeration and begin the batch. As mixture firms up and looks gravy, add in liquid chocolate and chips, turn off refrigeration and extrude finished product.

Mud Slide Cream Ice

INGREDIENTS

10-Qt Batch	20-Qt Batch	40-Qt Batch	
3 oz	6 oz	12 oz	Freeze-dried coffee (B)
½ oz	1 oz	2 oz	Cocoa (B)
32 oz	4 lb	8 lb	Sugar (B)
1 oz	2 oz	4 oz	Stabilizer CC–917 (B)
3 qt	1½ gal	3 gal	Water (B)
24 oz	1½ qt	3 lb	Ice cream mix (B)
1 oz	2 oz	4 oz	Vanilla extract (B)
4 oz	8 oz	16 oz	Liquid chocolate* (E)
1 lb	2 lb	4 lb	Chocolate chips (E)
1 lb	2 lb	4 lb	Graham crackers, broken (E)
1½ qt	3 qt	6 qt	Fudge (O)

*To prepare liquid chocolate, heat in a double boiler 5 parts chocolate to 1 part vegetable oil.

PREPARATION   Batch time: 15–18 minutes

Mix freeze-dried coffee with as little hot water as possible. Add cocoa and create a paste. Mix together sugar, 36 DE corn and stabilizer. Add in ½ of the water (hot) and blend well. Pour coffee mixture, liquefied sugar solution, ice cream mix, vanilla and remaining water (cold) into the batch freezer. Turn on dasher and run for 2 minutes, set timer to 15 minutes, turn on refrigeration and begin batch. When batch is complete, add in liquid chocolate, chocolate chips and graham crackers. As the mixture firms up, turn off refrigeration and swirl fudge into the tubs as you extrude the finished product.

Lemon Cream Ice

INGREDIENTS

10-Qt Batch	20-Qt Batch	40-Qt Batch	
3¾ lb	7½ lb	15 lb	Sugar (B)
½ tsp	1 tsp	2 tsp	Stabilizer CC–917 (B)
1¼ gal	2½ gal	5 gal	Water (B)
8½ oz	17 oz	34 oz	Lemon powder (B)
1½ qt	3 qt	6 qt	Ice cream mix (B)

PREPARATION   Batch time: 15–18 minutes

Mix together thoroughly the sugar and stabilizer. Add in ½ of the water (hot) and blend well. Pour all ingredients including the remaining water into the batch freezer. Turn on dasher, set timer to 15 minutes, turn on refrigeration and begin the batch. When the batch is complete, turn off refrigeration and extrude the finished product. Decorate tops of tubs with lemon slices.

248

Piña Colada Cream Ice

On a hot day, there's nothing better than a Piña Colada drink, ice cream flavor, or, now, a cream ice.

INGREDIENTS

10-Qt Batch	20-Qt Batch	40-Qt Batch	
26 oz	3¼ lb	6½ lb	Sugar (B)
12 oz	1½ lb	3 lb	36 DE corn (B)
1 oz	2 oz	4 oz	Stabilizer CC–917 (B)
3 qt	1½ gal	3 gal	Water (B)
24 oz	1½ qt	3 lb	Ice cream mix (B)
1 oz	2 oz	4 oz	Vanilla extract (B)
16 oz	1 qt	2 qt	Coconut fruit base (B)
24 oz	1½ qt	3 qt	Pineapple puree (B)
½ lb	1 lb	2 lb	Shredded coconut (B)

PREPARATION   Batch time: 15–18 minutes

Mix together thoroughly sugar, 36 DE corn and stabilizer. Add in ½ of the water (hot) and blend well. Pour all ingredients including the remaining water (cold) into the batch freezer. Turn on the dasher and run for 2 minutes to blend ingredients, set timer to 15 minutes, turn on refrigeration and begin the batch. As the mixture firms up and looks gravy, turn off refrigeration and extrude the finished product.

VARIATIONS

PIÑA BANANA COLADA CREAM ICE: For a 20-quart batch, add 5 pounds of peeled pureed bananas to the ingredients above before freezing. Adjust accordingly for other size batches.

CHA CHA CHA BERRIES COLADA: For a 20-quart batch, chop up 2 pounds of frozen strawberries into very small pieces and add it to the Piña Colada cream ice recipe before freezing. Adjust accordingly for other size batches.

 # Homemade Version

INGREDIENTS

6 oz	Sugar	8 oz	Crushed pineapple
24 oz	Water (hot and cold)	8 oz	Heavy cream
8 oz	Cream of coconut	2 Tbsp	Shredded coconut
8 oz	Pineapple juice		

PREPARATION

Thoroughly mix sugar with 12 ounces of water (hot). Pour all ingredients including the remaining water (cold) into an ice cream maker and freeze according to manufacturer's instructions. When the batch is complete, turn off refrigeration and extrude the finished product. Yield: 1½–2 quarts of cream ice

Peaches & Crème Cream Ice

INGREDIENTS

10-Qt Batch	20-Qt Batch	40-Qt Batch	
1½ lb	3 lb	6 lb	IQF peaches (E)
6 oz	12 oz	24 oz	Sugar (E)
12 oz	1½ lb	3 lb	36 DE corn (B)
26 oz	3¼ lb	6½ lb	Sugar (B)
1 oz	2 oz	4 oz	Stabilizer CC–917 (B)
3 qt	1½ gal	3 gal	Water (B)
24 oz	1½ qt	3 qt	Ice cream mix (B)
1 oz	2 oz	4 oz	Vanilla extract (B)
16 oz	1 qt	2 qt	Peach puree (B)

PREPARATION   Batch time: 15–18 minutes

Combine and marinate peaches and sugar for 8 hours. Mix together thoroughly sugar, 36 DE corn and stabilizer. Add in ½ of the water (hot) and blend well. Pour the remaining water (cold) and other ingredients *except* marinated peaches into the batch freezer. Turn on the dasher and run for 2 minutes to blend ingredients, set the timer to 15 minutes, turn on the refrigeration and begin batch. When the batch is complete, add in marinated peaches. As the mixture firms up and looks gravy, turn off refrigeration and extrude the finished product.

Pistachio Cream Ice

INGREDIENTS

10-Qt Batch	20-Qt Batch	40-Qt Batch	
26 oz	3¼ lb	6½ lb	Sugar (B)
12 oz	1½ lb	3 lb	36 DE corn (B)
1 oz	2 oz	4 oz	Stabilizer CC–917 (B)
3 qt	1½ gal	3 gal	Water (B)
24 oz	1½ qt	3 qt	Ice cream mix (B)
1 oz	2 oz	4 oz	Vanilla extract (B)
17 oz	34 oz	68 oz	Pistachio paste (B)
½ lb	1 lb	2 lb	Pistachios (E)

PREPARATION   Batch time: 15–18 minutes

Mix together thoroughly sugar, 36 DE corn and stabilizer. Add in ½ of the water (hot) and blend well. Pour the remaining water (cold) and other ingredients *except* pistachios into the batch freezer. Turn on dasher and run for 2 minutes, set timer to 15 minutes, turn on the refrigeration and begin the batch. As the mixture firms up and looks gravy, add in the pistachios, turn off refrigeration and extrude the finished product. Decorate tops of tubs with pistachios.

Peanut Butter & Jelly Cream Ice

INGREDIENTS

10-Qt Batch	20-Qt Batch	40-Qt Batch	
24 oz	1½ qt	3 qt	Peanut butter topping (B)
26 oz	3¼ lb	6½ lb	Sugar (B)
12 oz	1½ lb	3 lb	36 DE corn (B)
1 oz	2 oz	4 oz	Stabilizer CC–917 (B)
3 qt	1½ gal	3 gal	Water (B)
24 oz	1½ qt	3 qt	Ice cream mix (B)
1 oz	2 oz	4 oz	Vanilla extract (B)
1 qt	2 qt	4 qt	Grape jelly (B)
½ lb	1 lb	2 lb	Granulated peanuts (B)

PREPARATION   **Batch time: 15–18 minutes**

Thoroughly mix the peanut butter topping so the oil is evenly disbursed. Mix together thoroughly sugar, 36 DE corn and stabilizer. Add in ½ of the water (hot) and blend well. Pour all ingredients including the remaining water into the batch freezer. Turn on the dasher and run for 2 minutes to blend ingredients, set timer to 15 minutes, turn on refrigeration and begin the batch. As the mixture firms up and looks gravy, turn off the refrigeration and extrude the finished product.

 ## Homemade Version

INGREDIENTS

6 oz	Sugar
32 oz	Water (hot and cold)
8 oz	Peanut butter
2 oz	Granulated peanuts
6 oz	Heavy cream
12 oz	Grape jelly

PREPARATION

Thoroughly mix sugar with 16 ounces of water (hot). Pour remaining water and all ingredients *except* grape jelly into an ice cream maker and freeze according to the manufacturer's instructions. When the batch is complete, add in grape jelly, turn off the refrigeration and extrude the finished product. Yield: 1½–2 quarts of cream ice

Snickers Vanilla Chip Cream Ice

INGREDIENTS

10-Qt Batch	20-Qt Batch	40-Qt Batch	
26 oz	3¼ lb	6½ lb	Sugar (B)
12 oz	1½ lb	3 lb	36 DE corn (B)
1 oz	2 oz	4 oz	Stabilizer CC–917 (B)
3 qt	1½ gal	3 gal	Water (B)
24 oz	1½ qt	3 qt	Ice cream mix (B)
1 oz	2 oz	4 oz	Vanilla extract (B)
½ lb	1 lb	2 lb	Chocolate chips (E)
¾ lb	1½ lb	3 lb	Snickers bars, granulated (E)

PREPARATION   Batch time: 15–18 minutes

Mix together thoroughly sugar, 36 DE corn and stabilizer. Add in ½ of the water (hot) and blend well. Pour remaining water (cold) and other ingredients *except* chocolate chips and granulated Snickers bars into the batch freezer. Turn on the dasher and run for 2 minutes, set timer to 15 minutes, turn on the refrigeration and begin the batch. As the mixture firms up and looks gravy, add in chocolate chips and granulated Snickers bars, turn off the refrigeration and extrude the finished product.

Vanilla Cookie Dough Cream Ice

INGREDIENTS

10-Qt Batch	20-Qt Batch	40-Qt Batch	
26 oz	3¼ lb	6½ lb	Sugar (B)
12 oz	1½ lb	3 lb	36 DE corn (B)
1 oz	2 oz	4 oz	Stabilizer CC–917 (B)
3 qt	1½ gal	3 gal	Water (B)
24 oz	1½ qt	3 qt	Ice cream mix (B)
1 oz	2 oz	4 oz	Vanilla extract (B)
8 oz	1 lb	2 lb	Chocolate chips (E)
12 oz	1½ lb	3 lb	Cookie dough pieces (E)

PREPARATION   Batch time: 15–18 minutes

Mix together thoroughly sugar, 36 DE corn and stabilizer. Add in ½ of the water (hot) and blend well. Pour the remaining water (cold) and other ingredients *except* chocolate chips and cookie dough pieces into the batch freezer. Turn on the dasher and run for 2 minutes, set timer to 15 minutes, turn on refrigeration and begin the batch. When the batch is complete, add in the chocolate chips and cookie dough pieces. As the mixture firms up and looks gravy, turn off refrigeration and extrude the finished product.

Vanilla Chip Cream Ice

Without a doubt, one of the most popular cream ices flavors produced.

INGREDIENTS

10-Qt Batch	20-Qt Batch	40-Qt Batch	
3 qt	1½ gal	3 gal	Water
26 oz	3¼ lb	6½ lb	Sugar
24 oz	1½ qt	3 qt	Ice cream mix
1 oz	2 oz	4 oz	Stabilizer CC–917
1 oz	2 oz	4 oz	Vanilla extract
1 lb	2 lb	4 lb	Chocolate chips
4 oz	8 oz	1 lb	Liquid chocolate*

PREPARATION   Batch time: 15–18 minutes

Mix together sugar and stabilizer. Add in ½ of the water (hot) and blend well. Pour remaining water (cold) and all other ingredients *except* chocolate chips into the batch freezer. Turn on dasher and run for 2 minutes to blend ingredients. Set timer to 15 minutes. Turn on refrigeration and begin the batch. As the mixture firms up and looks gravy, add in chocolate chips, turn off refrigeration and extrude the finished product.

Vanilla Reese's Peanut Butter Cup Cream Ice

INGREDIENTS

10-Qt Batch	20-Qt Batch	40-Qt Batch	
3 qt	1½ gal	3 gal	Water (B)
26 oz	3 ¼ lb	6½ lb	Sugar (B)
12 oz	1 ½ lb	3 lb	36 DE corn (B)
24 oz	1½ qt	3 qt	Ice cream mix (B)
1 ounce	2 oz	4 oz	Stabilizer CC–917 (B)
1 oz	2 oz	4 oz	Vanilla extract (B)
1 lb	2 lb	4 lb	Reese's Peanut Butter Cups (B)
1 oz	2 oz	4 oz	Liquid chocolate* (B)

PREPARATION   Batch time: 15–18 minutes

Mix together sugar and stabilizer. Add in ½ of the water (hot) and blend well. Pour remaining water (cold) and other ingredients except the peanut butter cups and liquid chocolate into batch freezer. Turn on the dasher and run for 2 minutes, set timer to 15 minutes, turn on refrigeration and begin the batch. As the mixture firms up and looks gravy, add in the peanut butter cups and liquid chocolate,. turn off refrigeration and extrude the finished product.

*To prepare the liquid chocolate, heat in a double boiler 5 parts chocolate to 1 part vegetable oil by weight.

Strawberry Cream Ice

INGREDIENTS

10-Qt Batch	20-Qt Batch	40-Qt Batch	
26 oz	3¼ lb	6½ lb	Sugar (B)
12 oz	1½ lb	3 lb	36 DE corn (B)
1 oz	2 oz	4 oz	Stabilizer CC–917 (B)
3 qt	1½ gal	3 gal	Water (B)
24 oz	1½ qt	3 qt	Ice cream mix (B)
1 oz	2 oz	4 oz	Vanilla extract (B)
9 oz	18 oz	36 oz	Fragola paste (B)
1¼ lb	2½ lb	5 lb	IQF Strawberries (B)
5 oz	10 oz	1¼ lb	Sugar (B)
12 oz	24 oz	1½ qt	Processed strawberry base (B)

PREPARATION   Batch time: 15–18 minutes

Mix together thoroughly.sugar, 36 DE corn and stabilizer. Add in ½ of the water (hot) and blend well. Pour all ingredients including remaining water (cold) into batch freezer. Turn on the dasher and run for 2 minutes to blend ingredients, set timer to 15 minutes, turn on refrigeration and begin the batch. As the mixture firms up and looks gravy, turn off the refrigeration and extrude the finished product. Decorate tops of tubs with fresh strawberry pieces.

 # Homemade Version

INGREDIENTS

1 lb	Fresh, ripe strawberry pieces or frozen
8 oz	Sugar
32 oz	Water (hot and cold)
8 oz	Heavy cream
1 Tbsp	Lemon juice

PREPARATION

Puree the strawberry pieces. Thoroughly mix sugar with ½ of the water (hot). Pour strawberry puree, heavy cream, lemon juice and remaining water (cold) into an ice cream maker and freeze according to the manufacturer's instructions. When the batch is complete, turn off refrigeration and extrude the finished product. Yield: 1½–2 quarts of cream ice

Strawberry Cheesecake Cream Ice

A bite of this flavor is like eating a reduced-fat slice of great cheesecake.

INGREDIENTS

10-Qt Batch	20-Qt Batch	40-Qt Batch	
26 oz	3¼ lb	6½ lb	Sugar (B)
¾ lb	1½ lb	3 lb	36 DE corn (B)
1 oz	2 oz	4 oz	Stabilizer CC–917 (B)
3 qt	1½ gal	3 gal	Water (B)
24 oz	1½ qt	3 lb	Ice cream mix (B)
1 oz	2 oz	4 oz	Vanilla extract (B)
1 lb	2 lb	4 lb	Commercial cheesecake powder (B)
1 qt	2 qt	4 qt	Processed strawberries (B)
4 oz	8 oz	1 lb	Graham crackers, broken (B)

PREPARATION
Batch time: 15–18 minutes

Mix together thoroughly sugar, 36 DE corn and stabilizer. Add in ½ of the water (hot) and blend well. Pour all ingredients including remaining water (cold) into batch freezer. Turn on the dasher and run for 2 minutes to blend ingredients, set timer to 15 minutes, turn on refrigeration and begin the batch. As the mixture firms up and looks gravy, turn off refrigeration and extrude finished product.

VARIATIONS

BLUEBERRY CHEESECAKE CREAM ICE: For a 20-quart batch, replace the strawberries with 4 quarts of blueberry topping. Adjust accordingly for other size batches.

CHERRY CHEESECAKE CREAM ICE: For a 20-quart batch, replace the strawberries with 4 quarts of Bordeaux cherry halves. Adjust accordingly for other size batches.

RASPBERRY CHEESECAKE CREAM ICE: For a 20-quart batch, replace the strawberries with 2 quarts of raspberry puree at the beginning of the batch and 2 quarts of raspberry topping at the end of the batch.

11

ICE CREAM CAKE RECIPES

WHY MAKE ICE CREAM CAKES?

Turning an ordinary ice cream flavor into a dessert masterpiece without having to be a pastry chef or professional baker—and without a lot of time and fuss—is *a piece of cake!* And there are many reasons why you should consider doing so.

- You can build this part of your business 12 months a year—rain or shine.

- It's a business that thrives on holidays, special occasions and celebrations. Take the month of June as an example; besides June birthdays, consider selling cakes for graduation parties, bridal showers, anniversaries and Father's Day. What a great month to be selling ice cream desserts!

- You can offer a customized product to both a retail or wholesale customer.

- It provides limitless opportunities for growth both as a retail and as a wholesale business.

- It brings people into your retail shop.

- It's fun and creative for everyone involved in the process.

STEPS TO DESSERT SUCCESS

There are three basic steps to making successful desserts: buying the necessary tools; buying quality ingredients and keeping current on trends and ingredients.

1. **Buy the Necessary Tools and Equipment**
   Having the right tools can make the difference between success and failure. The proper tools will not only save you time and money, but will heighten the look of your final product. Examples: Proper temperature freezer for storing cakes and their ingredients; high-quality cake pans, pastry bags, decorating tips, spatulas, and so on.

2. **Buy Quality Ingredients**
   Don't skimp on your dessert case. Use the same quality ingredients as you do in your core product. This will separate you from the franchise retail store in your area. This will also help build your store's solid reputation.

3. **Keep Current on Dessert and Flavor Trends and New Ingredients**
   The world of desserts is constantly changing. What was popular in the 1990s is not "all that" in 2009! New flavors emerge, new fads appear out of nowhere and suddenly there are exciting new technologies that pave the way to a whole new family of dessert ingredients and decorations. The fun is in the journey of mastering what is happening now, and learning new things as they come into the mainstream.

So, have we sparked your interest? If you really want to pursue growing your ice cream business, then having an active ice cream cake business is a must. In many cases, the first choice for a birthday party is an ice cream cake. It's a very special treat, and it's the perfect takeout dessert. But you must remember one thing: the average consumer has just so much discretionary money to spend on meals, drinks, desserts and so on. You must establish your niche to motivate consumers to spend their "dessert dollars" with you. Ice cream cakes are a good motivator that brings customers into your establishment—**and it's a great repeat business!**

The most popular size ice cream cake for a birthday or anniversary is an 8- or 9-inch round that serves between 8–12 people. During graduation season, sheet cakes, either full or half, sell very well. When it comes to Valentine's Day, there is nothing better than a Chocolate Heart ice cream cake. And clearly two holidays, Mother's Day and Father's Day, are huge for cake sales, with a three-day span from Friday through Sunday. On average, the price of an 8-inch round made with hard ice cream goes for about $14.50–$25.00, and the average price for an 8-inch round made with soft ice cream goes for about $12.95–$16.95, costing approximately $3.00–$4.00 to produce (including packaging).

Pricing an Ice Cream Cake

If you use a 3.5 factor times cost, you will have a very fair markup. The cost used in the 3.5 times factor includes product, packaging and labor. Product cost includes ice cream, bakery base and decorating materials such as flowers and whipped cream. Material costs include cake circles, cake boxes and so on. Labor includes time taken to prepare, manufacture, empty the cake molds, decorate and box the cakes. Below is an example of what an ice cream cake really costs you and how the 3.5 factor cost figures into your selling price of an ice cream cake.

8-Inch Round Hard Ice Cream Cake

Ice cream mix	$6.50 per gallon
39 oz ($0.4½ per oz) ice cream mix	1.76
5 oz per cake, cake crunch (0.12 per ounce)	0.60
Manufacturing Cost	0.33
Labor	0.17
Decorating	0.67
Miscellaneous	0.20
Cake Box	0.45
Cake Circle	0.05
TOTAL	**$4.23 per cake**

TOTAL COST = $4.23 x 3.5 cost factor

SELLING PRICE = $14.80

- **Manufacturing Cost** 3 batches per hour, 2 employees, 60 cakes per hour, $20 per hour equals $0.33 per cake.

- **Labor** Includes cake-mold cleaning, sanitizing, removal of cake from mold, putting on circles and so on; 60 cakes per hour, $10 per hour, 1 employee.

- **Decorating** Varies from 15–30 cakes per hour depending on size of cake. Includes time for boxing, icing, whipped cream for trim; 1 employee, $10 per hour.

- **Miscellaneous** Includes flowers, leaves and so on, as well as labels on box.

Making a Fabulous Cookie Crumb Crust

Basic Recipe

80% Crumbs + 20% Butter (softened or melted) or some other type of fat to bind; could be as simple as graham cracker crumbs and butter—but oh, so ordinary!

Getting Creative!

- **Crunchy Chocolate Cinnamon Graham Cracker Crust:** Coarsely crushed chocolate-covered graham cracker crumbs + brown sugar + ground cinnamon

- **Peanut Butter & Chocolate Crust:** Chocolate cookie crumbs + warm peanut butter in place of some of the melted butter + miniature chocolate chips (4,000 count); try adding some cocoa powder or chocolate syrup for a flavor boost

- **Buttery Pecan Praline Crust:** Pecan shortbread cookies + finely chopped toasted pecans + butter pecan flavor extract

- **Coffee Toffee Crust:** Vanilla wafer crumbs + brown sugar + coffee syrup or extract + crushed toffee bits

- **Additions:** Vary the size of the crumbs from finely ground to big and chunky. Add chopped toasted nuts, toasted coconut, chunks of granola, melted nut butters, spices, candied ginger, brown sugar, chopped candies, chocolate chips and so on. Sometimes the best crusts are discovered when you use leftover ingredients from making gelato or ice cream. Have fun with it!

Using Store-Bought Cake Layers and Brownies to Make Bases for Ice Cream Cakes

Basics

- The cake layer should not be the focal point of the cake—the thickness of ice cream should be at least twice that of the cake layer.

- The cake layer should be moist and delicious. If not, doll it up by doing the following: 1) Soak one side of the cake in a flavored simple syrup—use your flavor extracts or bases to add depth to a basic simple syrup. Try making an espresso soaking syrup for a chocolate cake layer or an almond soaking syrup for a white or sponge cake layer; 2) Give the layer some "gooey stuff" by spreading on some fudge or a fruit variegate. Or sprinkle on a crunchy topping of nuts or candy at this point to add more flavor and texture.

Making a Chewy, Gooey Brownie Ice Cream Cake in a "Cold Molds" Pan

- Brownie crust

- Layer of fudge

- Top fudge with toasted chopped almonds

- Coffee gelato with toffee bits swirled with caramel variegate

- Freeze

- Frost entire cake with "peaks" of nondairy whipped topping, drizzle chocolate and caramel variegates over top and swirl with spatula to make the topping resemble toasted marshmallow meringue.

- **Tip:** There are many flavored nondairy toppings on the market—some are good and others taste very artificial. To create your own line of flavors, simply add the flavor yourself. The sky is the limit with espresso whipped topping, pistachio, caramel, chocolate, vanilla bean and so on!

Frosting an Ice Cream Cake in Ice Cream

Basics

- Use softened or freshly made ice cream or gelato without inclusions; this will create a silky smooth finish to your cakes.

- Choose an ice cream frosting that does not take away from the flavor of the ice cream inside your cake. Vanilla is always a good choice. Or use an ice cream frosting to enhance the other flavors of the cake—plain chocolate gelato frosting would be delicious and sophisticated on many cakes featuring chocolate, as would coffee ice cream.

- If you make your own Vanilla ice cream, you can create a whiter frosting by omitting the color. A white ice cream frosting can be tinted in pastel colors using food color pastes to create a whimsical touch to the finished cake, resembling the look of a fondant-iced cake. Again, have fun with this. A pink-colored ice cream frosting could be your signature look for heart-shaped strawberry ice cream cakes for a Valentine's Day promotion.

Tips

- If the ice cream frosting is too soft, it will melt too quickly and you will not have enough time to frost the cake. Try freezing the ice cream frosting for a few minutes.

- If the ice cream frosting is too hard, it will be chunky and difficult to spread. Stir it with a spade or rubber spatula until smooth and lump-free.

- Make sure your cake is frozen solid, at least 0 degrees or colder. You want your soft frosting to *freeze* onto the frozen cake as you apply it.

- It is easier to frost over ice cream than a cake layer, so it is best to have the ice cream at the top of the cake.

- For best results, cakes frosted in ice cream should be frozen before applying a border or final decoration.

Frosting a Cake in Ice Cream

- Secure frozen cake in center of board using a small amount of fudge or topping.

- Place correct amount of Ice Cream Frosting on top of cake. Use offset spatula, to quickly spread frosting over the surface of the cake to a thickness of ¼". Let remaining frosting hang over top edge of cake all the way around. Keep spatula blade flat against the surface of the cake as you work.

- Switch the angle of your spatula to a vertical position. Bring the excess frosting down the sides of the cake until it reaches the cake board. Molded cake and ice cream should be evenly covered with approximately ¼" thick frosting on all sides.

- Smooth sides by moving the spatula blade along the top edge of the cake, switching the spatula to a horizontal position, lightly touch the excess frosting and blend it into the center of the cake.

- If you want to use a cake comb or apply texture to the frosting, do it now.

Making Sure the Cake Is Served Well

Be sure that every cake customer is given an information card that explains how to serve and store the ice cream cake they have just purchased. This is very important, given that most people have problems cutting an ice cream cake, primarily because they don't take the time at home to temper it properly before serving. The card explains what must be done to serve it well. Using your batch freezer or soft serve machine, you are in a perfect position to produce a lot of cakes at any given time. What this means is that you can produce them in quantity and store them for an instant sale by a customer.

Our book *Ice Cream Cakes* thoroughly explains how to make an ice cream cake (and I highly recommend it). Reading the book will inspire you to be creative. The book has many recipes for ice cream cakes and pies, with specific instructions on decorating cakes and what ingredients are necessary to be really successful in this business.

So let's get started—**Right now!**

Basic Ice Cream Birthday Cake

This cake should be a main "staple" in your display case and you should keep a back stock available at all times, but "price" the cake to sell. If Stan Somekh, from our first Ice Cream Seminar, can make an ice cream cake, so can you!

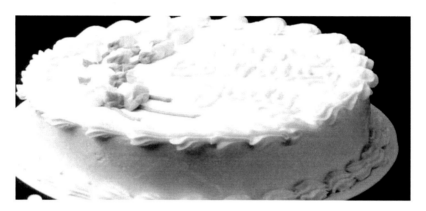

INGREDIENTS

18"	Chocolate or white cake layer, frozen (¾"–1" high, approximately 6.5 oz)
4–6 oz	Chocolate fudge, caramel topping or variegate of your choice (optional)
25 oz	Ice cream of your choice
9 oz	Nondairy whipped topping, divided
3–4	Edible flowers (optional)

PREPARATION

Place cake layer in bottom of 8" cake pan. If desired, spread chocolate fudge or other topping evenly over cake using a small offset spatula. Pour ice cream into pan and spread it into an even layer, making sure to eliminate any air pockets; then smooth the surface with the offset spatula. Freeze cake approximately 8 hours. Remove from pan. Place a small spoonful of nondairy topping in center of 10" round cake board. Place cake on board. Crumb-coat sides of cake, if necessary. Freeze cake briefly to set ice cream. Frost cake with 6 ounces of nondairy whipped topping. If time permits, freeze cake briefly before decorating to allow frosting to set. Put 3 ounces of nondairy topping into a pastry bag. Using tip #2-E, pipe a reverse shell border around top edge of cake and a regular shell border around base of cake. Decorate the cake as desired.

Makes 1 eight-inch cake approximately 45 ounces and serves 10.

Oreo Bomb Ice Cream Cake

The original idea for this cake came from Longford's Ice Cream of Port Chester, New York. Our version is slightly different from theirs, but both are terrific sellers. Remember, if your cake does not look terrific, it won't matter how wonderful it tastes. First impressions are extremely important and it will be the determining factor in making the first sale—or not. If you like Oreo ice cream, you'll love this eight-inch cake. It is simply all ice cream.

INGREDIENTS

25 oz	Oreo ice cream
9 oz	Nondairy whipped topping
1 oz	Oreo dry crumbs
12	Oreo cookies

PREPARATION

Take Oreo ice cream out of the batch freezer and pour it into a 9" cake pan. When the pan is filled up, use an offset spatula to smooth surface of the ice cream into a flat, even layer. Cover the "cake" with wax paper and blast freeze it for 6–8 hours. Remove cake from pan. Place a spoonful of nondairy topping in the center of a 9" cake board, and freeze briefly to set the ice cream on the board. Coat the sides of the cake with Oreo cookie crumbs. Spread nondairy whipped topping on the surface of the cake. At this point, you can keep the top surface of the cake clean or you can create a rosette pattern (13 in all) using tip #2-E. Next, place the 12 Oreo cookies all the way around the top of the cake, and sprinkle Oreo crumbs on top of the rosettes.

Makes 1 eight-inch cake approximately 48 ounces and serves 6–8.

Valentine's Day Chocolate Heart Cake

This heart-shaped ice cream cake looks and tastes just great. Be creative and give this cake a try. After all, Valentine's Day is a special day, isn't it?

INGREDIENTS

	Bay leaves
1	9" round sponge cake
2¼ lb	Chocolate ice cream
¾ cup	Belgian dark chocolate or bar coating
8 oz	Dark chocolate bar (for chocolate leaves)

Preparing the Chocolate Leaves

Disinfect a few bay leaves by soaking them for 5 minutes in 1/1000 solution of cold water, then another 5 minutes in a 1/100 solution of white vinegar and cold water. Drain and wipe dry. Using a brush, spread a thin layer of chocolate over the surface of each leaf. Allow to crystallize, then unstick.

PREPARATION

Using a heart-shaped cake pan, cut out a heart with the sponge cake. Place the cutout sponge cake inside the heart pan. Pour the ice cream into the pan. Freeze the filled pan for 6 hours. Remove cake from freezer and place it on top of a wire rack (place a pan beneath wire rack). Melt down ¾ cup of Belgian dark chocolate and ladle it into a measuring cup. Set aside to cool to 70° F, then slowly pour Belgian chocolate on cake. When cake is covered with chocolate, return the cake to freezer to harden. Before chocolate hardens, place chocolate leaves on top of the cake. Place the cake in the freezer to harden.

Makes 1 eight-inch cake approximately 48 ounces and serves 6–8.

Chocolate Chip Roll Cake

INGREDIENTS

1 full sheet	Chocolate layer cake, approximately ½" thick
96 oz	Vanilla Chip ice cream
2 qt	Fudge
18 oz	Chocolate nondairy whipped cream topping
12 oz	Chocolate chips or chunks

PREPARATION

Place the chocolate cake on a baker's tray with the waxed-paper side of the cake on the bottom of the tray. Using an offset spatula, spread 3 quarts of ice cream evenly throughout the sheet cake (like buttering a piece of bread). Allow ¾" space exposed at either end of the sheet cake. Standing in front of the pan, use your fingers to lift cake up and forward towards you, slowly peeling the loose wax paper from the cake until you have reached a form of a "C." Using very gentle pressure, keep peeling the wax paper away from the cake. Roll the cake towards you until it's in the shape of a cylinder. Place roll cake securely down on the pan with the seam side down. Cover the cylinder with wax paper and freeze the roll cake for 8 hours or overnight. Remove wax paper from the roll cake. Using a knife, cut a thin slice off each end of the cake (approx. ⅓"). Next, cut the cake either in half or in thirds. Spread a 1" wide strip of fudge down the length of a 6 x 9-inch cake board and secure the seam side of the cake to the fudge. Place the cake on a turntable. Spread the entire top of the roll cake with fudge. Pour chocolate chunks over the fudge, pressing slightly into the fudge. Fill pastry bag with nondairy chocolate whipped cream topping and using tip #4SR, pipe shells all around the base of the cake.

Makes 3 roll cakes, each 8" long; 2 roll cakes, each 12" long; or 1 very long 24" cake for that special holiday or birthday celebration.

Tartufo

An Italian chocolate-covered frozen dessert served at most Italian restaurants. Each is the size of a large ice cream ball (4 ounces) with an Italian Amarena cherry placed at the bottom. The ice cream can be either Vanilla, Vanilla and Chocolate combination or Gianduja. Once you get the technique down pat, they are a cinch to make. For anyone in the wholesale ice cream business selling to restaurants, this dessert is a great revenue source for you. Package them 36 to a box. You can sell them individually for about $1.50–1.75.

INGREDIENTS
To Make 1 Tartufo:

6 oz	Ice cream
1	Italian Amarena Cherry, raspberry or other filling
	Chocolate bar coating

PREPARATION

Place sheet of aluminum foil on baker's tray. Take a tub of ice cream out of the freezer, tempered so you can scoop out balls. Using a #10 ice cream scoop, scoop out a ball of ice cream, turn scoop upside down and place 1 Amarena cherry or raspberry inside the ball. Release the scoop onto the tray. Fill up the tray with 24 balls, 8 to a line in 3 rows. Place the tray back into the blast freezer for at least 6 hours. Heat up chocolate bar coating to 95° F, then pour bar coating into a large bowl (5–6 inches deep), large enough to enable a fork to be placed into the bowl. Remove the ice cream balls from the blast freezer. Place ball on fork, then dip it into the chocolate until completely covered. Remove ball from the bowl and place it on baker's tray. Before placing balls back inside the blast freezer, dip the fork into the chocolate and then wave the fork over the balls to give them a decorative chocolate look. Keep the balls inside the blast freezer for at least 1 hour. Remove from the blast freezer, pack each one individually with senior wax deli paper and place the Tartufos back inside a box (36 to a box).

ICE CREAM PIES

*An ice cream pie is the perfect takeout dessert for any ice cream store operation that does **not** make its own ice cream. Using your soft serve machine, it's an easy procedure that can only bring you success and revenue.*

The Crust

Pies are usually about 8" or 9" in diameter. Frozen ready-to-fill pie crusts can be purchased in graham cracker, chocolate and vanilla crumb. These premade pie crusts give you the opportunity to make pies very quickly, especially from ice cream freshly produced from your soft serve machine.

The Filling

Almost any ice cream, frozen yogurt or sorbet you produce in your shop will make an excellent pie filling. Just look at these combinations.

- Frozen yogurt can team up with a "healthier" pie crust such as granola or oatmeal cookie crumb.
- Sorbets can be swirled with creamy vanilla ice cream or frozen yogurt for a refreshing pie. Try decorating this with slices of glazed fruit, whipped topping and nuts.

Just how much soft serve ice cream does it take to fill a pie? This depends on the size of the pie crust, and how big and mounded you want the pie to be. Big, bountiful ice cream pies are currently the restaurant craze and can really attract a lot of attention. Of course, the bigger the pie, the more expensive it will be to produce.

Recommended Filling Weights with 8" or 9" Pie Crusts

24 ounces for a slightly mounded pie
32 ounces for a medium-size pie
36–40 ounces for a large domed pie

If you plan on layering a topping, for example, fudge, or mixing cookies or another ingredient into the filling, subtract that weight from the total ice cream weight.

The Decoration

Now is the time to get creative and have some fun. There are many delicious ways to finish a pie. Most pies call for a border of whipped topping, but a "zigzag" border of fudge looks luscious and tastes wonderful, too! Try using chocolate nondairy whipped topping for a change of pace. Or cover the entire pie with a meringue of fluffy white whipped topping swirls garnished with drizzles of chocolate, caramel or nuts. Don't be afraid to experiment and try new ideas.

Tips of the Trade

- If the ice cream filling is appetizing and colorful, don't cover it up completely. Be sure to show it off in your finished dessert.

- Use garnishes that relate to the flavor of the ice cream or crust; for example, Cookies 'n Cream ice cream garnished with chocolate cookie crumbs or whole chocolate creme-filled Oreo cookies.

- Give your finished pies fun names to make them more exciting; for example "Hot Fudge Sundae Splurge" or "Peanut Butter Passion."

- Make special holiday pies by featuring flavors that are popular that time of year. Decorate them lavishly with the spirit of the season.

- Try decorating a pie with colored sprinkles or edible confetti candies. These pies look particularly festive and appeal to children.

- Use 1, 2 and even 3 different flavors of ice cream in a pie. Different flavors can be swirled together or layered. If layering, let each flavor freeze before adding the next one.

- Keep a variety of pies in stock. If you sell them competitively priced and usually below that of a cake, you will sell pies all year round, and not have to wait for a "holiday occasion."

- If you plan on layering a topping, for example, fudge, or mixing cookies or another ingredient into the filling, subtract that weight from the total ice cream weight.

Basic Ice Cream Pie

Below is a very good example of what you can do decorating a simple ice cream pie. Use your imagination and create to your heart's content.

INGREDIENTS

1	9" Pie crust, frozen (approx. 6 oz)
24 oz	Ice cream
4 oz	Nondairy whipped topping
1–2 oz	Decoration (drizzles, nuts, chocolate shavings, etc.)

PREPARATION

Weigh the ice cream filling. Using a white rubber spatula, carefully mound the ice cream into a pie crust, placing most of the filling in the center. Place pie on a turntable. Using a small offset spatula, spread ice cream into the crust, making sure that there are no air pockets. Form ice cream into a slightly mounded dome shape with the highest point in the center and filling sloped downwards to the edges of the crust. The top edges of the crust should be visible. Smooth surface with offset spatula, making sure the dome shape is uniform all around the pie. Freeze pie until it is firm, several hours or overnight. Place frozen pie on a turntable. Using an 18" pastry bag and large star tip, make rosettes with whipped topping around the edge of the pie. Garnish the pie as desired.

Makes 1 nine-inch pie approximately 36 ounces and serves 8.

Mississippi Mud Pie

A Mississippi Mud Pie is simply a rich, stylish ice cream cake bursting with flavor.

INGREDIENTS

1.5 oz	Margarine
6.5 oz	Chocolate cookie crumbs (Oreo or Hydrox)
8 oz	Basic Cookie Crumb Crust
10 oz	Chocolate fudge, divided
4 oz	Graham crackers, crumbled
13 oz	Coffee ice cream
13 oz	Chocolate ice cream
½ oz	Dry chocolate cookie crumbs (for coating sides)

PREPARATION

Melt margarine. Blend chocolate cookie crumbs with margarine until thoroughly combined. Press crumb mixture evenly into the bottom of a 9" cake pan. Freeze crust briefly to harden crumbs. Spread 5 ounces of chocolate fudge on top of crust in an even layer. Pour Coffee ice cream into pan on top of fudge layer. Using offset spatula, smooth surface of ice cream into a flat, even layer. Freeze cake until the filling is frozen solid. Spread 5 ounces of chocolate fudge over the Coffee ice cream on the surface of the cake. Next place crumbled graham crackers on top of the fudge. Freeze at least ½ hour, or until topping has hardened slightly. Pour Chocolate ice cream over the fudge layer. Freeze cake approximately 1 hour, and then spread chocolate fudge over the top surface of the cake. Freeze ice cream 4-6 hours or overnight. Remove cake from pan and immediately coat sides of cake with chocolate cookie crumbs.

Makes 1 nine-inch cake approximately 50 ounces and serves 12.

Home Junkie's Ice Cream Cake

You can make a beautiful birthday or holiday ice cream cake or pie at home—it's a cinch to do. Even better than buying hard ice cream at the supermarket, make your own ice cream from scratch, and incorporate it into a fabulous-looking ice cream cake.

INGREDIENTS

1	8" Chocolate or white frozen cake layer cut horizontally into thirds (3/4"–1" high/approx. 6.5 oz)
4–6 oz	Hot Fudge or caramel topping
25 oz.	Ice cream or frozen yogurt of your choice
9 oz.	Nondairy whipped topping, divided
6–8	Raspberries or strawberries, if desired

Decorate by using any of the ideas that follow, or create your own.

PREPARATION: Ice Cream Cakes

Prepare cake base or cookie crumb crust and freeze in pan, if possible. Spread a layer of hot fudge on top of the cake base, if desired. Using a metal ice cream spade or scoop, remove thin layers of ice cream from the purchased ice cream, and place into the cake pan in overlapping slices on top of the cake base or crust. Keep filling the pan to the desired height. Freeze cake approximately 8 hours or overnight, until frozen solid. Remove cake from pan. Frost and decorate as desired.

PREPARATION: Ice Cream Pies

Follow the instructions above, but with the following changes:
- Overlap the layers of spaded ice cream as you build a large "dome" with the highest point in the center of the pie.
- Use a small offset spatula to carefully smooth the surface of ice cream into a lightly mounded dome shape. (Avoid getting ice cream on edges of pie crust.)
- Freeze pie before decorating.

NOTE: Any size cake pan may be used in the above recipe. The number of desired servings will determine what size cake pan to use.

Heavenly Chocolate Ice Cream Cupcakes

This wonderful cupcake recipe was created by my partner Lisa Tanner.

INGREDIENTS (per cupcake)

1.5 oz	Margarine
1 (2–2½ oz)	Baked dark chocolate cupcake, room temperature
1½ oz–2 oz	Chocolate ice cream, frozen yogurt or sorbet
½ oz	Chocolate sauce, fudge sauce or chocolate ganache
¼ oz	Miniature chocolate chips or chopped chocolate candies (optional)
1½ oz	Chocolate nondairy whipped topping or chocolate whipped cream
	Drizzle of chocolate ganache or chocolate bar coating, grated chocolate, chocolate "rose"

PREPARATION

Remove cupcake from paper lining, if used. Place cupcake on counter and carefully slice off top of cupcake using a serrated knife. Place base of cupcake in portion cup or serving cup, cut side up. (A clear 5½-ounce portion cup works well.) Use a small 1-ounce ice cream or cookie scoop to scoop ice cream; place ice cream on top of cupcake base. Drizzle sauce around ice cream, making sure it looks attractive in the cup. Top ice cream with chips or candies (if using). Replace "top" of cupcake, pressing lightly to secure to ice cream. Freeze filled cupcake until ice cream has set—at least ½ hour. Using a pastry bag filled with chocolate nondairy topping or whipped cream, pipe a large swirl "rosette" on top of cupcake, starting at outer edge and gradually tapering to a point as you build up the rosette. (A large round tip was used in photo.) Drizzle a thin line of chocolate ganache or bar coating over cupcake in a circular pattern. Garnish with grated chocolate and a pretty chocolate decoration in the center like the beautiful chocolate "rose" from Dobla.

APPENDIX: THE ICE CREAM PANTRY

SUPPLIERS

Equipment

Continuous Freezing and Filling Equipment

APV Ice Cream
9525 W. Bryn Mawr Ave.
Rosemont, IL 60018
888-278-9087
    Continuous freezing equipment

Autoprod
5355 115th Ave. North
Clearwater, FL 34620
813-572-7753
    Ice cream filling equipment

Cherry-Burrell/Waukesha
611 Sugar Creek Road
Delavan, WI 53115
414-728-1900
    Continuous freezing equipment

Frigomat
Via 1 Maggio
20070 Guardamiglio (MI)
Milan, Italy
0377-451170
    Gelato pasteurizing equipment

Gram Equipment of America
1212 N. 39th St., Suite 438
Tampa, FL 33605
813-248-1978
www.gram-equipment.com
    Ice cream continuous freezing and filling
    equipment

Northfield Freezing Systems
719 Cannon Road
Northfield, MN 55057
507-645-9546
    Ice cream freezing systems

Penn Scale Mfg. Co. Inc.
150 W. Berks Street
Philadelphia, PA 19122
215-739-9644
www.pennscale.com; sales@pennscale.com
    Digital scales

Processing Machinery & Supply/WCB
Waukesha-Cherry Burrell
625 State Street
New Lisbon, WI 53950
800-252-5200
    New & reconditioned ice cream
    continuous freezing equipment

Separators, Inc.
747 East Sumner Avenue
Indianapolis, IN 46227
800-233-9022
    Separators

Silverson Machines
P.O. Box 589
East Longmeadow, MA 01028
413-525-4825
    Batch and shear mixers

Tetra Laval Food (Hoyer)
753 Geneva Parkway
Lake Geneva, WI
262-249-7410
    Ice cream continuous freezing and filling
    equipment

Tindall Packaging
1150 East U Street
Vicksburg, MI 49097
616-649-1163
www.tindallpackaging.com
    Ice cream filling and packaging
    equipment

Walker Stainless Equipment Company
625 State Street
New Lisbon, WI 53950
608-562-3151
  Processing tanks

T.D. Sawvel Co. Inc.
5775 Highway 12
Maple Plan, MN 55359
763-479-4322
www.tdsawvel.com
  Ice cream filling equipment

Tri-Clover, Inc.
9201 Wilmont Road
Kenosha, WI 53141
262-694-5511
  Batch mixers

Batch Freezing Equipment

Carpigiani
Via Emilia 45
Anzola Emilia
Bologna, Italy
051-6505111
www.carpigiani-usa.com
  Gelato batch freezers and soft serve
  equipment

Electro-Freeze
2116 8th Ave.
East Moline, IL 61244
800-755-4545
www.electrofreeze.com
  Soft-serve freezers, batch
  freezers, blend-in machines

Emery Thompson Company
15350 Flight Path Road
Brooksville, FL 34604
718-588-7300
www.emerythompson.com
  Batch freezers

Stoelting, LLC
800-558-5807
www.stoeltingfoodservice.com
  Soft serve & batch freezers

Taylor Company
750 N. Blackhawk Blvd.
Rockton, IL 61072-9988
800-678-7084
www.taylor-company.com
  Soft-serve freezers, batch freezers, frozen
  drink machines

Technogel-USA
800-689-8819
www.technogel-usa.com
  Gelato batch freezers

Refrigeration

Beverage Air
P.O. Box 5932
Spartansburg, SC 29304
800-845-9800
  Refrigerators and freezers

Clabo Group-Oscartielle
33300 Central Ave.
Union City, CA 94587
800-672-2784
www.clabona.com
  Orion Gelato dipping cabinets

Delfield
P.O. Box 470
Mt. Pleasant, MI 48804
517-773-7981
  Refrigeration equipment

Detecto
P.O. Box 151
Webb City, MO 64870
800-641--2008
  Portion control scales

Excellence Commercial Products
P.O. Box 770127
Coral Springs, FL 33077
800-441-4014
www.stajac.com
  Freezer dipping cabinets &
  merchandising equipment

Hussmann Corporation
Convenience and Specialty Store Group
Gloversville, New York 12078
518-725-0644
www.hussmann.com
  Dipping cabinets

Kelvinator Commercial Products
864-369-1665
www.kelvinator.us.com
  Dipping cabinets, storage refrigerators,
  freezers, ice cream cake display cases

McCray Refrigerator
Grant Avenue/Blue Grass Rd.
Philadelphia, PA 19114
215-464-6800
  Dipping cabinets, storage
  refrigerators and freezers

Master-Bilt
800-647-1284
www.master-bilt.com
  Dipping cabinets; storage
  refrigerators,freezers; ice cream cake
  display cases

C. Nelson Manufacturing Co.
265 No. Lake Winds Parkway
Oak Harbor, OH 43449
800-922-7339
www.cnelson.com
  Ice cream storage chests and
  hardening chests

PrimoTec
4771 Arroyo Vista, Suite B
Livermore, CA 94551
800-284-1243
www.primotec.com
  Ranieri cabinets and café
  equipment

Wadden Systems
800-392-3336
www.icecreamflavors.com
  Mix-in flavors for soft serve

Trucks & Mobile Vending Carts

All Star Carts
1565D Fifth Industrial Court
Bayshore, New York 11706
631-666-5252
  Mobile vending carts

Custom Sales and Service
11th Street and Second Road
Hammonton, NJ 08037
609-561-6900
  Ice cream vans

David Cummings USA, Inc.
159 E. Lakeshore Blvd.
Kissimmee, FL 34744
407-301-4435
www.davidcummingsusa.com
  Ice cream vending trucks

Hackney Brothers Inc.
P.O. Box 2728
Wilson, NC 27894-2728
919-237-8171
  Mobile carts

Johnson Truck Bodies
215 E. Allen Street
Rice Lake, WI 54868
800-922-8360
  Refrigerated and freezer truck bodies

Workman Trading Corporation
94-15 100th St.
Ozone Park, NY 11416
718-322-2000
  Mobile vending carts

Sanitation Equipment & Supplies

Haynes Manufacturing Co.
24142 Detroit Rd.
Westlake, OH 44145
800-992-2166
www.haynesmfg.com
  Food grade lubricants

McGlaughlin Oil Company
3750 East Livingston Avenue
Columbus, OH 43277
614-231-2518
 Lubricating oil (Petro Gel) for processing
 equipment

Nelson-Jameson
2400 E. 5th St.
Marshfield, WI 54449
800-826-8302
 Sanitation and lab supplies

Purdy Products
379 Hollow Hill Drive
Wauconda, IL 60084
800-726-4849
 Sanitation supplies

Refrigiwear, Inc.
Breakstone Drive
PO Box 39
Dahlonega, GA 30533
706-864-5457
 Refrigerator and freezer plant clothing

Weber Scientific
2732 Kuser Road
Hamilton, NJ 08691
800-328-8378
 Lab equipment and supplies

Miscellaneous Equipment

American Soda Fountain
455 N. Oakley Blvd.
Chicago, IL 60612
312-733-5000
 Old-fashioned ice cream equipment

Blendec
1206 S. 1680 W
Orem, Utah 84058
800-253-6383
 Smoothie blenders

The Buddy System
3495 Winton Place, #209
Rochester, NY 14623
888-280-7031
www.thebuddysystem.com
 Cone dispensers and holders

Cal-Mil Plastic Products
4079 Calle Platino
Oceanside, CA 92056
760-630-5100
 Cone holders

Cold Molds
1025 Osgood Street
North Andover, MA 01845
800-906-7221
www.coldmolds.com
sales@coldmolds.com
 Molds for ice cream cakes

CRC
3218 Nebraska Ave.
Council Bluffs, IA 51501
712-323-9477
 Mix-in shake machines

Diamond Brands
1660 So. Highway 100, #590
Minneapolis, MN 55416
612-541-1500
 Ice cream novelty sticks

Flavor Burst Company
499 Commerce Drive
Danville, IN 46122
800-264-3528
www.flavorburst.com
 Soft-serve machine flavor injectors

Frozen Dessert Machine Cleaning
P.O. Box 554,
Jericho, NY 11753
516-731-8617
 Soft-serve cleaning maintenance

Echo Industries
61 R.W. Moore Ave.
Orange, MA 01364
978-544-7000
www.icecreamcans.com
  Metal cans

Geltecnica Machine
Salita Al Molinello, 32
Rapallo, Italy
0185-230339
  Italian novelty bar machines

Gruenwald Mfg. Co., Inc
100 Ferncroft Rd.
Danvers, MA 01923
800-229-9447
www.whipcream.com
  Whipped cream machines

Hamilton Beach Commercial
4421 Waterfront Drive
Glen Allen, VA 23060
800-572-3331
www.commercialhamiltonbeach.com
  Milk shake blenders and scoops

Innovative Marketing
9909 South Shore Drive
Plymouth, MN 55441
612-525-8686
www.goldengourmet.com
  5-gallon pail openers

ISI North America, Inc.
30 Chapin Rd.
Pine Brook, NJ 07058
973-227-2426
www.isinorthamerica.com
  Whipped cream dispensers

Lloyd Disher Company
5 Powers Lane Place
Decatur, IL 62522
217-423-2611
  Ice cream scoops

Novelty Baskets
1132 Heather Lane
Carrillton, TX 75007
972-492-4738
  Wire trays for novelties

Pelouze Scale Company
7560 W. 100th Place
Bridgeview, IL 60455
800-654-8330
  Weight scales

Ropak Corporation
20024 87th Avenue South
Kent, WA 98031
800-426-9040
  Plastic containers

Server Products
P.O. Box 249
Menomonee Falls, WI 53051
800-558-8722
www.server-products.com
  Hot fudge machines

Silver King
800-328-3329
www.silverking.com
  Hot fudge machines

Solon Manufacturing Co.
P.O. Box 285
Solon, ME 04979
207-643-2210
  Ice cream novelty sticks

Swirl Freeze Corporation
2474 Directors Row
Salt Lake City, UT 84104
801-972-0109
  Blend-in machines

T.J.'s Racks
1141 W. Swain Road, #132
Stockton, CA 95207
800-532-3917
  Ice cream can collars

The Zeroll Company
PO Box 999
Fort Pierce, FL 34954
800-872-5000
www.zeroll.com
Ice cream scoops

Flavoring Ingredients

Chocolates

ADM Cocoa
12500 W. Carmen Ave.
Milwaukee, WI 53225
800-558-9958
Cocoa, chocolate chips, coatings

Barry Callebaut
1500 Suckle Highway
Pennsauken, NJ
800-836-2626
Cocoa, chocolate bar coatings

Forbes Chocolate
800 Ken Mar Industrial Pkwy
Broadview Hts, OH 44147
800-833-1090
Cocoa, chocolate chips

Gertrude Hawk Chocolates
5117 Pine Top Place
Orlando, FL 32819
407-876-8673
Chocolate inclusions for ice cream

Guittard Chocolate Co.
10 Guittard Road
Burlingame, CA 94010
800-468-2462
www.guittard.com
Cocoa and chocolate chunks

Henry & Henry, Inc.
3765 Walden Ave.
Lancaster, NY 14986
800-828-7130
Fudge toppings, variegates

Kalva Corporation
3940 Porett Drive
Gurnee, IL 60031
800-525-8220
Ice cream cone dip coatings

The Masterson Company
P.O. Box 691
Milwaukee, WI 53201
414-647-1132
Cocoa, fudge, chocolate chips

W.L.W. Bensdorp Co.
1800 Westpark Drive #305
Westborough, MA 01581
508-366-9910
Cocoa

Fruit (Processed)

Bunge Foods
885 No. Kinzie Ave.
Bradley, IL 60915
800-828-0800
Ice cream flavor ingredients

Chiquita Brands
250 East Fifth Street
Cincinnati, OH 45202
800-438-0015
Banana ingredients and shapes

Coco Lopez
800-341-2242
Coconut cream

Extreme Smoothies
963 Worcester Road
Framingham, MA 01701
508-435-9058
Sells smoothies pucks, equipment

Fantasy Flavors/Blanke Bear, Inc.
611 N. 10th Street
St. Louis, MO 63101
800-886-3476
Ice cream production ingredients

Flavor Chem Corp.
1525 Brook Drive
Downers Grove, IL 60139
630-355-3013
Flavor extracts

Lyons-Magnus
1636 South Second Street
Fresno, CA 93702
800-344-7130
Ice cream flavor ingredients

Limpert Brothers, Inc.
P.O. Box 520
Vineland, NJ 08360
800-691-1353
www.limpertbrothers.com
Ice cream production ingredients

Milne Fruit Products
PO Box 111
Prosser, WA 99350
509-786-2611
Fruit purees

Ramsey/Sias
6850 Southpointe Parkway
Brecksville, OH 44141
800-477-3788
Fruit preps and purees

I. Rice & Company
11500 D. Roosevelt Blvd.
Philadelphia, PA 19116
800-232-6022
www.iriceco.com
Ice cream & Italian ice flavorings

SBI Systems
8 Neshaminy Interplex, #213
Trevose, PA 19053
215-638-7801
Ice cream flavorings & purees

Star Kay White
85 Brenner Drive
Congers, NY 10920
914-268-2600
Ice cream bases, fruits, nuts

Fruit (Frozen)

Clermont Fruit Packers
503-648-8544
Fruit purees

Global Trading Company
800-849-9990
Fruits from throughout USA and Mexico

ITI Inc.
3371 Route 1
Lawrenceville, NJ 08648
609-987-0550
Fruit ingredients

Oregon Cherry Growers
P.O. Box 7357
Salem, OR 97303
800-367-2536
Cherries: various sizes, kinds

Prima Foods International
1604 Esex Avenue
Deland, FL 32724
904-736-9138
Fruit purees

Ravifruit-French Food Exports
100 Manhattan Ave.
Union City, NJ 07087
201-867-2151
Fruit purees from France

Wawona Frozen Fruit
100 W. Alluvial
Clovis, CA 93612
209-299-2901
Frozen fruits

Nuts

Ace Pecan Company
900 Morse Village
Elk Grove Village, IL 60007
312-364-3250

Boyer Brothers, Inc.
821 17th Street
Altoona, PA 16603
814-944-9401
 Peanut butter paste and variegates

Peanut Corporation of America
800-446-0998
 Peanuts: all sizes, kinds

Pecan Deluxe Candy Co.
2570 Lone Star Drive
Dallas, TX 75212
214-631-3669
 Candy-coated nuts

Superior Nut Company
225 Monsignor O'Brien Hwy
Cambridge, MA 02141
800-966-7688
 Peanut butter variegate

Tracy-Luckey
110 N. Hicks Street
Harlem, GA 30814
800-476-4796
 Pecans

SNA Nut Company
1348-54 West Grand Ave.
Chicago, IL 60622
800-544-NUTS
 Pecans

Young Pecan Shelling Co.
1200 Pecan Street
Florence, SC 29501
800-829-6864
 Pecans

Flavor Extracts

Beck Flavors
411 E. Gano
St. Louis, MO 63147
800-851-8100
 Flavor extracts and vanilla

David Michael & Co.
10801 Decatur Road
Philadelphia, PA 19154
215-632-3100
 Extracts and fruit flavors

Edgar A. Weber & Co.
549 Palwaukee Drive
Whelling, IL 60090
800-558-9078
www.weberflavors.com
 Vanilla, coffee flavorings

Lochhead Vanillas
527 Axminister Drive
Fenton, MO 63026
888-776-2088
www.lochheadvanilla.com
 Natural vanilla extracts

National Flavor Products
269-344-3640
www.nationalflavors.com
 Extracts and fruit flavors

Nielsen-Massey Vanillas
1550 Shields Drive
Waukegan, IL 60085
800-525-7873
www.nielsenmassey.com
 Natural vanilla extracts

Virginia Dare Extract Company, Inc.
882 Third Avenue
Brooklyn, New York 11232
800-847-4500
www.virginiadare.ccom
 Extracts and flavors

Overall Flavor Ingredient Companies

Autocrat
10 Blackstone Valley Place
800-288-6272
www.autocrat.com
 Coffee paste and extracts

Carmi Flavor & Fragrance Company
6030 Scott Way
Commerce, CA 90040
323-888-9240
www.carmiflavors.com
Flavor extracts

CTL
514 Main Street
P.O. Box 526
Colfax, Wisconsin 54730
800-962-5227
Malt powder, serving merchandisers

Dippin' Flavors
1820 S. 3rd Street
St. Louis, MO 63104
800-886-3476
www.dipinflavors.com
Ice cream ingredients

Hershey Foodservice
14 East Chocolate Street
Hershey, PA 17033
717-534-6397
Chocolate candy, toppings

Ice Cream Outfitters
6260 W 52nd Street
Arvada, CO 8002
303-780-9820
www.icecreamoutfitters.com
Ice cream flavorings and equipment

Instantwhip Foods
2200 Cardigan Ave.
Columbus, OH 43215
800-544-9447
Whipped cream & toppings

Kraus & Company
Martin Road
Wallied Lake, MI 48390
800-662-5871
www.krauscompany.com
Ice cream ingredient flavorings

Leaf Inc.
500 N. Field Drive
Lake Forest, IL 60045
708-735-7500
Candy ingredients

M&M/Mars
Division of Mars, Inc.
High Street
Hackettstown, NJ 07840
908-852-1000
Candies

Nabisco Brands, Inc.
7 Campus Drive
Parsippany, NJ 07054
800-828-0398
Oreo cookies & candy ingredients

Nestle Foodservice
800 N. Bland Blvd.
Glendale, CA 91203
800-288-8682
Candy ingredients and toppings

Oringer-Concord Foods
10 Minuteman Way
Brockton, MA 02301
508-580-1700
www.concordfoods.com
Ice cream production
ingredients

A. Panza & Sons, Ltd.
60 Parkway Place
Raritan Center
Edison, NJ 08837
(732) 225-1314
Distributor of ice cream production
ingredients and associated supplies

Parker Brothers
2737 Tillar Street
P.O. Box 9335
Fort Worth, TX 76107
817-336-7441
Ice cream ingredients

The Perfect Puree
975 Vintage Avenue, Suite B
St. Helena, CA 94574
800-556-3707
  Fruit purees

Precision Foods
11457 Olde Cabin Road
St. Louis, MO 63141
800-442-5242
www.precisionfoods.com
  Ice cream production ingredients

QA Products
800-635-7907
www.qaproducts.com
  Ice cream ingredients & toppings

Royal Pacific Foods
800-551-5284
  Ginger cuts, ginger pulp, juice

Torani
233 E. Harris Avenue
So. San Francisco, CA 94080
800-775-1925
  Syrups for espresso

Yohay Baking Company
75 Grand Ave.
Brooklyn, NY 11205
800-255-9642
  Cookies for espresso bars

Gelato Flavor Ingredients

Berzaci, Inc.
635 McGarry Blvd.
Kearneyville, WV 25430
877-823-7922
info@berzaci.com; www.berzaci.com
  USA manufacturer of gelato & ice cream
  ingredients

Elenka-Howard Gordy
871 Shepard Ave
Brooklyn, NY 11208
www.howardgordy.com
  Elenka gelato flavorings

Fabbri North America
57-01 49th Place
Maspeth, NY 11378
718-764-8311
www.fabbri1905.com
  Gelato flavorings

Inter-Continental Imports
149 Louis Street
Newington, CT 06111
800-424-4221
  Gelato flavorings

Montebianco USA, LLC
954467-1883
www.montebianco-usa.com
  Gelato flavorings

PreGel USA
8700 Red Oak Blvd. #A
Charlotte, NC 28217
704-333—6804
www.pregelamerica.com
Gelato flavorings

Stabilizers

Tate & Lyle
246 West Roosevelt Road
West Chicago, IL 60185
800-323-9489
www.tateandlyle.com
  Stabilizers

Hercules Inc.
500 Hercules Road
Wilmington, DE 19808
302-594-4578/
  Stabilizers

ICE CREAM CAKE PRODUCTION

Bakery Crafts
9300 Allen Road
West Chester, OH 45069
800-543-1673
www.bakerycrafts.com
  Ice cream cake supplies

C. Carbon Co.
800-253-0590
www.goblenmalted.com
  Belgian waffles ingredients

Cold Molds
1025 Osgood Street
North Andover, MA 01845
800-906-7221
www.coldmolds.com
sales@coldmolds.com
  Cake pans & novelty molds

DecoPac. Inc.
5700 Thurston Ave
Anoka, MN 55303
800-332-6722
www.decopac.com
  Ice cream cake supplies

Inline Plastics
42 Canal Street
Shelton, CT 06484
800-826-5567
  Ice cream cake packaging

The Kalva Corporation
3940 Porett Drive
Gurnee, IL 60031
800-525-8220
www.kalvacorp.com
  Chocolate coatings

Kopycake Enterprises
3701 W. 240th Street
Torrance, CA 90505
800-999-5253
www.kopykake.com
  Cake decorating equipment

Lucks Food Decorating Co.
3003 S. Pine Street
Tacoma, WA 98409
800-426-9778
www.lucks.com
  Cake decorating equipment & Edible
  Images

Parrish's
225 W. 146th St.
Gardenia, CA 90248
800-736-8443
  Ice cream cake-making supplies

Rich's
1150 Niagara Street
Buffalo, NY 14213
800-45-RICHS
  Non-dairy whipped cream for ice cream
  cakes

Wilton Industries
2240 West 75th Street
Woodridge, IL 60517
708-963-7100
  Ice cream cake equipment and supplies

Ice Cream Cones

CoBatCo Inc.
11215 S Adams Street
Peoria, Illinois 61603
309-676-2663
www.cobatco.com
  Waffle cone batter and machines

The Cone Guys
PO Box 17614
Philadelphia, PA 19135
888-266-3489
  Flavored ice cream cones

Cream Cone
P.O. Box 1819
Columbus, Ohio 43216
614-294-4931
  Waffle, sugar, wafer cones: all sizes and
  varieties

Joy Cone Company
3435 Lamor Road
Hermitage, PA 16148
800-242-2663
www.joycone.com

Keebler Foodservice
One Hollow Tree Lane
Elmhurst, IL 60126
897-511-5777
Waffle, sugar & wafer cones: all sizes,
varieties

Matt's Supreme Cones
125 Byrd St.
Orange, VA 22960
800-888-2377
Ice cream cones

Novelty Cone Company
807 Sherman Avenue
Pennsauken, NJ 08110
856-665-9525
Wafer and cake cones

PDI Cone Company
69 Leddy St.
Buffalo, NY 14210
716-821-0698
Ice cream cones & sprinkles

Mixes: Ice Cream, Frozen Yogurt, Soft-Serve, Nondairy

AE Farms
2420 E. University Avenue
Des Moines, IA 50317
800-234-6455
Ice cream mixes

Bison Foods
196 Scott Street
Buffalo, NY 14204
716-854-8400
Soft-serve ice cream mixes

Classic Mix Partners
601 S. Commercial Street
Neenah, WI 54956
800-722—8903
www.classicmixpartners.com
Ice cream & gelato mixes

Colombo/General Mills
800-343-8240
Soft-serve frozen yogurt mix

Fresco Famous Italian Ices
1337-1 Lincoln Road
Holbrook, NY 11741
631-471-8434
www.frescoice.com
Italian ices, gelato, ice cream

Gise Creme Glace
6064 Corte Del Cedro
Carlsbad, CA 92009
800-448-4473
Nondairy frozen dessert shop

Greenwood Farms
Atlanta, GA
800-678-6166
www.greenwoodicecream.com
Ice cream mixes

Ice Cream Club
1580 High Ridge Rd
Boynton Beach, Fl 33426
800-535-7711
www.icecreamclub.com
Ice cream mixes

Kohler Mix Specialties
4041 Hwy. 61
White Bear Lake, MN 55110
800-231-1167
Ice cream mixes

Welsh Farm
55 Fairview Avenue
Long Valley, New Jersey 07853
908-876-3131
Hard ice cream mix

Packaging

Airlite Plastics
914 North 18th Street
Omaha, NE 68102
402-341-7300
Plastic cups: all sizes, kinds

Cardinal Packaging
1275 Ethan Ave.
Streetsboro, OH 44241
800-544-9573
    Plastic cup packaging

Douglas Stephans Plastics
22-36 Green Street
Paterson, NJ 07509
201-523-3030
    Plastic lids

Gelato Supply Co.
1025 Virginia Ave, NE
Atlanta, GA 30306
404-392-5115
www.gelatosupply.com

Negus Container & Packaging
888-241-7482
www.negusboxnbag.com
    Paper ice cream containers

Plastican, Inc.
196 Industrial Rd.
Leominister, MA 01453
978-537-4911
    2½-gal. plastic tubs for ice cream

PlasTech
800-544-2927
www.maltcollars.com
    Malt collars

Polar Plastics
7132 Daniels Drive
Allentown, PA 18106
215-398-7400
    Plastic cups and spoons

Spartech/Gen Pak Canada
260 Rexdale Boulevard
Rexdale, Ontario M9W 1R2
Canada
800-387-7452
    Plastic containers

Rynone Packaging
www.Rynonepackaging.com
    Corrugated ice cream containers

Sealright Company
9201 Packaging Drive
Desoto, KS 66018
800-255-4243
    Paper cups: different sizes & types

Sweetheart Packaging
10100 Reisertown Road
Owings Mill, Maryland 21117
410-363-1111
    Paper and plastic cups, lids

Menu Boards

Cow Tunes for Kids
P.O. Box 2445
Brentwood, TN 37024
877-269-8273
    Promotional ice cream CDs

www.imagedelight.com
847-288-9366
    Food photography

Mainstreet Menu Systems
1375 North Barker Road
Brookfield, WI 53005
800-782-6222
    Menu boards

Packaging and Storage Containers

Buckhorn
55 West Techcenter Drive
Milford, OH 45150
800-543-4454
    Storage handling containers

Polar Tech Industries
415 E. Railroad Ave.
Genoa, IL 60135
800-423-2749
    Insulated shipping boxes

Polyfoam Packers
2320 Foster Avenue
Wheeling, IL 60090
800-323-7442
   Insulated shipping boxes

ASSOCIATIONS

American Dairy Association
Dairy Management Inc.
10255 W. Higgins Rd. #900
Rosemont, IL 60018
847-803-2000

Dairy and Food Industries Supply
Associates
1451 Dolley Madison Blvd.
McClean, VA 22101
703-761-2600

Hazelnut Marketing Board
P.O. Box 23126
Portland, OR 97281
503-639-3118

Ice Cream University
79 Edgewood Ave
West Orange, NJ 07052
973-669-1060
www.icecreamuniversity.org
   Annual Gelato Tour of Italy; books;
   seminars; newsletters on batch freezer
   and ice cream cake production, retailing

International Ice Cream Association
1250 H Street NW Suite 900
Washington, D.C. 20005
202-737-4332
   Annual sourcebook, *The Latest Scoop*

National Ice Cream & Yogurt Retailers
Association (NICRA)
1028 West Devon Ave
Elk Grove Village, IL 60007
800-847-8522

National Pecan Marketing Council
Knapp Hall
Louisiana State University
Baton Rouge, LA 70803
504-388-2222

National Soft Serve and Fast Food
Association
9614 Tomstown Road
Wayneboro, PA 17268
800-535-7748

New England Ice Cream Association
P.O. Box 1677
Merrimack, NH 03054-1677
603-424-1410

Underwriters Laboratories
333 Pfingsten Road
Northbrook, IL 60062
847-272-8800
   UL approval for equipment

PRINT INFORMATION

- **Getting Started**
- **How To Succeed In The Incredible**
  Ice Cream Business
- **Ice Cream Cakes**
- **Ice Cream and Frozen Desserts: A**
  Commercial Guide to Production and
  Marketing
- **Ice Cream University News**
  (Newsletter)
- **Incredible Ice Cream: Making It Your**
  Way with Passion!
79 Edgewood Ave
West Orange, NJ 07052
973-669-1060
www.icecreamuniversity.org

Correspondence Course 102:
Ice Cream Manufacture
The Pennsylvania State University
Department of Independent Living
128 AG-Mitchell Building
University Park, PA 16802
814-865-7371

Dairy Field Magazine
Stagnito Publishing Company
1935 Shermer Road, Suite 100
Northbrook, IL 60062
708-205-5660

Dairy Foods Magazine
Cahners Publishing Company
200 Clearwater Drive
Oak Brook, IL 60523
303-470-4445

Dessert Professional
45 West 34th Street, #600
New York, NY 10001
212-239-0855

Food Production Management
2619 Maryland Ave.
Baltimore, MD 21218
410-467-3338

Ice Cream, Fifth Edition
Chapman & Hall
115 Fifth Avenue
New York, NY 10003
212-254-3232

The National Dipper
1028 West Devon Ave
Elk Grove Village, IL 60007
800-847-8522

Pastry Art & Design Magazine
45 West 34th Street, #600
New York, NY 10001
212-239-0855

Scandinavian Dairy Magazine
Frederiks Alle 22
DK-8000 Arhus C
Denmark
45-86-13-26-93

RECIPE INDEX FOR PROFESSIONAL ARTISANS

RECIPES FOR HOME ICE CREAM JUNKIES

SUBJECT INDEX